A HISTORY OF THE PARISH OF CHARDSTOCK AND ALL SAINTS

P. J. Wood
&
R.W. Carter

Published by P. J. Wood 26 Helliers Close, Chard, Somerset TA20 1LJ

First Published 1999

*A reprint with additions,
published by the Chardstock Historical Record Group, 2005 and 2009,
with permission of the authors.
Second reprint 2011 with a few minor corrections and additions
Third reprint 2016 with a few minor corrections and additions*

ISBN 0 9535341 0 3

The moral rights of the authors have been asserted.

*All rights reserved.
No part of this publication may be reproduced, stored in a retrieval system,
or transmitted in any form or by any means electronic, mechanical,
photocopying, recording or otherwise,
without the prior written permission of the copyright owners.*

Layout and typesetting by Chardstock Historical Record Group

Typeset in Garamond Premier

Reproduction by Axminster Print

*The oldest known illustration of the church
is in the background of a picture of
the Revd. Thomas Babb, Curate of Chardstock in the 1820s*

CONTENTS

		Page
Preface		iv
Foreword and Acknowledgements		v
Chapter One	Topography/Geology	1
Chapter Two	General History	4
Chapter Three	The Manor Court	12
Chapter Four	Stewards' Accounts of the Manor in the 15th & 16th Centuries	16
Chapter Five	Chardstock Sub - Manors	19
Chapter Six	Highways, Byways and Transport	22
Chapter Seven	Markets, Fairs, Shops and Trade	27
Chapter Eight	Land Use	34
Chapter Nine	Farms	38
Chapter Ten	Houses	44
Chapter Eleven	Education	46
Chapter Twelve	The Church	52
Chapter Thirteen	The Prebend of Chardstock	58
Chapter Fourteen	Ecclesiastical and Civil Courts	62
Chapter Fifteen	Nonconformity	68
Chapter Sixteen	The Poor in Chardstock	69
Chapter Seventeen	Charities	79
Chapter Eighteen	Inns and Ale Houses	83
Chapter Nineteen	The People of Chardstock	86
Chapter Twenty	The Influence of National Events	93
Chapter Twenty-one	Village Organisations	100
Chapter Twenty-two	Memories	105

Appendices

Appendix A	Building Surveys	111
Appendix B	Chardstock Parish Checklist	118
Appendix C	Field and Place Names	122
Appendix D	A Common Field at Alston	131
Appendix E	Prebendaries, Vicars and Curates	134
Appendix F	Perambulation of the W and NW Bounds in 1672	136
Appendix G	Some Occupations	137
Index		139

LIST OF ILLUSTRATIONS

Hoopers Farmhouse in 1856	cover
Revd. Thomas Babb	i
Rock Forms and Superficial Rock Cover, Maps 1 and 2	3
Prehistoric Enclosure, Cauldron Handles and Palstave, Plate 1	5
Topography, Place Names and Boundaries, Map 3	9
Prehistoric Sites and Find Locations, Map 4	11
Salisbury Diocese in the 14th Century, Map 5. Chardstock Manor House, Plate 2	13
Chardstock Manor at 1100 - 1500AD, Map 6	21
Bridges, Milestone, Tytherleigh Arch and Toll House, Plate 3	25
Coaches, Wheelwright and Blacksmith, Plate 4	29
Lime Kilns, Plate 5, Map 7	33
Mill Leat Systems, Map 8	35
Main Farms and their Land, Map 9	41/42
Structural Details found at some Farms, Plate 6	43
St. Andrew's School and College, Plate 7	51
St. Andrew's Church Features, Plate 8	59
Chardstock Village in 1781, Maps 10 and 11	61
St. Andrew's Church Features and Cello, Plate 9	63
Inns and Heraldry, Plate 10	87
Beacons, Plate 11 and Map 12	97
20th Century Wars, Plate 12, Map 13	98
Pictures, Then and Now, Plate 13	107
Smallridge, All Saints, Strong's, and Village Organisations, Plate 14	109
Commons Settlement, Wm. Bond, Thos. Palmer, Organisations, Plate 15, Map 14	110
Selected Fieldwork Features, Map 15	117
Plan of Alston Common Field in Medieval Times, Map 16	132
Plan of Alston Field in the Early 20th Century, Map 17	133

PREFACE
The Court Chardstock

We have no hesitation in recommending this book to those who are interested in History in general and Chardstock in particular. It has come about as a result of many hours spent poring over half-legible documents, often needing to be translated from Latin or Norman French or written in almost indecipherable Germanic script.

The difficulty with local history is that much of it has never been documented and has been passed down by word of mouth from generation to generation for sometimes hundreds of years. The main reasons for this were either illiteracy or fear of the consequences of the written word, should a change of Sovereign occur! The effect however was that much has been lost, changed and in some cases embellished, so that the truth is indeed hard to come by.

We feel that Mr. Wood and Mr. Carter have successfully blended these two elements in their work and that they are greatly to be thanked for their efforts on behalf of us all in Chardstock.

Kathleen W. Milford
Lord of the Manor of Chardstock

Maurice G. Milford

FOREWORD AND ACKNOWLEDGEMENTS

The recording of history is a continuous process with fresh discoveries and documents constantly appearing. These new sources of information often help to explain past events and confound well-established theories. Therefore this work can never be complete and, no doubt, many readers will find much to add from their memories, experiences and long-forgotten manuscripts.

Chardstock is a parish with an extensive and varied history, the recording of which is bound to be fragmentary. Of Prehistoric times, only conjecture, fieldwork, and a few buried remains can tell how the inhabitants lived and worked. This also applies to the Roman and Saxon periods and it is not until the coming of the Normans that written evidence begins to appear. It must be appreciated that this material was not compiled for the benefit of future generations but for contemporary society. Therefore it gives only part of the story, and a brief insight into the organisation of village life and the people living here.

Chardstock is fortunate in that many of these records survive, although they are widely scattered. This is mainly due to administrative reorganisation which has taken place. The county boundary changes which led to Chardstock being transferred from Dorset to Devon meant that records are held in both counties. The change of Diocese, from Salisbury to Exeter via Bristol, presents a further difficulty in tracing documents, some of which are held in Wiltshire. National records relating to the parish can be found in Birmingham, Lambeth Palace and the Public Record Office, now based at Kew. Printed sources and some manuscripts are held in Somerset and some are in private hands. Compiling the history has involved the collecting of information from as many sources as possible over a long period of time. The selection of the material to be included and when to write the history have been the greatest problems. It is hoped that the reader will find something of interest from the variety of topics in the chapters which follow.

During our research, we have received much help from many people. First and foremost, thanks are due to the Local Historian, Mary Parmiter, whose knowledge of Chardstock and its people is beyond compare. We are grateful for the help given by the staff of the Record Offices of Devon, Dorset, Somerset and especially Wiltshire (Trowbridge) and Somerset Local History Librarian, David Bromwich. Thanks are due to the landowners and farmers of Chardstock for permission to walk over their land during our field studies. We are grateful to fellow local historians Joan Tunstall, Ron Gilson, Colin and O-lan Style for their help and use of their reports. We thank the staff of the Chard and Ilminster News for allowing many hours of study of their records. The map of Salisbury Diocese has been reproduced by kind permission of the Canterbury and York Society, and the 1781 Manor Survey by permission of the late Lord Henley. It is believed that all Ordnance Survey and other maps used are out of copyright but, even so, the immense debt owed to those early surveyors who carried out such painstaking work should always be acknowledged. Finally we should like to acknowledge the help received from so many Chardstock people, in particular, Kathleen Chubb (for all of Chapter 22), June Wellington, Reg Brooks, David Eames, Adrian Goff, Frank Huddy, David Ingrams and Michael Moore. Mrs. C. East, J. Dallimore and Arthur Page have also provided information.

Peter Wood
January 1999
Roger Carter

FOREWORD TO THE FIRST REPRINT:

When the first edition of the History of Chardstock sold out, the Chardstock Historical Record Group felt that this important book should remain available to all those interested in the Parish. With the kind agreement of the authors, we have therefore undertaken the production of this reprint.

In a few cases, further research by the authors in specific areas has been incorporated, but no general revision has been undertaken. In particular, the current condition of archæological and other features mentioned has not been checked. However the opportunity has been taken to make some minor amendments and clarifications – for instance "this century" has been changed to "the 20th Century" – and the index has been extended. Improved computer and printing techniques have allowed us to improve the quality of reproduction of the illustrations.

Chardstock Historical Record Group. August 2005

FOREWORD TO THE SECOND AND THIRD REPRINTS:

The second reprint, published in May 2011, incorporates a few minor corrections and additions. The book title was also changed to include All Saints.
The third reprint, published in May 2016, incorporates a few further minor corrections and additions.

Chardstock Historical Record Group. May 2011 and May 2016

Chapter One
TOPOGRAPHY / GEOLOGY

The shape of Chardstock Parish, and the varied type of rock beneath the surface, is the result of the action of sea and weather over many million years. At least three times the sea has planed all off to a fairly level surface. Fractures (faults) and tilting have made unevenness and this has been modified by the action of freezing, wind and rain. The result is a complicated mixture of rock types, causing variations in fertility and drainage and also providing areas where useful minerals or construction materials could be obtained. The oldest rocks are in the valley bottoms, but there are areas where faulting has lowered an adjacent landblock or where erosion has formed later deposits. The interesting fossils and their value in identifying geological sequences in this area led the pioneering geologist A. J. Jukes-Browne to carry out a detailed study which he published in 1902 (Map 1). This map was made by noting the type, slope and height of rocks in the many farm pits, railway and road cuttings, and wells seen and dug in late Victorian times. To a trained eye, the valley sides give clues to faults and the junction between hard and soft rocks. A springline may show where porous rocks meet underlying clay. Jukes-Browne mainly studied the underlying rocks, but most of the parish is covered with drift, which is the clay and stones remaining after these rocks have been partly dissolved and sorted by weather. In addition, at times during the later geological periods, severe weather conditions led to the erosion which was largely responsible for the formation of the present landform.

Jurassic Rocks

These rocks are now in the lowest part of the parish. The blue clay has long been valued for tile and pottery making. The Romans may have used it to make roofing tiles at Woonton (c.200-300 A.D.). Large quantities of Medieval pottery have been found at Whitehouse and there was a Victorian land-drain, tile and brick works near Kitbridge. The weathered clay was also used for spreading on sandy soils to convert them to loam, a type of soil that is better for the retention of moisture and nutrients. Limestone occurs in slabs of varying thickness and has been used for floors and roofs. In Victorian times, it was used to make an early form of cement called hydraulic lime, which will set under water. This was made in kilns at the bottom of the valleys, such as at Castle Wood and Hell Bottom (this kiln is well preserved).

Cretaceous Rocks

The Jurassic rocks were later raised, tilted to the east and then planed off by the sea. Green sandy deposits were laid down by further erosion processes in the Cretaceous period, 110 million years ago, the age of the largest dinosaurs. These sands occur on the valley sides and, because they overlay the clay, a spring line is formed at the junction. While this causes boggy, acid and poor land, in the past it provided the power source and the clean spring water vital for farm life. Deposits of iron ore were also formed at this horizon and were used in small scale smelting. The upper greensand is harder and splits naturally into blocks which are favoured for building throughout the parish. This is not flint but a similar, slightly grainy, light brown stone called chert. Very early man (80,000 years ago) valued this for making into stone tools. These were fashioned from a core and then trimmed to form axes and scrapers. Good building chert was found in the many small pits which are now hollows, high up on the valley sides. On the hilltops, chert has become shattered by the action of frost. This is sharp and makes an excellent base for roads and foundations. The action of melt waters during the Ice Ages, 1,500,000 - 8,000 years ago, deposited great thicknesses of broken chert in the Axe Valley. At Broom Crossing, the former Charity Land called Holditch Hill has been quarried away. In the pit was a rail siding where the gravel was loaded for railway use in the 19th and early 20th Centuries.

About 100 million years ago, the land to the west had become desert and there were few rivers to deposit mud. A limy ooze was deposited at about a rate of one metre per 100,000 years. This formed the Upper Cretaceous period chalk deposits, which are now found mainly in the east of the parish. Chalky soils are fertile, well drained and easily cultivated: for this reason, early arable fields were preferably in these areas. The top surface of chalk becomes soft and decomposed; this is called chalk marl, useful for spreading on non-chalky areas to decrease acidity and thereby release nutrients for crops. Chalk marl pits, as at Burridge and Storridge became very large. In Victorian times, hydrated lime was preferred to marl (frost weathered chalk) because it is less bulky and quicker in action. This enabled much of the remaining common land to be brought into cultivation. Hydrated lime was made from chalk in the same way as hydraulic lime; the dangerous quicklime was left in heaps for the rain to hydrate slowly and safely. The newly-cultivated acidic land on Bewley Down was neutralised using lime supplied from kilns at Woonton and Bewley Farms.

Tertiary Period

This was 70 to 2 million years ago and was notable for volcanic action, the formation of the Atlantic Ocean and for the steady cooling of the climate. Chardstock has only traces of Tertiary rocks, but land movement resulted in a large fault which runs down the east side of the Kit Valley and formed a line of weakness, later eroded during the Ice Ages, to give the valley its present shape. The face of the fault can be seen as a steep slope at Cotley. Another double fault, forming the Burridge Valley, can actually be seen in section in the north face of Snowdon Quarry, west of Chard.

Ice Age

There were several Ice Ages, with the ice advances being interspersed with warmer conditions. Twice, advances took ice to the Somerset coast, blocking the rivers and forming lakes. It has been suggested that this water finally broke through a Chard fault line and eroded the valley to Tytherleigh. The severe freeze/thaw cycles eroded the hilltops leaving gravel and clay deposits that cap the hills and spill over into the valleys. Geological processes continue largely unnoticed at the present day. The land, recovering from ice pressure, slowly tilts westward and the sea level rises. The soft greensand rocks form a series of shelf like mini-faults above Husk Wood and in many other places. At Whitehouse, domestic deposits 800 years old are now up to 1.5 metres deep (see Map 2).

John Jones

From 1858 to 1860, the Headmaster of the newly formed Chardstock Middle School, taught Geology to his pupils. John Jones was careful to call himself no more than an "Amateur Geologist" but he was a pioneer and a great enthusiast. He was a leading member of the Chard Literary Institute and proposed the formation of the Chard Museum. By 1860, he had established a collection of fossils in his museum at the school and had written an attractive little book entitled "Rambles Round Chard with a Hammer". It could be bought, price 1s, from J. Nowlen & T. Young, Chard Booksellers, or from the author at Chardstock. This starts, as do many scientific books of the period, with a careful explanation that the Creation, as described in the book of Genesis in the Bible, is not disproved by Geological theory, if considered broadly. He describes passing by Chard Canal, which was about to be closed and partly converted into a railway. He mentions the new railway line at Axminster as having fresh brown embankments with ballast for it being dug from the pits at Tytherleigh Bridge (i.e. Broom Pit). He said that the road at Kitbridge was inconvenient, wretched, worse than most in England and full of protruding stones. The hedgebanks there were described as covered with a great profusion of wild flowers and ferns and he noted that the brick kiln nearby was in use.

Sources

Chard, a Geological Survey 1970 Chard History Group 3.
Jones, J. 1860 Rambles Round Chard with a Hammer.
Jukes-Browne, A. J. 1903 The Geology of the Country Round Chard Proc. SANHS xlix.

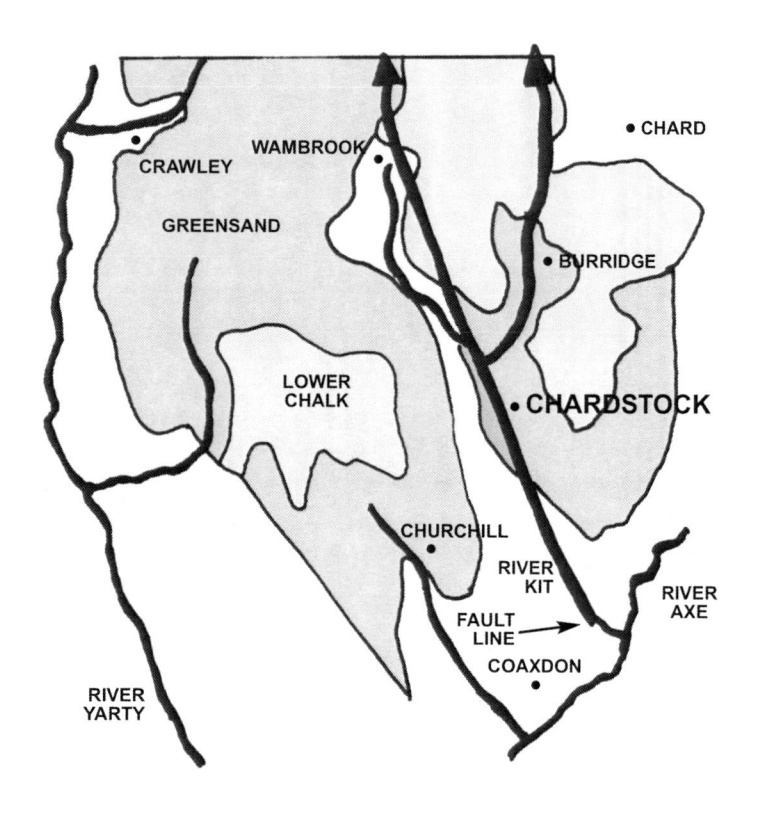

MAP 1. Rock forms in the Chardstock Area

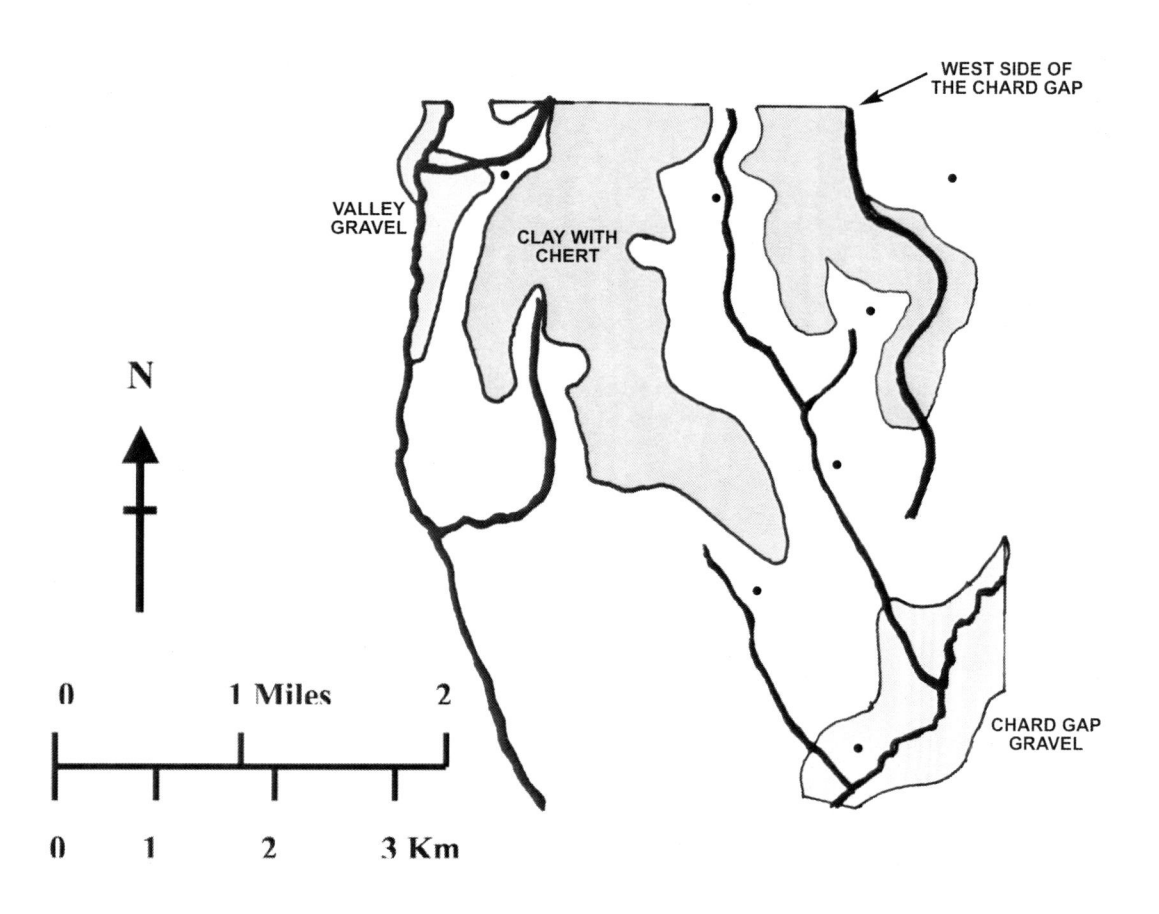

MAP 2. Superficial Rock Cover (drift)

Chapter Two
GENERAL HISTORY

Paleolithic (Old Stone Age)
Many Stone Age tools have been discovered, now as much as 10 metres down, in the gravel of Broom Pit. It is thought that these mainly hand-axes were made by migratory fisher/hunters at a summer camp by the wide gravel shallows of the early river Axe. This would have been during one of the interglacials, possibly as much as 1.5 million years ago. Examples of these famous tools can be found in many museums throughout the country.

Neolithic (New Stone Age)
The superb stone arrowheads, characteristic of this period, are difficult to find in the local stony soil. One tranchet type was found during fieldwork at the south end of Bewley Down and worked flint flakes were found nearby.

Bronze Age
Because the area has a high rainfall and is underlain by clay rocks, early settlement took place on sloping, self-draining land just off the hilltops. The earliest evidence for hilltop settlements was found by the Chard antiquarian Arthur Hull who, in 1850, was surveying the commonland on Bewley (pronounced Billy) Down in order to convert it into hedged fields or closes. He showed it to his friend George Pulman, an Axminster newspaper proprietor. Pulman states in his book, that five embanked circles were found and within one were hut and hearth remains. Some coarse black pottery was dug up. The circles were being destroyed for roadmaking. One oval enclosure described, has been re-discovered in a fir plantation on the eastern slope of the Down (see Plate 15). Its bank is 1 metre high and 27-37 metres in diameter. It is likely to be the remains of the enclosing bank of an animal fold of Bronze Age date, c.2000 - 1000 B.C. (similar circles were found at Worthiel Farm, Wambrook). Pulman and Hull also found two (nationally important) bronze cauldron ring handles (class A1) on Bewley Down and these are now in Taunton Museum. A survey of 1672 (Appendix F) mentions stone cairns or mounds in this area. It is likely that linear banks seen in the plantation nearby also date from this period and may be the remains of very early fields. The soil here is light but stony. Later cultivation was on the more fertile lower areas. Pulman also reported mounds near The Half Moon earthwork to the south. Bronze Age axes have been found at Woonton Farm nearby (now in Chard Museum) and at Cotley (now lost).

Iron Age
Evidence for settlement in the Iron Age period, c.500 B.C., appears, with varying degrees of certainty, in several locations. A possible one is at what is an apparently unfinished hill-slope enclosure called The Half Moon. This is about ½ mile south of the above sites but it has probably been much damaged in the 19/20th Centuries. Another is at Cold Harbour field (harbour meaning earthfort) beside Bounds Lane in the north of the parish. The single rampart of this survives for a quarter of its circuit. It had an outer ditch and a western entrance. Iron ore and slag have been found in and around it. At Cotley, a hoard of about 60 Durotrigian style coins were found in 1865 (now lost). Early forms of the place names of Burridge and Wambrook nearby, appear to contain the element "burh" meaning fort, this possibly referring to Cold Harbour. The general administrative structure of the country slowly formed over the following 1000 years and consisted of three or more tiers. Boundaries changed at times in function and importance. At the largest scale, the area was a boundary between the tribes called the Dumnonii (hence Devon), a loose agrarian community to the West and the more sophisticated Durotriges to the East. In Roman times these latter consisted of a southern section centred on Maiden Hill/Dorchester and a northern section on Ham Hill/Ilchester. On a smaller scale were the spheres of influence which encircled each local hillfort. As administrative areas, the use of these may have continued over a long period of time.

Roman Period
The Roman invasion in 43 A.D. took place to the east of England. A force under Vespasian moved westward during the next 10 years. It is believed that a frontier supply road was built through what became the east of the parish and ran from Axmouth to Lincoln. Another road from Dorchester ran west and crossed it near Woodbury Farm, Axminster, where a possible early fort has been discovered. Nearby settlements/estates followed at South Chard, Wadeford, Whitestaunton and possibly Membury. A spread of roof tile has been found on Woonton Farm but since there are clay pits on lower ground, the site may have been a tile factory. Access to the Woonton site could have been from a possible road running north to south along Bewley Down or from a precursor of the Farway (see Chapter 6). The use of Cold Harbour as a meeting place probably continued into Roman times and beyond. A sherd of mid-Roman period pottery (New Forest Ware) was found a few metres south of the rampart. A late Roman burial was found upon Beacon Hill in 1823. This consisted of a reddish 7 inch high urn containing coins of Faustina and Aurelius, black ashes and bone, and was surrounded by rounded pebbles and buried within a 20ft diameter (D) mound of stones. Beside it was a possible corn drying kiln, 4ft deep by 2ft D., walled and containing ashes and with a 1ft by 1ft D., grinding quern.

PLATE 1

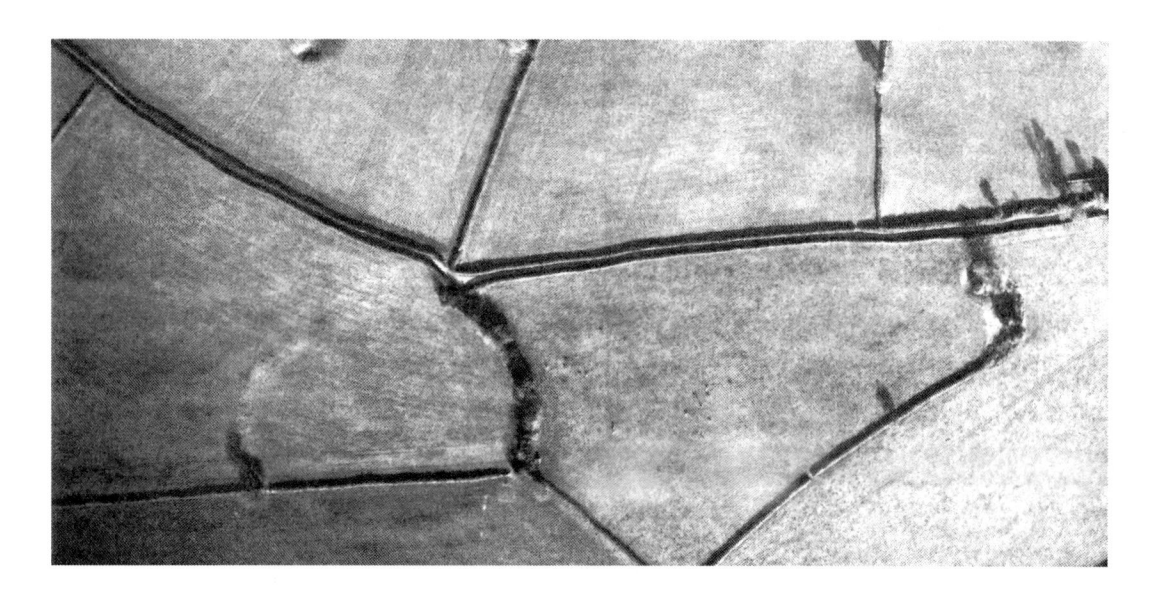

Prehistoric Enclosure called Cold Harbour, near Bounds Lane

Bronze Age Cauldron Handles found on Bewley Down

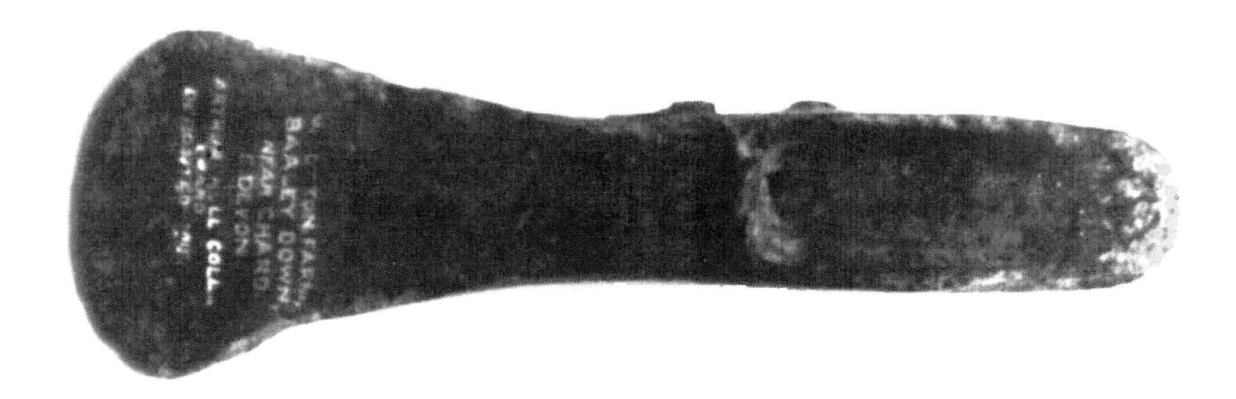

Bronze Age Palstave (with loop broken off) found at Woonton Farm

Sub-Roman, Celtic and West Saxon Periods

With the breaking of ties with Rome and the subsequent collapse of the economy, it is generally thought that the structure of estates survived to a degree. These ultimately came under the control of the kings of the emerging kingdom of the West Saxons or Wessex, as they slowly extended their areas of influence westwards. King Ine (688-726) carried out various campaigns into the Celtic Dumnonia. His successors for a while found it difficult to keep these lands. By 705, the bishopric of Winchester had been extended so far west that it was necessary to divide it and found a new one centred on Sherborne. Endowments were made to the Abbeys of Glastonbury and Sherborne while, nearer at hand, Muchelney Abbey was founded just north of Ilminster. Church land was sometimes preferentially established in politically unsettled areas. A very early charter of Cynewulf 757-86 (now lost) refers to Snarstock Treov (tentatively, snare-place plus the Cornish "trev" village/homestead). Its name may relate to snare (a trap). A comparable early grant is that of Abbamburh or A(l)ba(m)bruth by King Egbert (802-39) which may be Wambrook. In the 11th and 12th Centuries, Wambrook appears again as Wybrewurth and Wambroc.

The appearance of the countryside around Chardstock has been dominated by areas of furze and bracken-covered commonland until about 1840. This must have been a distinctive feature in about 700 A.D. when a language transition from early Welsh to early English was taking place. The name given for rough land was ceart, pronounced "chart" and this is likely to have applied to an area from Axminster to Combe St. Nicholas. A more likely reference to the Chard or Chardstock Manor is in another grant to Sherborne Bishopric by King Ethelwulf (839-58) where it is called C(h)erdel. This appears to mean "rough commonland valley". It is probable that the establishment of the County Boundary with Cold Harbour Hillfort as a boundary point, effectively dividing the estate, occurred just before this time. Presumably Chard Manor, being now in another county, was later granted to Wells when, or after, it was established in 910. This was later confirmed by King Edward in 1065, under the name C(h)erdren, which means, in Old English, cheart-renn or dwelling in a rough common. The extensive areas of wild land that is mentioned above, was not confined to Chardstock. To the east the wooded area of Wyld extended to Charmouth, across Marshwood Vale and north-east to Selwood. Northwest was Neroche Forest and to the west was another area of common (part of the names of Membury and Heathstock) while the Dalwood and Stockland names suggest earlier woodland.

The Manor in Norman and Later Times

The structure of the manor of Chardstock at the Norman conquest of 1066 was probably much as it had been for the previous 200 years. The Bishop of Salisbury's Reeve lived near what is now the Manor House and he would have been visited frequently by the Bishop's Steward. An early chapel would have been very close to the house, perhaps on the site of the present church, which is at least the third building to be located there. The manor was divided into two tithings, the boundary running through the village. Both tithings had a principal farm or "tuna". The northern one was Wilmington, close to the Roman tile site. This, in 1155, was known as the vill of Wilmintuna and was possibly the home of a person called Wighelm or Wulfhelm. The southern tuna was Alston, known as Alwoldeston in 1201, possibly being Alfwald's Tuna. An Alfwold was Bishop of Sherborne from 966 to 978 and a second Alfwold was the Bishop during the years prior to 1058. If named after one of these, the first is more likely, since in 1058, the manor was transferred to the new Diocese of Sarum, now Old Sarum near Salisbury. It must be emphasised that at this early date, the scattered farms were basically run by extended families (plus kinsfolk and slaves), these paying dues to the Bishop. By 1086, slaves were becoming tied peasants; complex Feudal tenures and co-operative strip-field cultivation systems were becoming established. King William I ordered that a detailed assessment be made of the tenures of England. Chardstock was visited by two separate teams and their reports were produced as a definitive version in 1086. The Domesday Book entry reads:-

The Bishop (of Salisbury) also holds C(h)erdestoche (Chardstock), and two men-at-arms, Walter and William, from him. Before 1066 it paid tax for 12 hides. Land for 20 ploughs, of which 4 hides are in Lordship; 4 ploughs there; 6 slaves; 45 villagers and 21 smallholders with 17 ploughs. There are 2 mills which pay 20s; meadow 10 acres; pasture 3 leagues long and 1½ leagues wide; woodland 2 leagues in both length and width; elsewhere underwood, 3 furlongs long and 2 furlongs wide. Value of the whole £16.

It is not known who the knights Walter and William were, but Walter could have had the surname Tyrel (because of later Tyrel ownership). The Manor was included in the Hundred of Whitchurch (Canonicorum) Gheld Assessment and was the property of the Bishop of Salisbury. Overall there was arable land for 20 plough teams to work, but there were only 4 on the Bishop's farm, which was worked by slaves, and 17 elsewhere in Chardstock. These ploughs were pulled by 4 or 8 oxen and guided by 2 men. At any one time, a third to half of the arable would be fallow, which would be grazed. The remainder of the manor (which may at this time have again included Wambrook and did include Crawley) was farmed by 45 tenants and 21 smallholders, all of whom owed dues and services to the Bishop. The corn crop was milled at two mills. One was probably near the village, at Town Mill, while the other may have been situated at Millway Farm, Hook or Lodge. The 10 acres of meadow were for a hay crop and grazing. The large area of pasture represents the furzy tract of Bewley Down, and the similar area of woodland ran from Smallridge to Cotley. Intriguingly, somewhere, there was a detached area of underwood (probably coppice supplying fuel and spars).

The bishop held the Manor until the reign of Stephen (1135-1154) when it passed to the king. During the reign of Henry I, the administration of the country had been controlled by Roger, Bishop of Salisbury. On the accession of Stephen, the bishop and his relations continued to exercise their authority, much to the displeasure of the king. After a rumour that the bishop was about to support Matilda, Stephen's rival for the throne, the king used a brawl at Oxford as an excuse to seize Roger, his son and their castles. On the death of Roger in 1139, the king retained all of his wealth and estates including, presumably, Chardstock. This is borne out by the granting of a charter of the Manor of Chardstock by Henry II in or about the year 1155 to Gilbert de Percy who became Sheriff of Somerset and Dorset in 1164/5. Shortly after receiving the manor, Gilbert de Percy made a gift of the church at Chardstock to the Cathedral of Sarum. Evidence of this is contained in a confirmation charter of Henry II, dated 1158, which lists amongst other gifts, "Ecclesiam de Cerdestok ex dono Gerberti de Perci". This created the Prebend of Chardstock and the prebendal stall which can still be seen in Salisbury Cathedral today.

The Percies may be related to the Lords Percy of Northumberland and Yorkshire but this has not been proved and it is more likely they are from a separate family originating in France. Gerbert or Gilbert had an estate at Tinchebray near Perci in Normandy from where the family probably took its name. They seemed to have quarrelled over the possession of the manor for, in about 1155, a settlement was made in the Bishop of Salisbury's court between Robert de Percy, his son Robert and Gilbert de Percy, whose grandfather, Walter Tyrel, was said to have held the manor and from whom Gilbert inherited it. In this charter, the two Roberts renounced all claims to the manor in favour of Gilbert, who went on to grant, during the reign of Henry II, Craulauee (probably the modern Crawley) and Chilcompton to his nephew Richard Gulafre. He also received his uncle's interest in the village of "Wlmintuna" (Wilmington), the remains of which have been found near Whitehouse, Holy City. The word "city" is a typical nickname for a shrunken or deserted village (the earliest documentary reference to "Holy City", occurs in an entry in the back of the Chardstock Poor Rate book dated 12th November 1773 quoting a deed of 1734). Gilbert also gave his nephew brushwood, all the forest and anything he had at La Rigge (Ridge), all his holdings in La Hoche (Hook), a mill and the park. The tenements of Eilaf de la Bere, Galfridum de Farneie (Farway), Walter son of Edward of Cleave, levegarum; the reeve, Walter Britonem, Elvefam wife of Fairi and Edward de Wdemul, were also included in the gift. Eggemore from the boundary at Tiderlege (Tytherleigh) as far as the broad pond went to Richard Gulafre. The deed goes on to list furlongs next to Eggemore, one above the road and another below, and names land near Anestathes (probably near Broom), Gotfurlong, Furnham, Birdfurlag, Stamerlege, and also at Huverstamerlege. The Lordship of Huntelege (Huntley) and various rights of common passed to Richard.

Gilbert, who died in 1179 without issue, does not appear to have held the manor for very long, because in 1160-61, William de Percy claimed Chardstock as his inheritance. The dispute was settled in favour of William in the court of Bishop Jocelin de Bohun. William held the manor until 1195-96, when in the court of King Richard I at Westminster, he quitclaimed (i.e. gave up) all rights to the "whole vil of Cherdestokes" to Herbert, Bishop of Salisbury. The bishop paid 20 silver marcs and one warhorse, worth 50 shillings, to William. Chardstock then remained in the possession of the bishops, apart from a short break during the Commonwealth Period when the bishops were out of favour with the king, until it was sold to the Henley family in 1873. Its importance can be judged from Map 5.

There were other early holdings. In 1201, Stephen Tyrrell gave up his claim to Chardstock and the bishop granted him one hide of land at Milnhale (now possibly the site of Millway farm) and land at Alwoldestone (Alston). The same year John, son of John of Wulmintone, gave up claims to mills in Chardstock and La Hok (Hook), to two furlongs of land at Chardstock, one furlong at Alwoldestone and half a furlong at Fugelescumbe (possibly Volscombe at Farway). In 1202, William, son of Robert, gave up his claim to one and a half hides of land at Brelege (Bewley). The bishop gave William 30 marks of silver. About 1226-1228, Ralph de Vaux, whose family was at Wood, near Ashill in Somerset, gave up all his rights to the manor but kept the land he held at Seneberg (now possibly Seaborough) and Tidderlega (Tytherleigh).

In 1278, another William Percy challenged the right of the bishop to the manor, contesting that the ancestor who had given up the claim to the manor was not the rightful owner, but someone from another family with the same name. This challenge does not seem to have been allowed as, in 1286, when Bishop Walter Scammel died, it was noted that there were 16 cattle on his land at Chardstock. In 1293, the Chardstock lands of the bishop were rated at £36 15s.

The bishops never lived at Chardstock, but appointed a steward to administer the manor on their behalf. The steward's reeve would prepare an annual account in the form of a roll of parchment, which was submitted to Salisbury. The earliest account we have is that of John Crown, for the year 1422/23. There are also Account Rolls for 1425/7, 1502/3, 1537/8 and when William Grange was Reeve in 1545. A deer park was included in the estate, the name and part of the bounds of which still survive in the land known as Parks. A grant was made by the king in 1294, to Bishop Nicholas Longespee, of free warren in his demesne at Cerdestok. The right of warren was really the right to hunt, usually restricted to the recipient's estate, which at Chardstock could have been the park. In early grants it is not specified which animals could be hunted. They may have been those considered harmful to the deer, possibly the fox and the wolf, though few wolves were left in England by the 13th Century. Other animals which could be hunted may have included the hare and the rabbit. Rabbits were considered a delicacy and it was not until 1880 that tenant farmers were allowed to kill rabbits on their land.

In 1298, a mandate was issued by the bishop to the Archdeacon of Dorset to excommunicate some persons unknown who had broken into the park. Four other specific references to the Park were in 1363, 1364, between 1388 and 1395, and 1432. In 1363, a complaint was made by Robert, Bishop of Salisbury, to a commission of oyer and terminer, which heard and determined cases of serious offences. The bishop complained that John Rale of Smalregge, Nicholas Rale, Wimund Rale, Hugh Rale, John Forde, John Besaunt and others, broke into his park and warren, hunted there and took away hares, rabbits, pheasants and partridges from the warren. They were also accused of assaulting the bishop's men and servants. In the following year there was a night attack on Thomas Broke's estate at Holdych by William Smyth of Cherdestoke and many others. On this occasion men were assaulted, closes and houses broken and trees felled and taken away. This attracted a 40s fine. In the same year the bishop complained of what may have been a revenge attack. He accused Thomas Broke and Constance his wife, Robert Haukere, William Haukere the elder, William Haukere the younger, William Cartere, John Pykharm, Simon Broke, Roger Grey and others of breaking into and hunting in his free warren at Cherdestoke. They also fished in his fishery and carried away fish, 6 young sparrowhawks nesting there worth 60s, hares, conies (rabbits), pheasants and partridges from the warren. They also, "trod down and consumed with cattle his crops and grass", and assaulted his men and servants. This merited the imposition of a 20s fine. At an unknown date between 1388 and 1395, a mandate was issued by Bishop John Waltham to the clergy of the Deanary of Bridport declaring that "unknown Malifactors and their abettors had incurred greater excommunication for poaching deer in Chardstock park". The clergy had to publish this during Mass "with cross held high, bells pealing and candles lighted, extinguised and cast to the ground". In 1432 Robert Hyndelley was appointed Park Keeper at a rate of 2d a day and a robe or 6s 8d at Christmas. In 1437, Robert Henley, possibly the same man as he was described as "parker", was accused of not appearing before the Justices of the Bench, "to answer Thomas Josep touching a plea of debt of 44s" (£2 4s).

Occasionally the bishops stayed in a manor house on the site of the Court. A document, noted in the Chartulary of Glastonbury Abbey, was signed at Chardstock in July 1270. It referred to the appointment of a vicar at Domerham and Merton (Damerham and Martin), south of Salisbury and in the county of Hampshire. This was when Walter de la Wyle was Bishop of Salisbury. It is not known if he was resident in Chardstock at the time, for he died in 1270. Simon of Ghent (Bishop from 1297 to 1315), issued a document dated 1303 from Chardstock, demanding that certain churches be consecrated, and Bishop Robert Wyville (1329 to 1375), summoned incumbents to appear before him, or his commissioners, at Chardstock in 1343. In 1338, he obtained permission from King Edward III to crenellate or fortify the house. His successor, Bishop Ralph Erghum (1375 to 1388), was also granted a royal licence in 1377 to "strengthen with a wall and crenellate" the city of Salisbury and various manors, including Chardstock, belonging to him. Whether this was carried out is not known, for very little of the original building remains. At least one other bishop stayed at Chardstock. In September 1390 at Chardstock, Bishop John Waltham, who followed Bishop Erghum, instituted Adam Cotheleston as Vicar of Bettiscombe. Later, the manor was let to a tenant on a lease for a term of years, the bishop remaining as the chief holder until 1836, when the Ecclesiastical Commissioners were set up to administer church estates. In 1501 the manor was let to William Shier, who in turn let it to a tenant named William Pynney. In 1544 it was let to Henry Brytayne, William Pynney possibly continuing to be the tenant. Bishop John Capon (1539 to 1560) granted the manor to Raff Henslow for 99 years at an annual rent of £52 2s in about the year 1547, and Edward Wilshire appears as tenant in 1566. In 1568, it would seem that Raff Henslow assigned the manor to Thomas Estmond and John Parrys for the remainder of the 99 years. John Parrys then died, leaving Thomas Estmond the sole possessor. The yearly revenue from the manor had originally been divided between eleven people. John Parrys's share was now given to his sons and brothers so that the number of people with holdings increased. New transactions and exchanges followed, until the situation became confused and strife arose. This ended with Hugh Culme of Wycroft and Thomas Estmond of Lodge, putting the whole matter to the Chancery Court Commissioners in 1578. The manor was then divided, and names and holdings set out in a document dated 1582.

During the time of the Civil War and the Commonwealth Period which followed, the manor was sequestrated along with the other property belonging to the Bishop of Salisbury. In 1646, it was sold to Laurance Maidwell and Matthew Pinder for the sum of £5242. At the restoration, it reverted to the Bishop, who in 1665 leased it to John Henley of Shadsdon in Southampton, for 21 years renewable every 7 years, which was according to the Customs of Leases held under Bishops. The Lease appears to have been renewed until 1870 by the Henley family, who sometimes used it as security for loans. In 1787, an auction of the Leasehold Estate was advertised in "Trewman's Exeter Flying Post" on the instructions of the co-heiresses of Robert, Earl of Northington, who had died in 1786. The auction was to take place at Garraway's Coffee House in Cornhill, London on 10th April 1787, and the annual value of the Manor was given as £1,210. It appears to have become the property of Frederick Morton Eden, Bart. who married Lady Elizabeth Henley, fifth daughter of the Earl of Northington and co-heiress to the Estate. Sir Morton Eden was created Baron Henley of Chardstock, in the peerage of Ireland, in 1799 and died in 1830. The lease of the Manor passed to his son Robert who became the second Baron Henley and in 1831 assumed the name of Henley only. When he died in 1841

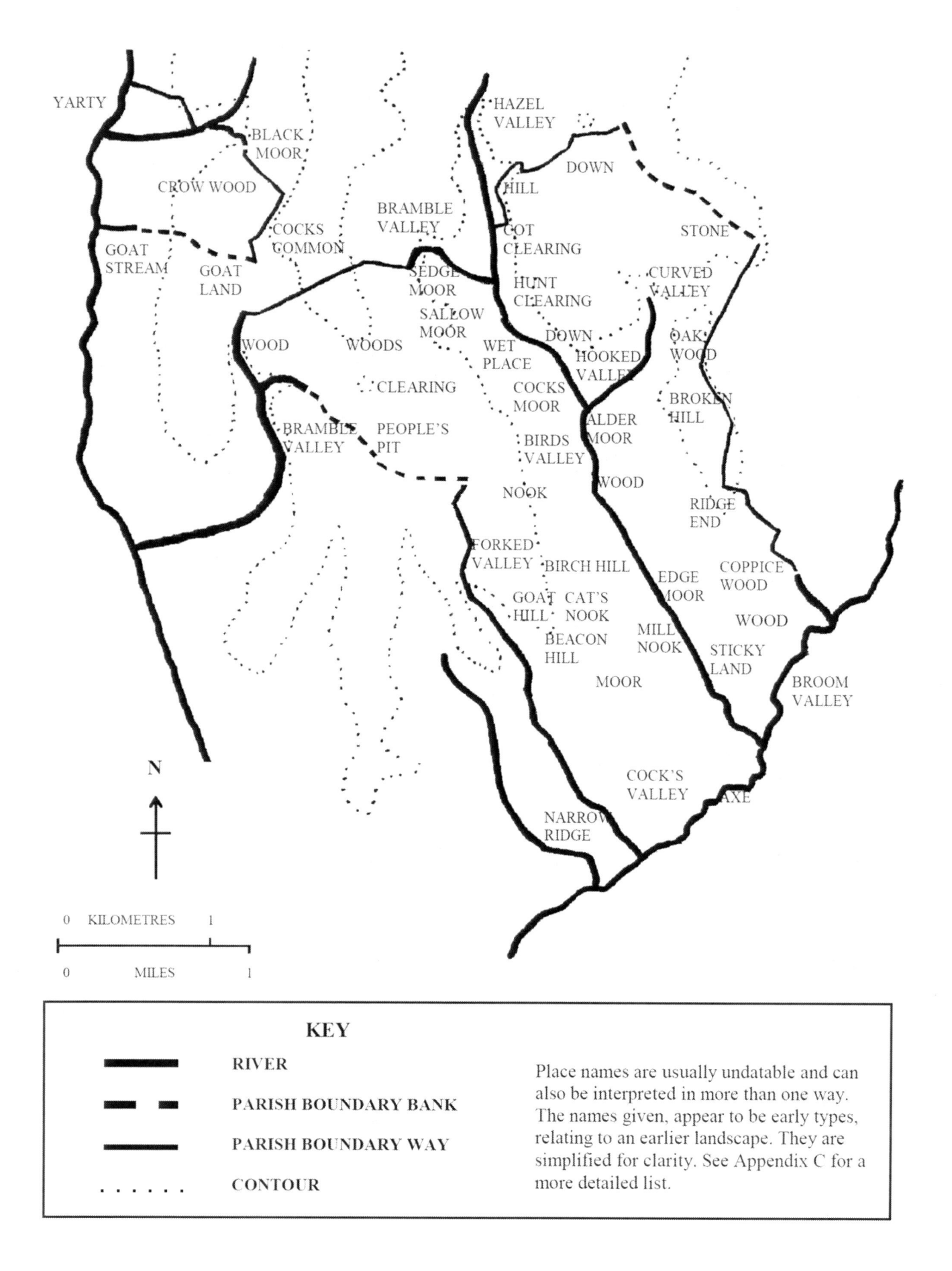

MAP 3. Topography, Place Names and Boundaries

his son, Anthony Henley, the third Baron Henley inherited the lease. On the death of Bishop Walter Kerr Hamilton in 1869, the manor was vested in the Ecclesiastical Commissioners and in 1870 an agreement was made that it should be conveyed to Baron Henley for the sum of £51,000. He immediately mortgaged it to the Corporation of the Sons of the Clergy for £52,000 and interest. It continued in the Henley family from the date of the conveyance in 1873 until 1915. During this time it was subject to many mortgages. Finally it was divided into lots and sold at two separate auctions in 1915 and 1916 by Frederick, the fourth Baron Henley, the son of Anthony. The central part of the estate together with the Lordship of the Manor was acquired by Isaac Lisle-Smith. He had married Maria Jane Wale whose family had farmed at Court Farm, the principal farm on the estate, once the demesne land. It subsequently passed to his son, Alick Lisle-Smith and then to his grand-daughter, Mrs. Kathleen Milford. On her death in 1999, the Lordship of the Manor passed to her son, Jonathan Milford, who now holds the title.

The Parish of Chardstock
The parish had its origins as an administrative area of the Church, but also fulfilled a civil function as part of the county structure. The area of Crawley was transferred to Membury in 1883 under the Divided Parishes Act. Chardstock civil parish was originally part of Dorset, but was transferred to Devon in 1896. At this time, the adjoining parish of Wambrook, once part of Chardstock, was added to Somerset. Chardstock ecclesiastical parish was originally in Salisbury Diocese. It was transferred to the Diocese of Bristol when it was formed in 1542 before returning to Salisbury in 1836. In 1840, the Consolidated Chapelry of All Saints was formed from Chardstock and Axminster Hamlets. During the 1970s, the Crawley portion of the Chardstock ecclesiastical parish was transferred to Yarcombe. In November 1978, Chardstock and All Saints ecclesiastical parishes were moved into Exeter Diocese and are now part of the Axminster Team Ministry. All Saints civil parish was formed from part of Chardstock and Smallridge in 1990.

Sources
Calendar of Patent Rolls, Somerset Local History Library.
Carter, R. W., Parmiter, M. & Wood, P. J. 1977 Parish Surveys in Somerset - Wambrook
Commonwealth Records, Birmingham Public Library.
Davidson, J. 1833 British and Roman Remains in the Vicinity of Axminster.
Division of the Manor of Chardstock, 1582 British Library.
Jones, W. R. and Macray, W. D. Sarum Charters and Documents.
Manor Court Rolls. Dorset Record Office.
Milford, Mr. M. G. Private Documents.
Morris, J. 1983 Dorset Domesday.
O'Donovan, M. A. 1988 Sherborne Charters.
Pearce, S. M. 1983 The Bronze Age Metalwork of SW England. BAR 120 ii, 507 no.20.
Poole, A. L. 1955 The Oxford History of England - Domesday Book to Magna Carta 1087-1216.
Pulman, G. P. R. 1875 The Book of the Axe.
Poor Rate Books - Chardstock. Devon Record Office. 2590A/PO.
Sale of the Manor of Chardstock 1646, Close Rolls, Public Record Office.
Sale of the Manor of Chardstock 1915, Catalogue.
Trewman's Exeter Flying Post newspapers.

MAP 4. Prehistoric Sites and Find Locations in the Chardstock Area

Chapter Three
THE MANOR COURT

Four Manor Court record books survive, covering a period from 1585 to 1787. The second volume, for the years 1672-1702, is written in 17th Century Latin and the others in English. Unfortunately it has proved impossible to obtain a translation of the Latin in the second volume. These books contain many interesting references to the land and buildings which belonged to the Manor. It is not clear who built these but it seems that the tenants and copyholders were responsible for the maintenance of their accommodation and holding or tenement as it was called. This Chapter deals with some of the responsibilities of the Manorial tenants.

Tenancies
Under the Chardstock Manorial System, most of the land and cottages were held on copyhold tenancy. An entry fee was payable when the tenement was let out, and an annual rent was collected. The copyhold was subject to "lives", the tenant having a copy of the entry in the Manor Court book. On the making out of the contract, up to three lives could be named, usually the copyholder and then two of his named children, usually the two eldest sons, but failing their existence, girls could be included. On the death of the holder, his widow, if any, would inherit, providing she did not marry again. She also lost the holding if she had a bastard child. Next came the two nominated lives in the order set out. If there were no survivors, the property fell again into the hand of the Lord of the Manor and would be re-let on a fresh copy. If new lives were needed, the property was handed in and taken out afresh with the new lives added. Normally in order to obtain a copyhold, it was necessary for the would-be holder to be born in the manor, but owners of "leaseholds" could also qualify. The leasehold method of landholding usually extended for 99 years and could be left in wills to any nominee. A much more usual method for a man to enter a copyhold was by marrying a female "life". All women's inheritance went to their husbands on marriage. There are many references in the Manor Records of Copyholds changing hands and an entry for 28th June 1762, provides a typical example.

Samuel Dommet of Chardstock, cordwainer, (shoemaker) took a tenement, orchard and two fields of 6 acres late in the possession of Francis Soaper, deceased, in the North Tithing. Two little plots of ground parts thereof at Huntley excepted. Held for the lives of Isaac Dommet aged 2, Sarah Dommet aged 7, and Ann Dommet aged 5, son and daughters of Samuel Dommet.

An example of a widow inheriting is taken from 12th April 1599. "Walter Denman died tenant of two cottages in Chardstock town and Syble his wife is admitted for her widowhood." When a widow died, no heriot was levied. A heriot was at this time a money payment by the heir and was, in effect, a death duty. It originated as the duty of an heir to return to his lord military accoutrements, perhaps a horse, harness and weapons supplied to the deceased. In the Norman period it became a gift to the lord of the best beast belonging to the late tenant of a property. In October 1600, it was recorded that "Margaret Woolmyngton dyed sithens (after that) last court tenant to a xv acre tenement and there is no herriot because she was a widow. William Woolmynton ought to have the tenement for his life."

Often before the Manor Court proceedings were recorded in the Court Book, there appears a list of the customs of the Manor. The following entries are taken from the Manor Court Book 4, covering the years 1750-1787.

30th April 1779
We Present that one Life upon a Copy in possession and Three in Reversion is Good and Warrantable.
We Present that no man by our custom can buy the Reversion of another man's Estate or Copyhold Tenement without the steadholder's consent which is the last life living on the copy.
We Present that a Reversion copy on a Reversion copy is a void grant.
We Present that no Amercement (i.e. a Manorial fine) can be gathered before it be affeered (or confirmed) by the Tenant.
We Present that no Tenant by our Custom can keep any more stock upon the Common in the summer than his Copyhold Estate can winter.
We Present the Northmoor do belong to the Copyhold Tenants and no other and it is to be lett out at Michaelmas old style to Candlemas for the use of the Copyhold tenants and no others.
We Present that no Copyhold tenant can lett or sell his Common Except he sell his whole Copyhold therewith.
We Present that Chillpitt Pitt, Green Lane Pitt, Hookfield Pitt, Bloody Pitt, to be the Common Pitts for the Copyhold tenants to dig marle and stone to be used upon the Premises and no others.
We Present that the Commons do belong to the Copyhold tenants and no others.
We Present that it is Contrary to our Customs for any person to dig Marle or Earth upon the Commons and carry it to the Leasehold Ground (and Freehold Ground - 1781 version).
We Present the Reeve shall drive the Commons three times a year between Mayday and Michaelmas.
We Present that any Copyhold tenant can cutt any tree growing upon the same Copyhold Estate to be used upon the Premises the Reeve to have a penny for the Delivery of the same if the Reeve refuses two or three of the tenants may deliver the same.

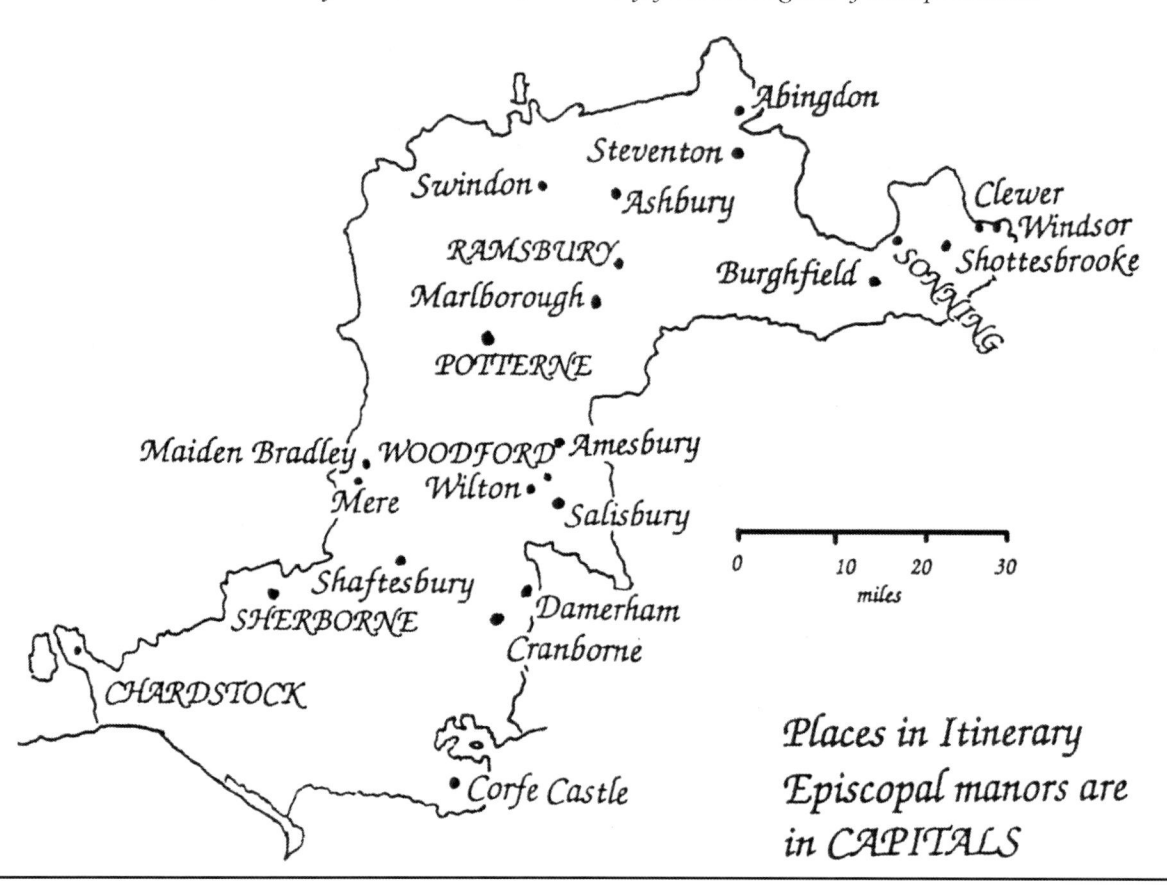

MAP 5. *Salisbury Diocese in late 14th Century, from the Register of Bishop Waltham*

Places in Itinerary
Episcopal manors are in CAPITALS

PLATE 2. *Chardstock Manor House*

Commonage

The Commons did not, as is popularly supposed, belong to everyone. They were the property of the Manor and were governed by the regulations of the Court. Only certain tenants were allowed to use them for pasturing, the number of animals being strictly controlled. In 1597, John Pynnye had to show the Court by what authority he was using South Common, and John Marsh was accused of using the common where he had no right. In 1603, Richard Turner of Membury was accused of depasturing and feeding 80 sheep on the waste of the manor. It was stated that he folded the sheep on land belonging to the Deans and Canons of Windsor, contrary to custom. He was amerced (fined). He must have been bringing his sheep from Membury to feed illegally in Chardstock. The next year, the Court noted that "Mr. Lowde doth use the common with horses and other beasts where he hath no right. Day given him to put them out of the common or else to show cause to the contrary." The same year, "John Clode doth overcharge common with wether cattle and sheep amerced (fined) 1d." and William Pouldon "doth overcharge the common with his cattle amerced xii d." The tenants were not allowed to cut the furzes growing on the commons and there are numerous instances of offenders being fined for this practice. In 1597, Robert Pitcher and his family were brought before the Court accused of felling furzes on the common to bake sale bread. This was probably surplus bread to sell, either in or out of the Manor, rather than for the tenant's own consumption. In 1602, Thomas Willse was one such offender. He "doth fell furzes in the common at Bewlydowne and doth bring the same home to his house and doth sell the same to some of Charde. He is amerced xx s (£1) and a payment of xxxix s xi d (£1 19s 11d) is given him to have the same (i.e. he also had to buy the furzes) and not to fell any more furzes there to sell." Furze was used as fuel, particularly for baking, and the young growth as fodder for horses and cattle.

Repairs

With so many houses roofed with thatch, fire was always a worry. In April 1750, John Chard, the elder, customary tenant, surrendered ground "where a cottage lately stood destroyed by fire lying in Chardstock Town." John Chard, the younger of Chardstock, yeoman, was granted the land. There are numerous references to fireplaces, known as mantels, being in decay and needing repair (also see Chapter 10). In 1595, Mary Seward's mantel was in decay. In 1597, John Welsh of Chardstock and Nicholas Westofer of Alston were ordered to "amend" their mantels. In 1598, Widow Seward, Widow Strong and others, were forbidden to make fire before their mantels were amended. In 1597, William Vincent, a tenant of the Manor, was instructed to make stiles on a footpath behind a barn leading to Chard. Hedges and the control of water were a constant problem. In 1598, Nicholas Chubb was ordered to repair a hedge at Townsend "in the inside" and John Parris had to do the same. The Court decided to view the hedges of William Hellends at Ostham to see "whether they be noisome to Mr. Bowditch and also Mychell's houses." The hedges in the whole of Hountely Lane were overgrown and those tenants who had ground against them were to cut them before Christmas. The same trouble occurred at James Lane in Crawley, and Christopher Bonde and John Baylys were told to "amend their hedges." Ditches were also the responsibility of the tenants and in 1600, the Court noted that Alice Parrocke ought to scour her ditch against Robert Atkings. In 1603, an entry reads "The ditch of Johane Staple against her meadow is very much in decay and the way is much decayed thereby. Therefore she hath a day given her to scour and ditch sufficiently the same ditch." Another entry for the same year instructs "The widdow Denman and Thomas Turner to repair their hedge agynst the waye and keep in the water by the hedge belowe the churchyard toward Mill." In 1602, the water at Bramblecombe had been "turned out of his course" by William Parris. He was given a day "to turn the same into his ancient course." In 1604, it was noted that "All Wolmyington Lane is foundrous by the water running there at flood time in the default of the tenants of Wollmyngton Farm viz. Mary Parris, Robt Parris, Thomas Parris, John Parris Therefore day is given them to turn the water there into their ground and continually there to keep the same to amend the said land and also to cut the hedge adjoining thereto before the first day of May next upon pain of viii s iiii." (8s 4d). In 1755, the Vicar was in trouble with the Court, and the entry in the record reads "Wee present the Revd. Mr. Hele for turning the water at Viccaridge Shoot out of its course into his Fishpond." Throughout the years there are many more examples of overgrown and poorly maintained hedges and ditches.

Licences

The tenants were granted various licences by the court. One of these gave the holder the right to dig marl. Marl was decayed chalk obtained from pits and spread on the ground as a fertiliser. The following examples illustrate how important it was to hold such a licence. 1595, "Licence to John Turner to make a pit in Eggmore to make good his tenement which he holds by the service of a capon to be paid at the audit next after Michaelmas." April 1598, "Licence to George Harvey to dig marl in common by Knights house and carry it out of Manor to his tenement at Rudge." October 1599, "Licence to Christopher Collynes to dig and make a marl pit on Bewly Down near Bremalcome (Brimblecombe) and to carry marl thence to Bewly Ground called Broadecrofte and Collynes Close paying a fat capon at the next audit." Some tenants did not bother to obtain the necessary licence and in the margin of the records for October 1601 is written "no marle pitt to be digged without license". Andrew Parrocke was one of the offenders who annoyed the court officials in 1601. "The tythingman of the South doth present that Andrewe Parrocke hath digged a marl pitt on Eggemore without lycence Amerced xv s (15s) or a good fat capon."

Licences to allow legal action to be taken were also granted. In April 1602, a licence was granted to Thomas Pears, a customary tenant of the manor, to sue John Baylye who was another customary tenant. The cause of the dispute is not given and the matter is not referred to again in the records. If a tenant wished to let his cottage or tenement he had to apply to the court for permission. The following example is taken from the court records for April 1599, "Licence granted to George Wilse to let his cottage lying near Farway Marsh to Richard Wollmyngton for eight years."

Estrays
Animals appear to have strayed over considerable distances from their owners, and there are a number of references to claims for repossession. In October 1597, Thomas Pears had "a ram hog in his custody one year of age came as a stray." In April 1602, James Hill and Peter Cope of Staplegrove and Abraham Graunte of Lawrence Lydeard, both in Somerset, came to the court to prove that a colt which had appeared in Chardstock belonged to James Hill and was not "thief stolen". The following October, Thomas Pears of Wambrook proved that "a strayer colt colour black being in the Hayward's possesion to be his own proper goods and not thief stolen." A similar claim for a horse in the custody of John Chubbe was made by William Fenner of Taunton.

Later Courts
Most of the entries in the later Manor Court Books refer to the letting of the various tenements and copyholds. There are some records of property "out of repair", for example in 1739, John Newberry's barn, George Grubham's dwelling house and Mr.Gare's stables at the Five Bells were all out of repair. An unusual entry in 1744 states, "We present the Axminster Summer House (?) is out of repair." There are also a number of entries relating to the deaths of copyholders, when the copy would be handed in and the next holder, whose name is very often given, admitted. For example in 1718, Nicholas Chubb was admitted to a cottage and garden on the death of Thomas, his father. In May 1732, Isaac Dean on the death of Sarah Dean, was admitted to two tenements in the North Tithing called Ridge, 52 acres. April 1746 Deaths, "Joan Crabb next taker Mary Godwin. John Bragg next taker his widow." The copyholders were required to attend the Court and in 1785, several tenants were fined 2s 6d each for non-attendance. There are, of course, many other entries too numerous to mention but of great assistance when tracing people and property.

During the 19th Century, the Court became a shadow of its former self and was reduced to meeting twice a year to collect the rents from the tenants. By 1877, it had become known as "Lord Henley's half yearly Rent Audit." A report in "The Chard and Ilminster" newspaper dated 10th November 1877 is typical of what was really a social occasion. "On Monday Lord Henley's half yearly rent audit was held at the George. After business Lord Henley, as usual, sat down to dinner with the tenants. Toasts were given to the Royal Family by Lord Henley and to Lord and Lady Henley by Mr. R. Wale. Lord Henley thanked the tenants for regular payment of rent and hoped agriculture would be more prosperous. He said "Good cottages near the farm and a good plot of garden ground near the cottage would be thought more of by the men than a shilling more a week." Lord Henley left and a sociable evening followed. Bells rang out and in the evening a bonfire was lighted in a field near the village.

In 1887, the newspaper reported that only the more important tenants attended the meeting presided over by Lord Henley. On the following Saturday at the George Inn "about 40 of the smaller paying tenants" were given a supper over which Mr. Robert Wale, the Steward, presided. It was also reported that "Lady Henley during her short stay in the neighbourhood has been busy visiting the farmers' and labourers' wives in the parish. Her Ladyship being a great favourite among the cottagers." The last court was held in 1925.

Sources
Chard & Ilminster News, Som. Local Studies Library.
Manor Court Books, Chardstock. Dor. R.O.

Chapter Four
STEWARDS' ACCOUNTS OF THE MANOR IN THE 15th & 16th CENTURIES

The earliest Account surviving is for the year 1422/3 and was that of John Crowne, who was the Reeve or Steward of the Manor of Chardstock. The Accounts deal with items under various headings. Some of these are given below, together with examples taken from the two similar accounts of 1422/3 and 1426/7. The preamble to the second of these accounts records that owing to the death of John Chaundler, Bishop of Salisbury 1417-26, the episcopal seat was vacant and King Henry VI, as feudal overlord, was paid instead the sum of 100s 6d. It is possible that John Chaundler stayed in Chardstock in August 1422. In the section of the account devoted to hospitality, John Crowne, Chardstock Steward, spent 3s 2½d in providing lodgings for the Bishop, and Richard Fyton, Bishop's Steward, submitted a bill of 3s 1d for his "expenses of hospitality."

Income of the Manor
(a) Rent paid by the Tenants
This included various fixed rents amounting each year to £28 7s 11¾d. Other rents were for pasture and a sheeprun holding on Beledowne. John Smyth of Membury rented land, "for common of pasture which he holds for 80 sheep on Beledowne". Some of the land was in the process of being enclosed. One entry reads "rent from Thomas Glover for one piece of enclosed land he has containing 2 acres, and that assart (rough land, cleared and hedged) enclosed lately formerly belonging to Robert Crokhole". 12d. was paid by Robert Geol (or Eoel) for Common of Pasture he has on Beledowne formerly William Osinere's (or Osmere) in Deneworth. Rents were paid for gardens, one being called "La Strete Orchard". Matilda Stille paid 4d for three meadows in the lord's demesne (land retained by the lord for his own use, i.e. the Manor farm) in the Oldeland. This was a holding which had no common rights attached to it. She held it for a term of 60 years. William Wagge (of Wagg's Plot?) paid 8s for 10 acres of land at Furseham which he held for the term of his life.

Chief rents, of 3d and 4d, were paid to the lord as a form of poll tax by freeholders described as "native born". Robert Farewey should have paid 4d in 1422, but paid "nothing this year as he is a fugative from the lord." William Knap paid nothing because he was in the lord's service at Sherborne Castle. Other rents were not paid for a variety of reasons. These were called defaulted rents and they amounted to 13s 3½d in 1422. One of these was from tenements which must have been held by the Manor at Lyme Regis. The relevant entry reads, "In defaulted rent for flooded tenements at Lym drowned by the waves of the sea ... 6s." Obviously the coast was receding in 1422 as it is today. There was a defaulted rent "for common of pasture in Beledonne of which William atte Water was formerly tenant, now the said William has died and nobody can be found to take care of the said pasture, therefore there is a defaulted rent of 12d." John Smyth had given up his cottage "and it lies in decay", so the annual rent of 4d remained unpaid.

A number of rents were not paid in money but in kind. Examples of such rents are 9lbs of iron paid by John Crowne for a tenement, and 9lbs of iron paid by William Fareway for a tenement formerly John Cakebread's at Farway. This may have been at the holding now known as Brockfield, where there was a field called Colliers in 1781. Possibly charcoal was being made there and used in the production of the iron. The total of rents in iron was 67lbs. 2lbs of wax was the rent from Robert Pope for a tenement formerly that of John atte Yerde. 4 horse-shoes were the rent from Elizabeth Joce for a tenement. Nothing was received this year "because the said Elizabeth has relinquished her tenancy and it lies decayed and no-one can be found to care for it." Some rent had even been paid in nuts, although by this time most had been commuted to money payments.

(b) Payments of money, called Threshings
These were made by tenants instead of performing the customary service to the lord. Examples of this are 2s for customary work for harrowing from John Elyot for one tenement formerly John atte Hakes in Chatteshole. 4d for the services of William Deth for sowing part of Mullhele taking the labour as cash this year. 4s for ploughing 8 acres of customary land this year for winter sowing for 6d per acre. In 1426, 6d customary work from William Deth for the liberty of boar in the meadow of Mullehele which he has fixed in pence. For a year's boar rent 2d and for half his customary rents and for this year's rent 4d.

(c) Profits from Miscellaneous Sales
Various detailed accounts of sales made, include the iron received as rent, wool, sheep skins, corn, an ash tree and underwood from Eggmoor. 5s 11d was received for pannage for pigs. The 2 lbs of wax received in rent was sold for 12d and the 67 lbs of iron was sold at ¾d a pound for 4s 2¼d. 4s 10d was received for ox hides, and a note was added explaining that two of the animals died of disease and one bullock was slaughtered. William Page was charged 3d for pressing apples and making one cask of cider at the lord's mill called La Musemull. The account notes that there would have been more, but the fruit was defective this year. The site of the "Musemull" is not known. Presumably it was the lord's cider mill! One old ploughshare was sold for 6d, and 4s was charged as rent for 8 hens per annum. 4s 8d was received for 8 quarters of lime, 6d for fattening bullocks and 6d for selling dung from the sheepfold at Axmede. The total profits for the year were £5 17s 1d.

(d) Profits from Sales of Pasture, Corn and Stock

The sales of Pasture were not very profitable in 1422/23, as it would appear that the lord's sheep and oxen "depasture" most of the available land. That which was sold, or let, was at a reduced amount owing to "the lack of a buyer". Other land was lying fallow during the year and therefore could not be let, and so the total income was only £2 4s 5d. 1426/27 seems to have been a better year, the income having risen to £4 7s 10½d. The income from sales of corn and stock was greater, amounting to £23 15s 1¾d. Wheat was sold at 6s a quarter, oats at 2s 4d a quarter, a mare at 3s, a bullock at 9s, a cow at 6s, a sheep at 10d, a ewe at 8d, a pig was valuable at 2s, a capon at 3d and a hen at 2d.

(e) Fines and Heriots

A fine was a payment by a tenant on entering a property. A heriot was a gift of the best beast or in later times goods, or a money payment, by the heir to a manorial property, paid at the death of the copyholder. William Tornor paid 3s for entering a messuage (a house and the land around it) and land at "Tiderlegh". Robert Tornor, the previous holder, had died and his widow, Agatha, had given the lord two cows as the heriot when handing in the tenement. A fine of £1 6s 8d was paid by John and Thomas Wagge, natives of Chardstock, "for a licence to hold land at marriage".

Expenditure of the Manor
(f) Miscellaneous Expenses of the Manor

New iron shoes costing 5s were bought for 18 bullocks used for the sowing of winter corn. Pit coal, worth 2s 4d, and wood coal (probably charcoal), worth 12d, was bought for use in "steeling" ploughs. This may have been for edging wooden shares. A carpenter was employed to make plough boards and sharebeams, to which the shares were fixed. Payments were made for ploughing, sowing and harrowing the lord's land and for grease, whipcord and harness for the waggons used on the Manor. A "roofer" was employed to work on the roof of a cow shed. He also worked on walls between the long stable and the churchyard, between the chancellor's room and the lord's bakehouse, and the kitchen and the bakehouse for 8 days at 4d a day. He was also given a dinner costing 2d each day. We do not know if the villagers were expected to obtain their bread from the lord's bakehouse in the same way that they had to mill their corn at the lord's mill, or at a "customary mill". As late as 1602, a Licence was granted, by the Manor Court, to Robert Pitcher "to sue all the Clevehill tenants and other customary tenants that ought to grind at his mill for not grinding there".

A tiler was paid 5d a day for tiling the latrine of the chancellor's room. This took him 2½ days and he spent a further 2 days working on the corn barn. 1200 tiles for roofing several houses cost 3d each but stone tiles for the sheepfold were only 2d each. Sheep were important; 19d was expended on just under 2½ gallons of tar for tarring the sheepfold and 2s 4d "on grease for the same". The steward notes the cost of bread, beer and meat "bought for various men and women, and handed out at the request of the reeve, for the lord's sheepfold, this year given out 3s 7d". A new key for the door of the chancellor's room cost 2d and 10d was spent in buying a wheelbarrow. A man was paid 3½d a day for fencing part of the lord's park, and another 3d a day for cutting and carting wood at Mullhele. Weeding the crops cost 10s 8d and was expensive "because of the great multitude of thistles this year". It was also a wet year for haymaking, and the hay had to be turned 5 times. At harvest, 24 men and women were employed in binding sheaves and carrying the corn. They consumed 30 gallons of beer at a 1d a gallon, but it is not clear from the accounts if this was for the whole period or every day! The carter, the drover and the shepherd were each paid 6s 8d a year, and the bailiff's salary was £1 a year.

(g) Livestock, Corn, Nuts, Apples and Cider etc.

(This and the following section, which appear under expenditure, seem as though they should form part of the assets of the Manor).

The accounts give details of the numbers of animals kept on the demesne of the Manor. There were 5 horses and 1 mare which had been received as a heriot from Edward Tilie. There were 21 oxen and 6 cows, one of which was lame. The accounts of sheep, pigs and chicken are complicated, showing how important these animals were. As far as can be ascertained, there were 161 sheep, 2 rams, 61 ewes, 54 young rams and 106 lambs. 435 fleeces were recorded. The accuracy of the figures of 1 boar, about 12 pigs, 20 piglets and 117 chicken is doubtful. Corn grown on the Manor's arable land was listed as wheat, barley and oats. Various amounts of hay, nuts, malt and apples, from which 3 pipes of cider (each containing about 126 gallons) were made, are also included in the account. Of these three pipes, two were sold.

(h) Farm implements

There were 2 ploughs with all the necessary apparatus, 2 furravers of iron, 2 summer plough shares, 2 coulters, 8 yokes with keys and irons for the same, 2 harrows with iron teeth, 1 pulley for a horse collar, 4 collars, 4 harnesses, 2 new carts made from the lord's wood, 1 cart bound with iron, a glue pot for use with the carts, seed baskets, a long plank table with 3 trestles, an iron bucket bound with iron catches for drawing water, 1 tub, 1 wheelbarrow and 2 forks for dung! There were 2 furnaces, 1 in the kitchen and 1 in the bakery. 1 mill with 2 stones was included in the list.

1537/8 Accounts

An account made in 1537/8 by John Clerke, Steward of the Manor, survives and follows a similar pattern to that of 1422 but is not so detailed. It deals mainly with the rents received, and does not include payments made or an account of animals, crops and farm implements.

1545 Accounts

The 1545 account also survives and is similar to that of 1537/8, referring to many of the same people and much of the same land. The Reeve or Steward was William Grange, his immediate predecessor being Nicholas Stedham. The Assise or fixed rents are stated as being £40 9s 3½d "from free tenants and customary tenants paid for four years". 20s was also collected as rent for various lands and tenements in Lyme and elsewhere. At the end of this section the following note appears, "And the account of this rent does not know where it should be levied .... 10s". In another part of the document mention is made, as in the 1422 accounts, of "rent of the lord's tenants at Lyme for the waste of the sea ... 6s". No increase had been made in the sum of 6s for over a century, but this is perhaps because in 1537/8 it was headed "Loss of rent"!

Elizabeth Forde rented, for 2s, a parcel of land lying on the common between Hooke and Bowdiche, above which William Shere had built a fulling mill. The Churchwardens of St. Andrew's were charged 3s 4d rent, 16d of which was for a stable called South Orchard. It is not known what else they rented. In both accounts, the Vicar, Thomas Hobull, rented land, formerly Robert Wyat's, in the lord's park. Also, in both accounts, John Pytt the Chaplain, pays a rent of 16d yearly. In 1537/8 it is for "one room situated within the manor house", but in 1545 this is changed to read "one ....? within the area of the manor". The room referred to may have been a private chapel for the Bishop. Perhaps the change was due to the Reformation, or to a scribe's error, or because the accounts are in Latin and difficult to read, or to a mistake in translation of the word "camera" which can mean ecclesiastical law-court held in a private house. Perhaps John Pytt was the Chancellor and the room was the one mentioned in 1422. In 1545, four courts were held and bills received by the Steward for expenses totalled 29s 1d.

In both accounts the total rents obtained from the letting of pasture is given as 72s. The names of the tenants and of the holdings are almost identical. When compared with the account of 1426/7, the amount of pasture let appears to be less, and the rent received has fallen by 15s 10½d. According to the 1537/8 account, John Player from Beere was paying a "tax" (possibly this was a rent) of 4d, Walter Pady of Crakern (Crewkerne) 12d and Henry Player of Haulechurch (Hawkchurch) 4d. However, the 1545 account states that John Player had to pay 4d to move, it is thought, to Salisbury and 12d was paid by Walter Pady for a licence to move to Crokehorn (Crewkerne). These appear to be the same people and the same amounts paid, but the wording of the entries is different. There is no mention of Henry Player in 1545.

The old manorial system was still in evidence in Chardstock in the middle of the 16th Century, although the obligation to work on the lord's land had been commuted to money. The practice of "taking the labour as money" was established long before this, as noted in the 1422 accounts as Thresshyng Silver. Following the Chardstock Manor accounts in 1537/38 is a section headed "Wutton" (probably the sub-manor of Wilmington). It would appear from these accounts that to plough an acre of ground in 1545 cost between 3d and 4d, the money being paid by the tenants instead of performing the work or "customary service". 10d was received from the customary service of harrowing by five customary tenants, each one harrowing for two days, i.e. 2d from each. There were also payments for customary work in sowing, mowing, haymaking and reaping, all on the lord's land. These were all listed under the heading "Sales of Customary Services". The Steward's Accounts suggest that life in Chardstock in the early 15th/16th Centuries remained unchanged. The inhabitants were still dominated by the manorial system, though its earlier constraints had been to some extent modified. The value of money seems to have remained about the same during the 123 years under consideration, and although there is no reference to living conditions, they may not have improved to any great extent.

Sources

Accounts of John Clerke, Reeve, 1537/8 Dor. R.O. KG1155.
Accounts of John Crowne, Reeve, 1422/23 & 1425/6/7 Dor. R.O.
Accounts of William Grange, Reeve 1545, Wilts. R.O. D1/34.

Chapter Five
CHARDSTOCK SUB-MANORS

Until 1290, the Lord of the Manor (or tenant in chief) was able to grant part of his manor, if he so wished, to another in return for knight service, thus creating sub-manors. Things became so confused that this practice was halted in 1290, except for grants made by the King. Associated with Chardstock Manor were several sub-manors. To the northwere Bowditch or Burridge, and Cotley, to the south Coaxden, to the west Wilmington and to the east Tytherleigh. There was also a small area known as the Manor of Ford. Most of the following properties were held by the same families, the Percys, Brooks Lords Cobham, Blounts Lords Mountjoy, Putts, Deans and the Eames. The Brooks and Blounts tended to lose and regain their lands as they fell in or out of favour with the monarch.

Bowditch or Burridge

In 1315/16, John, son of Richard de Bouedich, acknowledged that certain tenements, which may have been at Bowditch, belonged to his daughter Matilda and her husband, Adam Golafre. For this, Adam and Matilda paid John 100 shillings of silver. This is the first mention of the family although the name Buudihe occurs in the 13th Century. An entry in the 1332 Lay Subsidy Roll shows that Agnete Bouedych paid ii s (2s). In 1372, Robert Snouk granted land for grazing and pasture at Boneditch in the parish of Chardstock to John de Chydioke. This deed, given at Cotteleigh, also bears the name William Bakelford (Battleford). The Manor of Burridge or Bowditch was held for many years by the Brooks family, Lords Cobham, who also held Holditch Castle and Weycroft Manor. Burridge Manor passed to Charles, Earl of Devon in 1509 on the break up of Lord Cobham's estates. It must have returned to the Brooks, for in 1516, Sir Thomas Brook conveyed it to Thomas, Earl of Surrey (of the Howard family). In about 1547, the manors Bowditch, Coaxden and Wilmington were all in the possession of Catherine Parr, Queen Consort of Henry VIII. In the 18th Century, Bowditch belonged to Sir Thomas Putt (of Tom Putt apple fame) and is now part of the Cotley Estates.

Cotley

The Manor of Cotley was closely associated with that of Bowditch. In 1309/10, Geoffry de Cotteleagh and Isabella, his wife, acknowledged that the manor belonged to William de Stratton, Vicar of Chardstock. William then granted the manor, in fee, back to them. In the 14th Century, Philip Perci of Buidihe (Bowditch) granted to Nicholas, Lord of Cottelegh (probably the son of Geoffry), one acre and one perch of land in the furlong of Stapelweye which lay to the east of Motweia next to Stapelweye. Nicholas also had 3½ acres of land for which he had paid one mark (13s 4d). The rent was a rose at Midsummer for all service except, "royal service as much as belongs to so much free land in the manor of Cotteleigh".

On 7th August 1331 Simon [Meopham], Archbishop of Canterbury, granted Isabel de Cotteley a licence to celebrate divine service in a private chapel in her manor house at Cotteleye, provided the parish church of Cherdestock was not prejudiced. Isabella de Cottelegh is listed in the Lay Subsidy Roll for 1332 as paying xiii s iiii d (13s 4d). John de Chidyok, of Chideock Castle, who died in 1388, held the manor of Cotteley by knight's service, from the Bishop of Salisbury in the same way as his manor of Chardstock and Buckham. His son, also John de Chidyok, inherited the manor and granted it to John Wathecomb, Vicar of Chard, and Robert Crosse by a deed of 1388. Cotley was worth 8 marks (£5 6s 8d) a year at that time. In April 1389, John de Chidiok is recorded as making a gift to Richard Chidiok of all his goods, movable and immovable, animals, corn, ploughs etc. and household utensils, in his manor of Cotteleigh. At his death, in 1418, Sir Thomas Brook held the Manor (which was worth £10) jointly with his wife Joan, from the Bishop of Salisbury and it continued largely in the hands of the Brooks family for many years. It appears to have passed from their ownership in 1603, when an account of a dispute between the tenants of Chardstock Manor and the tenants of Lord Cobham over the ownership of a bank and ditch at Cotley is found in the Chardstock Manor Court records. The way in which these disputes were argued is interesting. The Bishop's tenants stated, "that we have commonly heard our forefathers ... and it is reputed among us that the ditch or trench which made the bank was and is also the land of the bishop ... we further say and present that the use of our country is that in whom the inheritance is, the bank is, the same is also lord or owner of the ditch or trench out of which the bank is made ..... and we do further present that there was a tree or oak, three parts of which oak or thereabouts, did stand upon the said bank and the fourth part of the said oak did stand in the inner part of the said ditch or trench, close to the said bank." The tenants then claim that only they took acorns and wood from the oak and that Lord Cobham's tenants did not stop them. The account concludes that these facts prove the bank, ditch and tree belong to the bishop. Finally we learn, "the said oak hath lately been felled by the appointment of the asssignees of the said bishop of Sarum". In 1625, the Manors of Cotley and Bowditch were conveyed by Mountjoy Blunt, Esq. to William Gardener, Gent., and later passed to Sir Thomas Putt. In 1864, the Revd. W. H. Marker, his descendant, was the owner. As with Burridge, Cotley became the property first of the Deans and then of the Eames family.

Coaxden

Little is known of the early history of the Manor of Coaxden. The Lay Subsidy Roll of 1332 lists Clemente de Cokkesden as paying iii s ix d (3s 9d) and Willelmo Cokkesden as paying xii d (12d). In 1563, John Cockesden, Gent. conveyed to Robert Crayford and Hugh Pearson, lands in Chardstock. These lands may have been part of the manor of Coaxden and in 1572, William Cockesden conveyed the Manor of Cockesden to Robert Freke and others. In 1602, Richard Simonds owned the manor, and on his death it passed to his grandson Simonds D'Ewes who was, at that time, under age. Simonds father, Paul D'Ewes, administered the property and let it to various tenants. Simonds married twice, his second wife was Elizabeth Willoughby and their son Willoughby D'Ewes is thought to have inherited the Coaxden property. The Cogans, originally stewards for Simonds D'Ewes, lived there as tenants and eventually bought it. In the middle of the 18th Century, Sarah Cogan married John Wills bringing the Coaxden property with her. Part of the house was burnt in the latter 18th Century, when it passed to the Conway family and later to the Knight family who lived there at the beginning of the 19th Century.

Tytherleigh

The first mention found of Tytherleigh is in 1155, when Gerberus de Perci left lands in Tytherleigh to his nephew Richard Gulafre, "all Eggemore from the boundary from Tytherleigh as far as the broad lache". It would seem that this manor belonged, in very early times, to the Bishops of Salisbury in their own right but it was later held on the same terms as the other sub-manors. In 1226/28, the Manor of Chardstock was quitclaimed by Ralph de Vaux to the Bishop of Sarum except the lands in "Tidderlega". In 1235/36, an agreement was made between Ralph de Tyderling and Richard de Musegros and his wife Grecia, whereby half a virgate of land at "Tyyderly" was warranted to Ralph for one pair of gloves or one penny at Michaelmas. In 1254/5, an agreement was made between William, Bishop of Salisbury and Eudo de Rocheford and Grecia his wife, for half a carucate of land in Tyderlegh, the rights being due to the Bishop in return for 60 marcs of silver. Richard de Tyderlegh appears on the Subsidy Roll of 1327, when he paid xii d (12d) and in 1332, when he paid iij s (3s). In 1380, a member of the Tytherleigh family (possibly named William) did homage to the Bishop for lands held in the Manor of Chardstock. After the Dissolution of the Monasteries, the Manor was held by Henry, Duke of Suffolk, who conveyed it to William Coxton, gent. The Daccombe family became owners and in 1606, William Daccombe sold it to Henry Henley of Leigh, Somerset. For many years the Tytherleighs were leaseholders, and they ultimately acquired the freehold. In his will of 1577/8, Robert Tyderlegh leaves, "proffitts" of his property of Titherlegh for the education of his children. A profligate descendant of the Tytherleighs dissipated his inheritance and in the 18th Century, the property was sold to Henry Coddrington and then to Thomas Pitts. It passed to John Stuckey in 1780, and later to his descendant John Churchill Langdon. The house later belonged to Sir Peter Emery, M.P. for the Honiton Constituency until 2001.

Wilmington

The first reference to this area again occurs in 1155, when John de Wlmintuna was a witness to Gilbert de Percy's deed which also mentions, "anything pertaining to me in the vil of Wlmintuna". Alicia de Wolmyngton paid 5s in the Lay Subsidy Roll of 1332 and in 1368, Elias de la Lynde granted to Trustees all his lands and tenements, rents etc. in Wolmyngton. In 1431, it was held by Sir Thomas Brouk. Almost a century later, in 1516, another Thomas Brook conveyed the manor to the Earl of Surrey, the eldest son of the Duke of Norfolk. The Wulmyngton Manor Court Roll for the year 1502/3, states that a Court was held on 9th June of that year. Other names and dates associated with Wylmyngton include, 1545 Elizabeth Mountjoy, 1560 Thomas Henneage, 1585 Richard Williams and Edward Wotton and 1625 Mountjoy Blunt and William Gardener. In the 18th and 19th Centuries, Woolmington belonged to the Putt family, and through the Deans it passed to the Eames family, and is now called Woonton.

Ford

The only known document to have survived from the Manor of Ford is a Court Roll for 1502/3. The manor probably lay in the Fordwater area and east of the present Chard to Axminster road. Included in the entry for June is a 4d. fine levied on John Phelpes for not repairing his hedge between Holdyche Park and Le Moreland. Sir Humphrey Stafford (the Earl of Devon) is mentioned as Landlord, and the tenants are admonished for allowing "their pigs to go about at large not ringed".

Sources

Court Rolls, Woolmington & Ford, P. R. O.
Deeds various, Dor. R. O.
Lay Subsidy Roll, Dor. R. O.
Manor Court Rolls, Chardstock, Dor. R. O.
Sarum Charters & Documents, 12/13th Cent. op. cit.
Som. & Dor. Notes & Queries, Various refs.

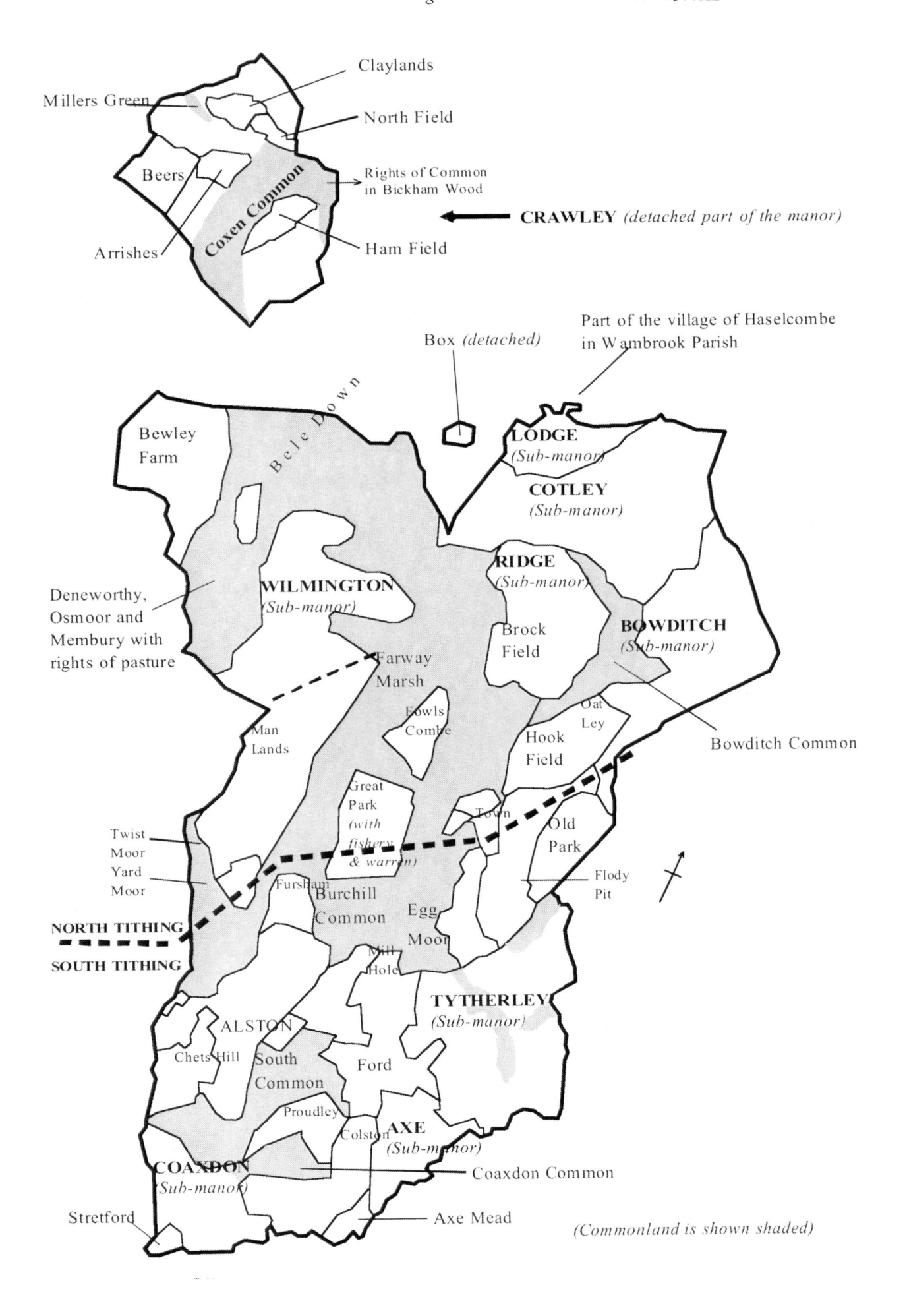

MAP 6. Chardstock Manor showing its Main Subdivisions at 1100 - 1500AD

Chapter Six
HIGHWAYS, BYWAYS AND TRANSPORT

Just as they are today, roads have always been of various ages, types and serving different purposes. For various reasons, sections would be abandoned, new ones come into use and the structure and alignment of the road be changed. This can readily be appreciated when the appearance of motorway, trunk road, country lane and footpath are considered relative to their use. Only in the last two centuries can new roads be safely dated by reference to actual records. It can be stated with reasonable certainty that many roads in modern use have an origin in the distant past, but in only a few cases can this be identified. One method is to find the earliest mention and then to speculate on what an original use or destination might have been.

In early times, travelling along the hilltop ridges may well have been the easiest, quickest and safest way, even if not the most direct. If the purpose was hunting, movement of cattle or packhorses, lower routes were sometimes preferable. Saxon charters give a very good impression of what the highly varied road network was like in this area 1000 years ago. Many Harepaths are to be found. This name means army routes, and while not only used by the army, they would have been maintained to a standard providing relatively quick and easy travel. In many cases, they originated as pre-Roman ridgeways between hillforts. The main local route, through what later became Chardstock parish, runs north from the Axe estuary. It leaves the area of Membury Hillfort and then meets what was probably a defensive cross dyke called the Grey Ditch (now the southern boundary of Chardstock parish). It passes along Bewley Down, past the Half Moon earthwork, Pulman's Circles, Wolfern Ball barrow, Whitewall ringwork (in Wambrook) and finally joins the White Way (the main Blackdown Ridgeway) at Combe Beacon barrow. The present straight appearance of much of this road is due to the 19th Century enclosure of the common land and this belies its ancient origin.

A358 Road

The most important road in this parish is now the A358 between Chard and Axminster. It was formerly a road of national importance and may have started as a Roman military frontier supply road running from Axmouth/Axminster to Lincoln, constructed in about 45 A.D. It may have possibly started near to the Roman fort of Woodbury (Axminster), where the Dorchester/Exeter road crossed it. This road, now called the Fosse Way, had regular forts along its length, the nearest to the north being probably at Ham Hill and to the south at Woodbury. It does not appear to have greatly affected the later parish development, but this would be expected, since post-Roman settlements tended to avoid Roman roads for reason of safety from raiders. Part of this remained as one of the main routes to the West Country until only 200 years ago, along the line, Windwhistle Hill, Axminster, Honiton and Exeter. All this was on Roman roads. As far as Chardstock is concerned, the road approaches the parish from the south by Weycroft (weg - a road in 1066) and crosses the meadow from Stretford (street - a paved way) to where the railway bridge is now. The first straight section then steadily climbs the hill spur in a carefully engineered way. It passes several semi-industrial sites of various ages. On the right is a meadow called Salternfearne in 1598, where formerly salt may have been made or stored. Next comes Coaxdon Mill, pit and limekilns, known to have been there in 1840 (Map 7). Finally Coaxdon (Cochesdene in 1155) is passed. The name is derived from "coccs" which were possibly charcoal kilns in a dene (or valley). Also in this short stretch is a field called Coalpit Close, the name again associated with charcoal burning. Another field nearby is named Rack Close, where cloth stretching racks would have stood. Passing Goldsmith's Lane, the road reaches the hill crest and with Tytherleigh hill in sight, turns 7° east, running straight for a mile. In doing so, it passes Red Gate and Red Lane, again names possibly to be associated with the colour of unrefined salt. Passing through the old gravel pits at Grubhams and crossing the river Kit by a ford (1423) and causeway (Forde Causey, 1600). Tytherleigh Hill is now mounted. A slight Z bend half way up deviates around an old wet area which was used to grow withies (Wallage Plot, 1781). From there, the Roman road probably originally ran in a straight line across what are now fields, to the top of the hill (Wateland 1423, Waytehill 1648) where it left the parish, turning 6° east and beginning the next mile-long straight down to Perry Street (Per - eg may possibly be the name of the river). It must be said that apart from its engineered quality, nothing has been found in the parish to confirm this part of the road as Roman. It is likely that it has always taken very heavy traffic and travellers and even armies on it, no doubt, sometimes caused problems. The two "wet spots", Ford and Red Lane are mentioned in Manorial records as being difficult to pass.

The road was taken over for maintenance by the Yeovil Turnpike Trust in 1753, as part of the Lower Compton, Yeovil, Crewkerne, Chard, Axminster, Turnpike Road. In 1800, the section from Haselbury Bridge was transferred to the care of a Chard Trust. Milestones were placed at Red Lane (2m) and Tytherleigh Hill (3m). These consisted of two cast iron plates fixed to a triangular stone and were probably made in the parish by John Bonfield at Crawley Foundry. The hill at Tytherleigh caused a severe maintenance problem because steepness, wet spots, a ford and heavy traffic, combined to cause severe erosion of the surface. Arthur Whitehead was paid £4 4s in 1840 for a survey and map of the hill improvement. The bridge was then widened and road "inequalities" removed by Thomas Brown. The hill was widened in 1844 and Noah Bishop was compensated for loss of land. The Trust was experimenting with the use of graded stone, laid according to the famous McAdam's principles. Sections of the most highly stressed areas were relaid by the licensed contractor, John Channing or Channis, at 4s 6d per rope (20 feet). Further ballasting was done in 1863 and further widening in 1871, when the hedges were straightened at the foot of the hill, for Mr. Langdon (of Stuckey's Bank - the Trust's Treasurer). In the early 20th Century, a road gazetteer described the hill as "extremely dangerous"!

In 1830, it was decided to improve a spur road through Tytherleigh, down to Broom. In 1840, John Bonfield built a Toll House, gate and bar by the Manor House, plus a timber bridge over the Axe, for £250. A full toll was charged by the gatekeeper, who in 1851 was John Channis's wife Ann. The adjacent farmers, Mr. Cuff and Mr. Bailly, were exempted tolls. John Channis and his son, also named John, would have been a familiar sight by the road, examining flints and cracking them to size. The new bridge was underpinned with rough stone pitching, and ten culverts were also added. The Axe was a severe river to bridge. Repairs to the bridge and the approaches were needed in 1856/8, and in 1863 the building of the new railway crossing provided an opportunity for Mr. H. Howell to put in 2000 loads of stone, two new bridges and a culvert on the Chard side for £145. A new linhay was built at Tytherleigh. At Colston, the main turnpike road crossed common land. When this was enclosed in 1863, it was reported that Mr. Keech was erecting his fences 3 feet from the road. The Clerk was instructed to remind him of the regulation, 30 feet from the road centre. Keech offered compensation of £5 but not less than £100 an acre was acceptable to the Trust. Henry Keech also owned a factory at the east end of Chard, where his unloading of goods was a hazard. A final composite deal involved the purchase of land in Chard at £30, and the provision, by Keech, of a new factory entrance and gutter cover. The construction of the railway in 1858, involved co-operation with the company engineer, Mr. Galbraith, while the bridge at Coaxdon was built. In 1869, a crisis arose when the land slipped by the limestone pits. The L. & S. W. Railway Co. wanted to divert the road around the slip, but the Trust insisted that either a retaining wall across the slip was built or a major diversion, up to the bridge, was made. The river was also flooding the road beyond the bridge. The bank was repaired and a footway constructed to Weycroft Bridge. The end of the Trust came suddenly in 1875, when the franchise was not renewed by the Government. The Tytherleigh Toll House, which resembled that on Snowdon Hill, Chard, was sold to Mr. J. C. Langdon for £10 and the gates and posts to Mr. Single for £1. Sadly, it was finally demolished in the 1950s.

A30 Road

The A30 is another ancient road in the original parish, also of national importance. It ran through Crawley, which in 1150 was Craulanee, in 1155 Cranlaneie and in 1332 Cralleweye. This is a complex name in origin, suggested as crawe-hlaw-weg, road to crow hill. It entered the parish from Yarcombe at a ford over the river Yarty, just north of the present modern Crawley Bridge. Fieldwork indicates that a pre-19th. century bridge also stood there. Proceeding over Miller's Green, it continued up the hill as James Lane (1598), although it is not known who James was. After bisecting a small medieval open field, it reached Salter Hill, by Hares Farm, which again suggests a salt route. Prior to 1817, there was no road along the Crawley valley, Crawley Farm being reached from James Lane at a higher level. Other clues to the use of this old road are provided by the unique picture of a pedlar in the stained glass of Yarcombe church, and also possibly by the clear spring (Fishern Well?) high on Bewley Down which is still leated to Linnington Farm. For the early foot traveller, the normal way from Chard to Honiton was via Lower Wambrook touching the edge of the parish at Money Pit Lane (coins were found there in the 18th. Century), and on to Longbridge (called this in 1575). In 1724, it was described as "a very bad road of stones and sand over brooks and spring heads and barren downs". In 1776, much of this road was adopted and improved by the Chard Turnpike Trust, but the route by Spittle Pond at Higher Wambrook was preferred. The sections of new hedge planted in beech at this time can still be seen along Causeway Lane near Money Pit Lane. The Ilminster/Honiton Turnpike was constructed to the then most modern and highest standard, and this ran across the Down above Yarcombe. It was therefore decided in 1817, to abandon the Stockland section of road and build a totally new and carefully graded road down through Bickham Wood, along the Crawley valley to James Lane, and then to improve the road to the Devonshire Inn on the Ilminster Turnpike. A new bridge appears to have been built south of the old one and consisted of a segmental arch with projecting keystones and a circular flood opening in each haunch. The section from the River Yarty at Miller's Green to Crawley Farm was known as the New Turnpike Road, but the subsequent twisting sections to Chard proved unpopular. A replacement embankment and deep cutting was finally built through Bickham Wood in 1829. Part of the road, in Crawley Bottom, was recorded as stolen by an encroachment in 1865. Then three years later, a series of complaints prompted the Trustees to instruct the Contractor, Mr. Gardner, that unless the cause of the complaints was removed, his contract would be suspended. The route became the A30 trunk road, and was for many years the main road from London to the West of England. Finally it was reduced in status again, in favour of the Ilminster road, the A303. Crawley bridge was swept away by floods in the 1960s and a new one now stands on the spot.

Other Ancient Ways
Another ancient road is the Farway (Farneie, Faiei 1155, Farewey 1332) which probably implies "busy road used by wayfarers". It appears to have led westwards from the top of Stockstile towards Bewley Down. In 1600, it was the Farway Bridge Road called Style. Battleford (Bakelford 1332) was possibly Baccela's ford. A steep way from Smallridge crossed the river there, and then divided into Coaxden and Chardstock branches. The latter passed through Alston as Alston Street, and then is mentioned in 1582 as Alston Causeway. The branch to Chardstock village continued to Kitbridge, where in 1599, the Kitbridge was to be rebuilt. Another early bridge out of repair, was Charne Bridge (1596) by Axe Farm. Charne possibly alludes to foaming water in the river Kit.

In 1101 there is a reference to the demesne fields between Eggmoor and the top road. This presumably refers to a Chardstock/Tytherleigh road. One old road ran from Chardstock Green, along the top of Eggmoor to the lane just below Tytherleigh Manor House, continuing as the road to Holditch.

Haleway is mentioned in 1332. There are five or more "Hales" in the parish, now known as Sharks Hole (Chattoshale 1422), Holy City (probably La Hole 1422), Hell Bottom (no early reference), Hole Hooke 1582 (unidentified) and Mulnehale 1201 (Mill-hale, unidentified). The name means hollow, which in this area is generally wet, e.g. as Halewell 1426 (unidentified) "spring in a hollow", testifies. It is uncertain where Haleway was, but Holy City seems likely. Parkway is mentioned in 1422 and may have run to, or was in, the area of Park/Parrock, names south of Cuckolds Pit. Churchwey occurs in 1422 and is presumably Dead Man's Lane, to the south of the church. Stapleweye occurs in 1327, and possibly passed near a large stone or staple. These may have been the outcrops beside the lane east of Burridge. Various other way names occur after 1500 but are not listed here. The roads in the centre of the village must have existed from very early times, and that to Huntley is mentioned in the Manor Court Rolls of 1598 as being overgrown. An entry for 1600 states that, "There is a common footpath leading from the top of Green Lane on 'thold parkes' and then directly to Stockham (Stockstyle) for all the Queen's subjects". The layout of roads on the 1781 Estate Map is much the same as that of today. In 1743, a road from Burridge Common (and from Chardstock?) to Chard was described as "the King's Highway".

River Axe
Just north of Broom Bridge is a field called Great Ernest. In 1155, this was Anestathes and in 1515, the other side of the river Axe was Avernas. This appears to be an intriguing reference to the river being used for transport, the name meaning single landing place. The probable site of this has been found, and it is interesting that Broom Lane appears to have run to it and not across former meadow strips as it does now. The use of the Axe for navigation was seriously considered in various schemes for an English/Bristol Channels Ship Canal that were planned in great detail between 1769 and 1824. Use of Beer as a natural harbour, Chard as a top pound level and construction to Bridgwater Docks was planned. A plan exists showing a feeder arm following the Kit Brook up to Cotley Wash and then tunnelling under Bewley Down to the Yarty. Whether this was to be navigational is not known.

Railway
The railway to Exeter was built as a branch or extension of the London and South Western Railway, running from London to Yeovil Hendford. The Contractor, Taylor, employed 3000 men, 600 horses and 2 locomotives to construct the many cuttings, embankments and bridges. The life-style of the Irish navvies so alarmed the clergy that a special mission to them was organised. Eventually, in pouring rain, the Directors left London for Exeter on 18th July 1860, in a special train of 20 carriages pulled by 3 locomotives. It stopped for speeches from local dignitaries at each decorated station. Ballast sidings were built just south of Broom Crossing, and a signal box controlled the gates and the points for the tracks into the gravel pit. This pit became of national historical importance owing to the large number of Paleolithic stone tools found there. It was worked until after the Second World War. Another crossing is at Axe Farm, and a single spur siding was at the Dorset Blue Lias Lime and Cement Works, just beyond Coaxdon. The track was doubled in 1861, but reduced to single again in 1967. At Chard Junction was a notice indicating that it was the station serving Chardstock College.

Coach Roads
It should not be thought that early roads were not busy. The rural population was much higher and what is carried by one lorry today was carried by many carts or even more packhorses. Similarly, animals were driven to market in great droves. Minor ways became eroded into deep and dangerously boggy holloways. The turnpike roads were eventually a great improvement, and allowed the growth of scheduled coach, mail and carrier services. In 1600, long before the turnpikes, John Pinney was mentioned in the Manor Court Rolls as the Chardstock carrier. In Chard in 1797, the Daily Post arrived at 10 am and left at 4 pm. Pigot's Directory in 1830, said that this was the great mail road and was the original line over which letters were conveyed prior to the establishment of mail coaches. At that time, letters from London arrived at Chard at 11.50 am and left at 2.45 pm. Going westward via Axminster, they arrived at 2.45 pm and left at 11 am daily on the Royal Mail. In January 1839, a Post Office was opened in Chardstock and by 1840, a mail cart ran directly between Axminster and Ilminster. By 1852, this had become a mail coach continuing to Taunton to connect

PLATE 3

Broom Bridge

Historian Mary Parmiter at Fordwater Bridge

Kitbridge in c. 1920

Churn Bridge, at Axe

Limit on Axe Bridge

Old Arched Entrance to Tytherleigh Manor House

The Tollhouse at Tytherleigh (demolished)

Milestone near Waggs Plot turning (the mileplates, which were probably made at Crawley Foundry, have since been stolen)

with the railway. In 1792, the Royal Clarence stage ran east/west on alternate days, stopping at the Red Lion in Chard for meals. By 1830, Chard was said to have been built up and changed amazingly. Coaches called the Devonport Mail and the Traveller ran daily on the Exeter/London route, and the Despatch and Subscription on the Axminster/Bristol run. The railway quickly killed the coach service, and by 1842 the Railway Coach ran from Axminster to Taunton. This became the omnibus service, firstly horse drawn and then motorised.

Carriers, Packhorses and Drovers
Long distance goods could be sent by carrier. In 1842, three companies provided a daily service east/west using waggons. These also ran regularly between the harbour at Lyme, Axminster, Chard, Chard Canal Wharf and the railway at Taunton. Very heavy goods travelled on the roads from early times. In 1246, stone blocks were being sent from Whitestaunton to build Newenham Abbey in Axminster. In 1851 two miles of turnpike road were stated to have been seriously damaged by Capt. Henley's timber waggons. A "hit and run, drink and drive" accident occured in April 1851, "John White, a Tatworth carpenter, who had a wife and ten children, was returning from Chard Great Market in a somewhat intoxicated condition, carrying a sack of potatoes. He was knocked down and killed on Two Ash Hill by a furiously riding horseman. Subsequent inquiries established that George Dawe, a miller from Coaxdon Mills, who was also intoxicated, had been responsible. He denied the charge, but was found guilty and sentenced to twelve months imprisonment". A correspondent writing about the roads from Chardstock to Chard in the Nowlen's Weekly Chronicle in 1859 complained, "Our village roads …. are in a disgraceful state the rough stones gives one a good idea of what they were a century or two ago when wheelcarriages were not in such general use. The hedges in some places are almost grown together and persons walking are in danger of losing their eyes. The Chard Parish district is quite as bad if not worse. A meeting was held about a year ago to have the lanes widened but nothing has been done yet". In the same year there is a report of an accident to the Taunton & Lyme Regis mail cart near the railway bridge at Coaxdon, where someone had placed large heavy stones in the road. The cart hit the stones, pitching Mr. Priddy, the driver, into a "small cavity". Fortunately he only slightly injured his knee, and was able to continue his journey. On another occasion, a horse drawing a gig from Axminster bolted after being frightened by something in the road. It ran into the Weycroft turnpike gate, which was closed at the time. This was broken in pieces, as was one of the shafts of the gig. The horse continued madly along the road, until the driver managed to get out of the gig and hold its head.

In the 19th Century, numerous brick works were making bricks, tiles and field drains to meet the greatly increased demand. The many limekilns in the area required regular supplies of cheap coal called culm. Even exotic goods such as Spanish Indigo, Woad and Madder were carried from Lyme to the dyeworks in Crimchard. Stoned roads were avoided by packhorse trains, owing to the danger of hoof damage. Drover's roads also existed and were used for a variety of animals. Oxenways is just between Chardstock and Membury, and may have been on such a route which possibly passed along Membury and Chardstock Commons.

Salt works lined the South Coast. There were eleven at Seaton in 1086, for example, and this product was carried inland to be used for food preparation etc. Typically, a packhorse way ran along the valley bottoms, avoiding as far as possible, excessively wet areas. From the packhorse bridge at Beckford, Membury, a way can be clearly traced going west for several miles. The route to the east is less clear but may have joined the Farway, previously mentioned. It was considered to be dangerous to meet a long line of linked horses laden with packs in a narrow lane.

Sources
Chard in 1851, 1969, Chard History Group.p5.
The Story of the Roads of Chard, 1968. Chard History Group. p2.

Chapter Seven
MARKETS, FAIRS, SHOPS AND TRADE

Chardstock Fair

There is not much documentary evidence of Markets and Fairs in Chardstock. An entry in the Pipe Roll of 1219 records a payment, apparently of a palfrey, owing from the Bishop of Salisbury for holding a weekly market on Wednesdays in Chardstock. Later, a fair was added and the entry in the Calendar of Charter Rolls reads, "Grant of special grace to William, Bishop of Salisbury, and his successors, of a weekly market on Wednesday at their town of Cherdestoke, co Dorset, and of a yearly fair there on the vigil, the feast, and the morrow of St. Michael, in September by King and of the said date by authority of parliament." The grant was dated 10th April 1441 at Windsor and was renewed in 1462 by Edward IV. The Fair may have continued as late as in 1859 for, in a list of fairs published in the Chard Illustrated Magazine for that year, Chardstock Fair is given as being held on "Old Michaelmas Day".

The Chardstock fair, and indeed the market, when it was concerned with animals rather than goods, may have been held on the outskirts of the village. In 1597, "The market way from Chardstock to .....?" was stated to be impassable suggesting the market, at that time, was not in the village. It is possible that fairs may have been held on Burridge Common or on land at the north end of Huntley Lane where, on the map of 1781, there were two fields called "Plaisters". The name may have come from the Old English word "plegstow" meaning "playing place".

Both the market and the fair have long since disappeared and, according to Pulman, the old market house and shambles, with the market cross, were pulled down at the beginning of the 19th Century. The site of the buildings and the cross, to which this is the only reference, is unknown. They could have been in the square in front of the George Inn, but there is no indication of this in any document so far discovered. The shambles (the meat market), is mentioned in the Manor Court Roll of 1608, when Thomas Strong and William Tyatt were presented, at the Manor Court, "for lyeing of soyle at the Shamells end in the high way". Thomas Strong lived in the east of the village in the house which was, until recently, the village shop, and is still known as Strongs. The Shambles could have been in the centre of the village, where the former police house now is. It is twice mentioned in the Poor Books. The first time is in a record of a Parish Meeting held on 19th December 1758, when it was agreed "to contract with Mr. John Leat for repairing the Shambles which he is to keep in good repair for the Term of twelve years for which he is to receive of the Parish one Pound sixteen Shillings at Easter next". The money was to be paid by the Overseers of the Poor. At the end of John Leat's contract, the Shambles was again in need of attention, and on 8th October 1773, the matter came before the Vestry Meeting. It was agreed "that Mr. James Hore shall forthwith build the Shambles wall with stone and sufft. (sufficient) quantity of Lyme and Sand and repair the roof of the Shambles and Thatch the same for the sum of three guineas and half". Unfortunately the Shambles is not identified on the Estate Map of the manor, made only about 10 years after the above entry. There is, however, on this map, a building drawn in the form of a barn or shed, which may have been the Shambles, standing on a piece of ground called Court Orchard at the corner of the road leading to Kitbridge, It is also possible that this was the old market house referred to by Pulman.

A reference to a market is to be found in Dean Chandler's Register of 1412 (see Chapter 14), when offenders were ordered to be beaten through the market. Sunday trading must have taken place in nearby towns or villages during the 15th. Century. In 1405, several villagers were accused of going to markets and fairs on Sundays, to the detriment of their attendance at church. At this time, much of the food must have been grown by the villagers themselves. Bread would probably have been baked by most people. Many things for everyday use would have been produced in the village, but obviously there was the opportunity to travel to markets held, perhaps in Chard and Axminster. In the 18th Century accounts of the Poor House, mention is made of Chard Market when, in 1792, worsted was bought there for 2s 4d. Other necessities appear to have been purchased directly from individuals in Chardstock, for example, in 1790, one hundredweight of cheese was bought from Richard Dening at a cost of £1. Soap and candles were obtained from Thomas Palmer, the candle maker, and wheat, beans and plants were bought from William Leat, the miller. Coal for the Poor House was brought from Langport and Lyme wharfs.

Chard Market

In the absence of information about Chardstock Market and Fair, the following account of Chard Market is of interest. It was originally granted on a Sunday, although from early times it was held on a Monday, and was one of the most important markets in the West Country. In 1838, the meat, butter, poultry and egg stalls were in the shambles in the new Market House, now the Guildhall, the front of which was reserved for the seed and corn market. The issue of the "Chard Union Gazette" dated 4th November 1839, contains a long description of the Monday market day from which the following information is taken. "Throughout the morning the streets resounded with the noise of carts and waggons, the tramp of horses and the lowing, bleating and squeaking of the livestock". Most of the purchases of animals, meat and vegetables seem to have been made before noon when the ringing of the town hall bell signalled the opening of the corn market. The corn was displayed in tubs and sacks from which the purchasers would use a wooden receptacle to obtain a sample for inspection. The "market house-wives" and the farmers selling the corn would then begin the bargaining process which resulted in eventual agreement of the day's price and the week's supply of corn bought. The main business of buying and selling between the farmers appears to have been carried on in the various inns, accompanied by a liberal supply of alcohol. Not only was food on sale but also a whole range of household goods and clothing much the same as in a modern market". The writer of the article in 1839 was quite surprised to find a "book-stall" providing "food for the inner man". This was a rather recent addition which he attributed to the fact that "the schoolmaster has been abroad"! The whole proceedings were presided over by the "Market-Man" or "Toll Collector" who superintended the erection of the stalls or "stannings" as they were called. He then proceeded to collect the rents or dues which was not a very popular occupation especially on a cold, wet and windy day. Apparently he could "as easily express his meaning without misunderstanding, by a certain position of his right hand, as by the use of his tongue".

In 1874, prices in Chard Market varied slightly from season to season. In July of that year, Beef was 9s 10d a lb, Mutton 8½-9½d, Pork 9d, Veal 7½-8½d, Lamb 10-11d, Bread was 7½d a loaf, butter 13-14d a lb, bacon 6s 10d a lb and new potatoes were 7lbs for 6d. Eggs sold at 1s a dozen. Note that wages were, probably, not much more than 10s a week.

St. White Down Fair
As with markets the villagers would have attended other fairs. One very important fair for the area, which began in 1361, was that known as St. White Down Fair which was held at Whitsuntide, on land adjacent to the modern entrance to Cricket St Thomas estate. The date given for Whitedown Fair in the Chard Illustrated Magazine for 1859 is 13th and 14th of June. The records of those buying and selling animals and leather from 1637 to 1649 have survived and contain several Chardstock names. However, the years 1643-1645 are unrecorded, probably due to the disruption of the Civil War, when the armies of the King and Parliament were active in the area. The following are some of the more interesting entries:-

1637 Margret Mathew of Chardstock sold to Trustrum Larkham one heifer & calfe .... iiij li 00s 00d (£4)
1639 Nicholas Turner of Chardstocke sold to Thomas Fry 21 yeawes & 19 lambes warrented sound from ye cough prize ... xi li (£11)
1641 Robert Gaylard of Cotly sold to Richard Pinny two oxen .... 9 li 12s (£9 12s)
1648 John Turner of Titherly sold a sparked heyfer & Calfe with a white starr in her forhead to William Abott of West Chinnick .... 4 li 9s 00d (£4 9s)
1649 Thomas Bond of Chardstock Bought one Black Cow & Calfe of one hee canot nominate...... 3 li 8s 0d (£3 8s)

The records of leather sales do not mention anyone coming from Chardstock.

At the Somerset Quarter Sessions held at Ilchester in 1628, John Bond of Chardstock was accused of buying and selling live cattle contrary to the statute then in force. It is not clear if this occurred at a market or if there was a private sale.

Chard Fair
The following account of Chard Fair, which was held in May, August and November each year, appeared in the "Chard and Ilminster News" for 6th May 1874. "The cattle and sheep came in early and in large numbers so that by 10 o'clock the streets were fairly crowded with the stock exposed for sale. The buyers, however, were not so eager as the sellers and business was decidedly slack". The account goes on to say that by midday all the cattle had gone and the rain began "helping to wash the pavements clean". The Gingerbread stalls did brisk business and "the lasses and lads seemed to get their share of holiday enjoyment without paying much regard to the state of the weather". The Chard November Fair held in 1907 attracted 1,500 sheep, 150 cattle and 50 horses and colts.

Musbury Fair
Some of the spirit of the traditional fair can be caught from the following unfortunate incident that was reported on 15th October 1859, by "Nowlen's Weekly Chronicle". Apparently, the wife of Mr. Miller, Confectioner of Chardstock, who was at the fair, "opened a tin of banghops (which boys buy)". It exploded and she was stated to be in a dangerous state. It is probable that these were homemade percussion fireworks that were sold as practical jokes for startling other fairgoers.

Shops
In 1599, Thomas Vyoncombe was baking bread which was not according to Assize. The Assize of Bread was an attempt to lay down standards for the weight of various kinds of bread. 16th Century Manor Court references to "sale" bread, the illegal sale of furzes for fuel, to Chard (mentioned elsewhere) and John Pynnye as the carrier, suggests trade was a continuing part of Chardstock life. It is not until the advent of the Commercial Trade Directories in the 19th Century that shops are mentioned. At this date, many shop products would have been made on the premises. In 1845, Bridget Deane, Richard Long and Robert Deem are listed as shopkeepers. Robert Deane was a bootmaker and shopkeeper, Robert Pope was a butcher, shopkeeper and farmer, while William Sumption was a grocer and draper.

PLATE 4

The Village Outing

*Pratt's Garage at Tytherleigh
(now remodelled)*

Wakley's Buses from Membury

B. Parris, Wheelwright, with his Threshing Machinery

Mr. Bonfield the Blacksmith

29

A Post Office was established in the village in 1839. This was the result of a representation to the Postmaster General by the vicar, the Revd. Woodcock. His efforts were reported in the Chard Union Gazette, which stated in January 1839, that there would be "a daily communication to and from the neighbouring town of Chard. This will be a great convenience to the inhabitants". In 1851, John Woodmelish was the sub-postmaster and in 1859, William French, who was also grocer, linen and woollen draper, a dealer in British wines and agricultural seeds, Huntley and Palmer's Biscuits and Martin & Co's Wellington manures. He was also agent for the West of England Fire and Life Insurance Company and was licensed to let horses and traps for hire. His shop was at Yew Tree Cottage. One of his advertisements, published in "Nowlens Weekly Chronicle" in 1859, is reproduced as follows:-

POST OFFICE, CHARDSTOCK.
GENERAL DRAPERY ESTABLISHMENT

WILLIAM FRENCH returns his sincere thanks to his Friends and the Public generally for the liberal support he has received for the last ten years, and begs to say that he has JUST RETURNED FROM LONDON, with a choice assortment of New, Fashionable and Plain Goods, and at such prices that will give satisfaction.

A new and great variety of Mantles, Cloaks, Black and Coloured Silks, Fancy and other Dresses, Ribbons, Flowers, Parasoles, Hosiery, Gloves, Hats, Caps, Umbrellas, &c.

An early inspection is respectfully invited.

Funerals completely and economically Furnished.

Post Office, Chardstock, May 18th., 1859.

The French family continued to run the Post Office for many years and in 1901 William French, aged 80, was the sub-postmaster. By 1906 it had moved to the Laurels, opposite the George Inn, and formed part of a grocery and draper's shop opened by Albert Brett in 1898. It remained at the Laurels until at least 1935 with the sub-postmaster/mistress being Albert Brett (1906 and 1910), Thomas Parris (1914), William Searle (1919) and Mrs. Elizabeth Searle (1923 and 1926). The telegraph came to the village in 1913. Between 1935 and 1939 Albert Brett gave up his business, the Laurels (later renamed Peperharow) was converted to a private house and the Post Office moved to Turner's Cottage in Kitbridge Lane. In 1939 the sub-postmistress was Maud Apsey. It remained at Turner's Cottage until 1988, when it was transferred to a new combined village shop and post office attached to No. 8 Westcombes and next to the Community Hall.

In 1914, Albert Brett had a grocery business at the Laurels opposite the George, and William Harris was a grocer at Strongs. This business was, by 1922, taken over by William Lentell, whose daughter, Mrs. L. A. Hodge ran the shop until it closed in 1978. There was also William Miller's bakery, in the 1940's, which became a grocer's shop in the 1950s run by Frank Huddy, and then by Mr. and Mrs. Woolford until the 1970's. It was known as "Chardstock General Stores". It was on the road to Kitbridge, on the site of the pound.

Water
The original water supply was from open springs. Pumps and wells gradually replaced these and with the coming of the mains water they also fell into disuse. A plaque on the wall of Little St. Andrew's claims to mark the site of the Village Pump. An important extraction facility for mains water is now at Hook, and a reservoir is at Ten Acre Gate.

Gas & Electricity
Gas was made in the village at a gas works situated to the west of the present vicarage. The Gas Works was erected by Mr. Henry Willey, Gas Engineer of Exeter, in 1868, and this produced gas for the church, school and for some street lights (one is now in Chard Museum). Electricity came to the village in the 1920s.

Weaving
Although Chardstock has always been represented as an agricultural village, this is only partially true. Industry has also played an important role in the development of the area. As indicated in Chapter 4 on the Steward's Accounts, iron was produced in the 15th Century. Samples of iron ore and slag waste have recently been found at several locations in the parish. Other industries were connected with the cloth trade. The will of John Parris of 1551, states that he was a weaver and that he left his "payre of Lowmes (looms) with all thy apparell therof" to his son John. Flax was grown and retted (soaked) at various sites, and there was a Dyehouse in the village in 1588. This house and Dyehouse Mead are marked on the 1781 Estate Map as being just West of the Old Vicarage. Much of the spinning and weaving was done by workers in their homes, and some of the finished products were sold as far away as London. In 1638, a Chardstock clothier, John Chard, "vented all such clothes as he hath made in London" but he gave no details of the way the transactions were arranged. In 1643, at the time of the Commonwealth, Philip Gillett supplied cloth for the use of army officers under the command of Lord Inchiquin in Ireland. In 1645, he complained that he had not received the £52 0s 11d owing to him for the cloth, neither had he been paid any interest. His complaint appears to have been upheld, but whether he actually received his money is not known. In 1741, James Welch, a clothier of Chardstock, valued his mill at £400 for insurance. In the manor survey of 1671, Thomas Marks is listed as a tenant of a fulling mill.

He had a dwelling house, garden and 2½ acres of moor. This is thought to have been on Burridge Common and was probably typical of many of the semi-industrial habitations to be found in the commons settlements such as Cuckolds Pit, Farway or Sycamore.

Lime Burning

Lime was needed for fertiliser and building mortar, and there was a flourishing lime burning industry with kilns at many locations, notably at Chilpits and Storridge. At Coaxden (near the road bridge over the railway) there are four kilns and an overgrown limestone quarry. A tramway brought stone from the quarry and also took lime from the kilns, under the main line railway and to a warehouse by the river (see Map 7). In 1865, lime and cement was manufactured by William Wheaton. By 1885, the business had become the Dorset Lime, Cement and Stone Co. having C. T. Titterton as its proprietor. In the 1890s, Samuel Mallatt was the manager and the site was known as the Dorset Blue Lias Lime and Cement Works. From 1914 to 1925, it operated as the Exeter Brick & Tile Co. Limeburning was a most dangerous occupation, and there were many accidents. One such was the subject of a report in "Trewman's Exeter Flying Post" in 1836. George Rice, a lime burner employed by Mr. Pryer, was overcome by an escape of gas while working in the kiln. Simon Pearce and William Clark went down to rescue him but they also collapsed, and a labourer named Collins attempted to save all three. He descended into the kiln with a rope tied round him and a handkerchief over his face. After returning with two of the men he was overcome while fixing a rope round the third man. On being raised to the surface he revived in the fresh air, but the other three men were dead.

Mills

Paper making was carried on by Henry Rose, who was followed by Betty Potter, at the water mill near Hook Cross in the middle of the 18th Century, and then by Thomas Apsey in the 19th. There were, of course corn mills, and the Churchwardens' presentments for the years 1599/1600 contain the following entry, "Item we present that our myller John Lange doth grinde one the Sabathe Dayes but uppon greate necessety". In the Division of the Manor document of 1582, John Coxe, John Trott and Robert Pitcher were listed as holding grist mills and John Parrock as holding a blade mill.

In 1590 a dispute arose between Christopher Stone, a barrister of the Middle Temple, who held Ford Mill, and George Cate, a copyhold tenant of Churchill. Christopher Stone complained to the Court of Requests that George Cate and other customary copyhold tenants from Alston, North Coxdon, Tytherleigh and Churchill refused to grind their corn at his mill, much to his financial loss. He said George Cate was "a frowarde and Evill disposed man" who incited other copyholders to grind elsewhere even out of the manor. In his successful reply George Cate stated that there were three ancient mills in the manor, the Town Mill held by John Cox, Hook Mill held by Robert Pitcher and Ford Mill held by Christopher Stone. It was the custom for the tenants to grind at the mill of their choice. He said that Stone's mill was worked by inexperienced boys and youths who spoiled the grain and that double and treble tolls were often charged. He also contended that the case should have been tried at the Manor Court as it was a local dispute. He insisted that he had never influenced any of the other tenants on where to grind their corn.

In 1602 Robert Pitcher, who held Hook Mill, was granted a licence to sue all the Clevehill tenants and other customary tenants that ought to grind at his mill for not grinding there. The outcome of this case is not known.

The 18th and 19th Century millers at the Town Mill were successively John Leat, his son William, John Collier, William Turner and Arthur Zeally. There were also grist mills (e.g. Minson's on the Kit upstream), fulling mills and a blade mill (for wheat?). In the 1790s, and at least to 1812, snuff was also milled in Chardstock. There is one reference, in 1829, to a lace mill.

Smiths and Metalworking

The blacksmiths, of whom there were several, included one at Tytherleigh. The smithy in the village, opposite the George, by what is now the entrance to the Court, was operated by the Bonfield family. The Bonfields were also machine makers and ironfounders in Crawley in the 19th Century. Oven doors bearing the Bonfield name have been found, including one, dated 1858, at Bridge Meadow, Crawley (see Appendix A). The business was sold in 1881 after having operated for upwards of 50 years.

Clocks

In the late 17th Century and during the 18th Century, clocks were made at Honey Hill by John Mitchell and Thomas Drayton. The clocks made by John Mitchell had fine engraved dials and frets, probably the work of Philip Levermore, who had married Elizabeth, the daughter of John Estmond of Lodge. Thomas was the son of the Vicar, the Revd. John Drayton and he married Ann, the daughter of John Mitchell. He eventually took over the clockmaking business, and later James, his son, moved to Chard where he also became a successful clock and watchmaker and was succeeded by his son Thomas.

Bricks and Tiles

There was a tile works at Kitbridge, owned in 1851 by William Haygate and Charles Chouler, manufacturing land-drain pipes. In 1859, it was called a brickfield, and was owned by Lewis Paull, but was sold at auction in December of the same year. An advertisement in "Nowlen's Weekly Chronicle" for 22nd December 1860, states that Mr. L. Paull was the foreman, and the proprietor was Mr. William Turner, Coal Merchant of Chard. Bricks, field drainage pipes and tiles were made there, and possibly associated with this industry were two men who were land drainers. The scale of this operation can be judged by the stock of 20,000 unfired bricks and tiles left when it was sold in 1859.

Other Occupations

Another occupation was that of cordwainer (shoemaker), one of the last being Harold Bond of Waterloo Cottage, opposite the Town Mill. Ropes and brushes have also been made in the village, and at Smallridge where tow was picked. Amongst the many other occupations listed in the late 18th and early 19th Centuries were those of cooper, sawyer, mason, clothier, tailor, milliner, dress-maker, weaver, flax and thread spinner, basket-maker, hurdle-maker; straw chair, mat and beehive maker, thatcher, dairyman, horse-dealer and gamekeeper. A carpentry, wheelwrighting, and undertaking business was situated in sheds behind the George Inn. There were, of course the farmers, cider apple growers, nurserymen and their labourers. In 1880, Elias Miller was recorded as a confectioner and farmer. As examples of farm products, as early as 1286, it was recorded that 16 head of beef had been left from one bishop to his successor on the Manor of Chardstock. In 1801, a Return of Crops made to the Government showed that 227 acres of wheat, 135 of barley, 94 of oats, 39 of potatoes and 28 of turnips and rape had been grown that year.

During the 20th century, successful building businesses were established, one by A. J. Strawbridge, another by the Chubb family and a third by the Bonfields. Threshing contractors Thomas Parris & Son and J. R. Pratt were in operation using traction engines and threshing boxes, but with the change in farming methods, both have long since closed. Recent years have seen the growth of several small industrial sites in the village. J. R. Pratt and Son also owned Broom Quarry which was producing gravel and sand from 1927 to 1942. Many tons were used in the construction of camps and runways at Ilton Airfield during World War II.

Sources

Chard, a Geological Survey, 1970 Chard History Group 3.
Chard and Ilminster News, op.cit.
Chard Union Gazette, Som. R. O.
Manor Court Rolls - Chardstock, Dor. R. O.
Nowlen's Weekly Chronicle, Som. R. O.
Pipe Rolls and Calandar of Charter Rolls, Som. Local History Library.
Poor Law Books - Chardstock, Dev. R. O.
St. White Down Fair records, Som. R.O.
Survey of the Manor of Chardstock, 1671, Dor. R.O.
Trade Directories, 19th/20th Century County Record Offices & Local History Libraries.
Trewman's Exeter Flying Post, West Country Studies Library.
Will of John Parris 1551, P.R.O.

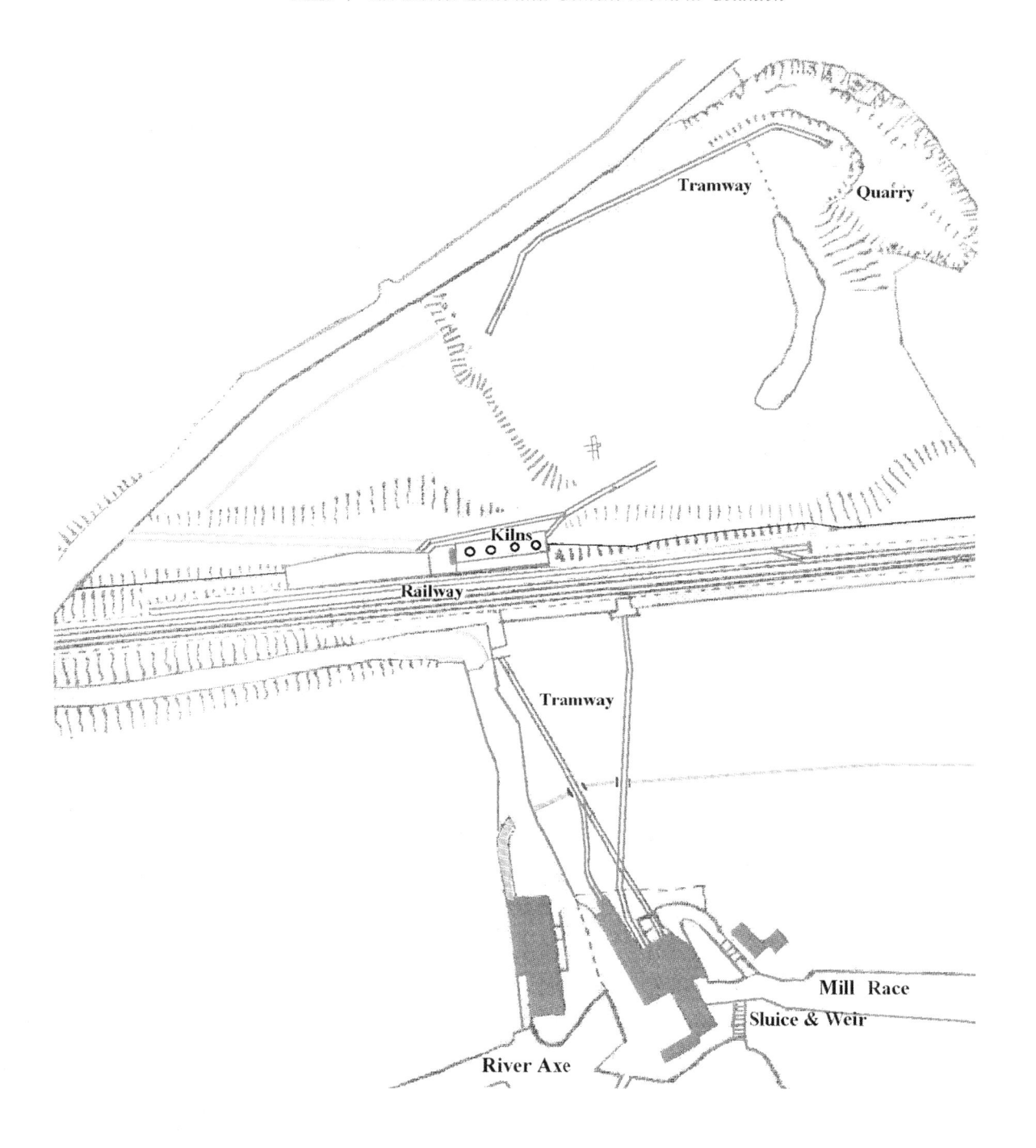

MAP 7 The Dorset Lime and Cement Works at Coaxdon

PLATE 5

Kiln at Bewley Farm with wooden arch support

Kiln at Hell Bottom with stone arch

Chapter Eight
LAND USE

Early Land Use

Early indications of land use are slight and difficult to build into a dated general picture. A probable Iron Age enclosure in the extreme north of the parish appears to have an associated lynchet bank which may form a pasture and/or territorial boundary. Similar banks elsewhere are placed on the top of scarps and often, in later times, formed the boundary between lower rough woodland/pasture and higher better pasture or arable land. Some of these banks leave the scarp while on some scarps there are no such banks. Map 4 shows the relationship between banks, springs, contours and known ancient sites. If there was a cultivated area associated with the Iron Age enclosure, then it might be surmised that area "C" later to become Burridge common field, probably has the best, well drained soil in the area. Cotley Down is bordered on the west by a lynchet bank under which was found an Iron Age coin hoard. Across the Kit valley to the west again is Bewley Down. This has a Bronze Age ringwork. The surrounding area was probably mainly used for pasture as it was much later in the Medieval period. However, cultivation traces may be seen as some old field banks next to the ringwork. Another early possibility is the ancient island of cultivation called Broad Croft, from which Bewley Down may have got its name. It is not known what was the economic basis of the Roman site nearby but, close to this, at a later date, was the Wilmington common field, which was on well drained and fertile chalky soil.

Hunting and snaring formed part of the ancient economy. A Neolithic arrowhead was found on Bewley Down. Huntley is likely to be a pre-9th Century place name and probably referred to a long hunt clearing, later called a "lawn". By 1101, this area was stated to be for hare hunting. Place names can form another source of pre-conquest information about the landscape. Unfortunately, the earlier names are difficult to identify and dating is likely to be impossible. The Place Name list in Appendix C, dates the earliest mention of names and from this group in particular, early name forms can be separated. The possible earliest names (pre-1200) relating to topography and early land use are given on Map 3. It is suggested that the overwhelming nature of the parish in the pre-conquest period was woodland, with signs of a rapidly expanding degree of exploitation. Even the possible areas of early pasture (above) seem to have reverted to woodland having early type of "leah" names. For example, Cotley suggests some sort of woodland dwelling, Bewley (correctly Beley) suggests a clearing in a long stretch of waste. In areas of original woodland, Crawley was probably totally wooded. Exploitation here began with the enclosure of areas for pigs (Beers) and goats (Haveland) and for trapping deer (deer hamms, Deerhams). Wood names also abound in the Tytherleigh area, but so do woodland exploitation names indicating, coppicing, clearance, charcoal burning and withy cultivation.

Medieval Period

The first comprehensive picture of the economy of Chardstock Manor is in the Domesday Survey of 1086. Compared with nearby manors, it was both large and wealthy. Twenty plough teams were in use, this implying approximately 120-160 draught oxen and a total of 3600 acres. The corn was ground in two large mills. An area of 10 acres of meadow was hand cut for hay and, like the arable, would have been periodically grazed. There are no details of stock but surrounding manors had mainly sheep plus some goats and pigs. As might be expected, there were large areas of rough pasture and woodland. Unusually, there was a considerable area of coppice wood, enigmatically stated to be "elsewhere" (detached from the parish?). The produce of the manor at these times is likely to have included corn, fish, meat and skins, wood for construction (timber and poles), iron and salt (from the connected manor of Colway in Lyme Regis).

Other sources of this type of information in the medieval period are a deed of 1155 and the steward's accounts (after 1422). This information can again be augmented by place name evidence and by the inventory of the sale of the lease of the Manor in 1566. The manorial land is described as being "dispersed" (in strips) in (the common fields?) of Estham, Notashe, Wythespit, Fursham and Flodypit and also in the furlongs (field subdivisions) of Berre (beer) and Bewspit. Enclosed pasture/meadow was in Axmeade, Millill Slade, Mow Furlong, North Mow, Meadham and Oteley. Most of these cannot be identified now. Some suggestive present day major names, such as Brockfield, do not appear. A medieval reconstruction of major manor divisions is given in Map 6. It can be seen how "ham" names refer to islands of cultivation surrounded by waste. In nearby parishes, these would be more frequently called "hays", although there may have been a subtle difference between the two. Many later "ley" names refer to crops or fallow arable. Meadow was also divided into strips or "doles", as was some woodland. One field is called Halfendole. In the Steward's accounts appears the reckoning for tasks of ploughing, threshing, winnowing, weeding and mowing. Sales of corn, stock, hides, wax, iron, cider, hay, apples and nuts also appear. There is mention in a court case of the Bishop's park, fishery and warren containing valuable rabbits, hares, pheasants, partridge and hawks. Near the manor court was a dovecot and a garden/orchard containing hazel, ash and nettles, all of which were utilised. Some crops and produce are mentioned by the Steward in surprising detail, for example, coarse wool, lambs wool, wool locks and fells, sheep and lamb pelts, oxhides (some diseased) and parchment. The Musemill (cider mill) contained apples, casks and cider. Ash loppings were used for plough stakes (to mark out the strips). Nolayash, Flodypit and Honeyell (common fields) are mentioned as being fallow in 1422. The pasture next to Egmor was sown with wheat and 2½ bushels of oats were surplus. Oxen were in the Deer Park in the summer and sheep were periodically folded in Axmede. The dung was removed and sold.

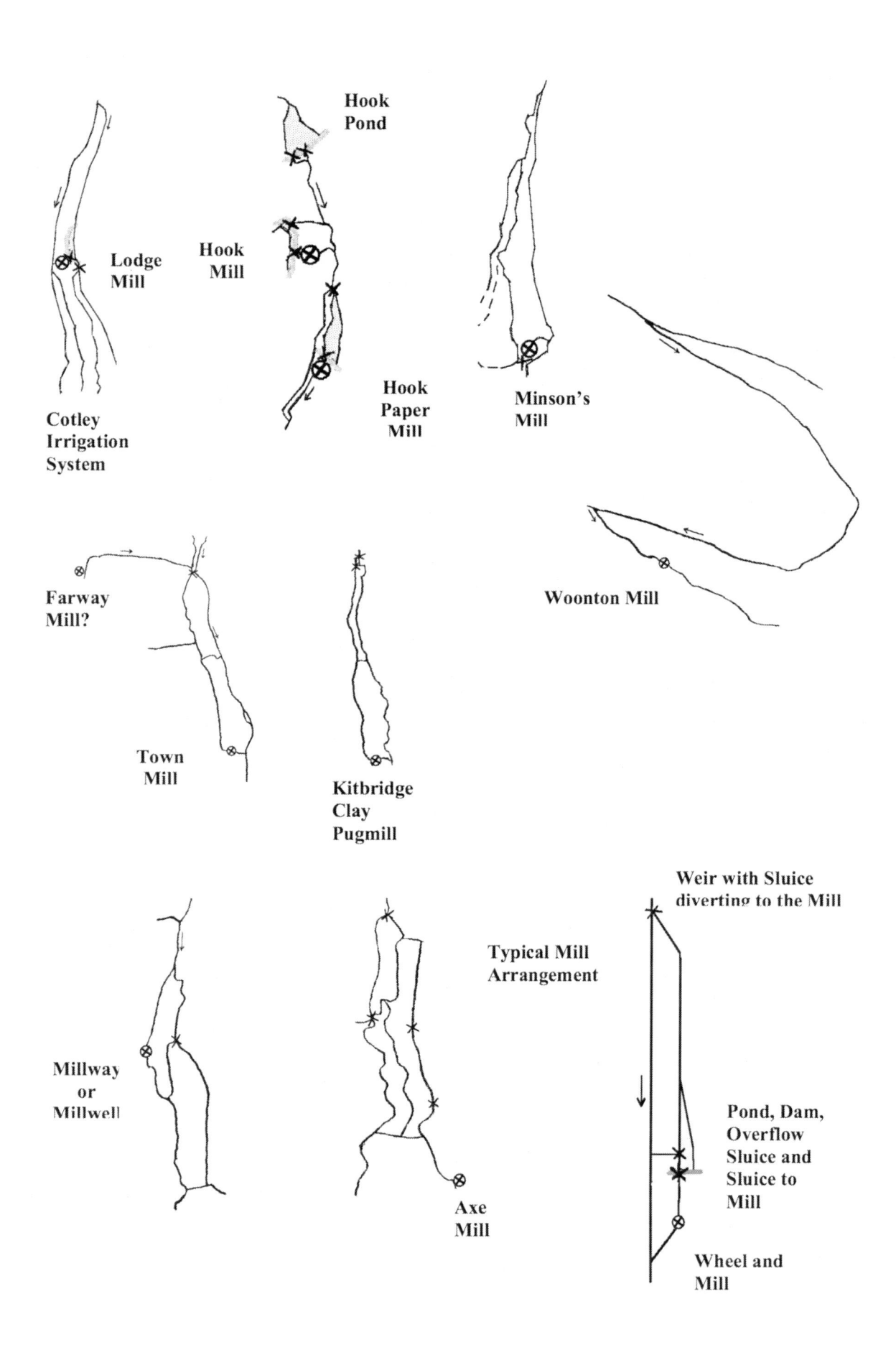

MAP 8 Mills of Chardstock (see Map 7 for Coaxdon Mill)

Lodge Mill

Hook Pond

Hook Mill

Cotley Irrigation System

Hook Paper Mill

Minson's Mill

Woonton Mill

Farway Mill?

Town Mill

Kitbridge Clay Pugmill

Millway or Millwell

Typical Mill Arrangement

Axe Mill

Weir with Sluice diverting to the Mill

Pond, Dam, Overflow Sluice and Sluice to Mill

Wheel and Mill

35

One of the most attractive features of the parish is that each part has a distinctive character and much has survived for more than 500 years. Crawley, Tytherleigh, Axe, Ford and Coaxdon most resemble the Devon style of scattered settlements, grown slowly by reclamation from woodland. The South Tithing, based on Alston, is of early Medieval type, still with evidence of the Feudal System of management. Burridge is a small version of it and some of its strips were in Tatworth. The North Tithing appears to be composed of later tenements or blocks of land. Bewley and Woonton are farms composed of fairly large regular fields. Cotley and Lodge appear to be of even later formation, probably the result of 16th/17th Century enclosure of downland and sheep runs, although they may have had more arable in mid-medieval times. It is a combination of topography, soil type, former use and economics that governs the land use at any one time.

Post-Medieval Land Use
It is apparent that, by the time of the Division of the Manor in 1582, most of the former large open common fields had been enclosed into closes. Only a few amalgamated strips survived, e.g.:-
    in Hookfield Agnes and Thomas Dallye 1 acre
    in Bluddie pytt John Welshe 1 acre
    in Hountley Thomas Dallye 1 acre
    in East Field John Bentley 1 acre

On the commons, however, manorial control continued. In 1596, Nicholas Wollmington was presented to the court for overcharging (over stocking) the common. There was a great temptation to steal firewood etc. from the new hedgerows. Thomas Martyne, a child, was encouraged by his mother in pickering and was whipped in open assembly. Some statements make even this earlier countryside still sound familiar. William Vincent was to make stiles on the footpath to Chard, behind the barn. Richard Parrock grubbed up hedges in Alston in 1598. Hountely Lane, from end to end, was overgrown with hedges. In 1641, a short piece of verse quoted by Robert Freeke, one time Steward, reveals his attitude to good land husbandry:-

    "A man in words and not in deeds
    Is like a garden full of weeds."

The Steward had a small army of officials to help reinforce regulations - Tithingmen, Constable, Hayward, Woodward, Pinder and Reeve.

In Tytherleigh, place names reveal what a degree of clearance of former woodland was taking place, e.g. field names like Ruds and Ridley. In 1595, it was stated, in somewhat scandalised tones, that the lord of the (sub) manor had enclosed all the common. The Chardstock commons were regularly cleared of stock by appointed drivers in order to cull, treat and identify animals. Five drives of the common took place in 1595. For many hundreds of years the commons had gates, closely controlled, kept in repair and possibly attended by Dormen. It is possible that the two places called Dinnetts were connected with these people. We hear of the gates at Alston, Challenger, Ten Acre, Churchill (Clapper Gate) and Crawley. Those using Fennye Lane at Alston were told to make a gate for it. Sheep and cattle (bulls, rothers, bullocks, heifers and calves) were taken to fairs. Many other activities took place on the commons, furze was cut for the baking of bread, licence was granted to dig marle (weathered chalk) near Brinscombe for spreading in Broad Croft. Great attention was paid to trees as there were few of timber bearing size. Vermin were also removed. In 1603, it was stated that there was not a rook in the whole manor! As far as arable crops are concerned, an example in 1600 is given by the growing of wheat, rye and beans in Crawley. References to land (arable), pasture and meadow are frequent and are usually in "closes", suggesting enclosure by hedges into smaller units. In days when so much work was by hand and before the introduction of land drains, there was great pre-occupation with the maintenance of hedges and ditches. An inspection of field ditches today will show how skilfully they were made so that they have a constant fall in level. The Accounts state that it is the custom of the land that a property's boundary is marked by the far edge of the ditch from which material for the bank has been dug (traditionally 4 feet from the centre of the bank). Ditches on higher land often lead to small ponds shared between several fields. Hedges were sometimes made by a hedger, who was contracted to make and plant hedgerow by the "rope" (20ft). Hedging slips were chosen to suit the locality and were usually available to hand, beech on Bewley Down and sallow willow on lower moorland. The local hedge-laying tradition consisted of pleshing in opposite directions into two parallel rows tied into round bundles, pinned down by forked branches. A hedger's axe and gloves can be seen on a Donyatt church bench end.

The late and post-medieval period saw a steady decline in arable and growth of pasture. The common pasture/woodland was late enclosed (1856) in Chardstock, but well before that there had been an increase in orchards, plantations and tree nurseries. Much of Bewley Down was only suitable for trees and even much of the present arable was only reclaimable after the advent of clay tile land drains, steam ploughs and lime fertiliser. At first, orchard trees were planted on ridged land for drainage. The acid moorland soils required neutralising with something more effective than chalk marl. Limekilns were built and hydrated lime produced. A typical limekiln built to provide lime for newly enclosed land can be seen at Hell Bottom. Early grass crops in the 18/19th Century were obtained by the construction of Catch Meadows. These were of flat meadow or hillside type, and had a clever system of weirs, sluices and channels (called gutters) designed to provide a c.20mm. sheet of flowing water. Husbandry in the 19th Century was a peculiar mixture of tradition and resounding new practices. For example, wassailing the cider apple trees still continued, even up to the 1920s when a ceremony similar to that of Somerset was recorded (i.e. cider libations on roots etc.) but the following Dorset song was sung:-

"Standfast root! Bear well top!
Pray God send us a good howling crop!
Hats vull, caps vull, dree busel bags vull!
(cres.)   Now, Now, Now!"   (firearms discharged)

It is not known if this particular song was used in Chardstock.

20th Century

From 1921 to 1951, two areas of land, for growing vegetables, were let as allotments by the Parish Council. There were 19 plots at Parks (by Cuckolds Pit) at a rent of 6s. per annum and 18 plots at Townend (Green Lane), at 7s. per annum. The last parts of the commons, for which no title could be found, were sold in 1955 by the Parish Council. Two were Tytherleigh Green and part of Burridge Common, which, on enclosure by an award dated 29th December 1857, had been allotted to the churchwardens and overseers of the poor in trust as allotments for the labouring poor. The other two pieces were the (now) recreation ground at Farway and a pit at Burchill, which had been used for supplying stone and gravel for road repairs.

Sources

Brand Committee of the Folklore Society. Proc SANHS, 93, p254.
Division of the Manor, 1582, P. R. O.
Manor Court Rolls, Dor. R. O.
Parish Council Records, Chardstock P. C.
Tatworth Middle Field, 1996 Chard History Group.

Chapter Nine
FARMS

Court Farm
Although the modern concept of a farm at first sight seems clear, originally they varied from former complete sub-manors like Cotley, to long lived and ancient farm/settlements like Bewley. The very word "farm" has changed, its original meaning was to let to a tenant for a fixed rent. Scattered groups of fields, let as a unit, also existed. These may have never had a farmhouse. The earliest mention of the main farms comes from place names. Chardstock Manor itself, will have had a home farm or demesne. It might be expected that this was centred on the present Manor House. A nearby spring of plentiful and good quality water would be considered essential for an early farm site in this area. Also near, should be naturally well drained and fertile arable land. The 1781 map shows Court House Farm immediately south-east of the manor house, but by 1852 this had gone and in the beginning of the 20th Century the Early English wagon roof barn was dismantled and sold to the U.S.A. In 1646, it was called Courte Farme, described as at the gate of the manor house, containing 3 acres. It lay by the church, enclosed "partly by the churchyard, partly by a quicksett". The Lord's garden (orchard) is mentioned in 1422. In the Domesday Survey (1086), the home farm (demesne) employed 4 of the 20 manor plough-teams and kept 6 slaves to augment the boon work of the villagers. At this time the farm was managed by the Reeve, who was elected by fellow villagers.

Chubb's and Woonton Farms
It is very likely that the above home farm existed at the time of the possible earliest mention of Chardstock Manor (see Chapter 2), although at that time it was probably an independent farm receiving dues from other subservient holdings in the manor. The manor was divided into two halves, each having a principal farm called a "tuna". The one in the South Tithing was probably named after its tenant Aelfwold (Alston) and in the North Tithing was Wulfhelm's tuna (later Wilmington, now Woonton). Aelfwold's farm was probably on the site of what is now called Chubbs Farm. In 1781, this was tenanted by James Hoare. It is not known when a Chubb held it. A spring rises to the east of the house and the original farm lands, probably called Fernhayes were to the west. This land was later extended to the south and divided into strips (see Appendix D) as Alston village grew in the 11th Century. Wulfhelm's farm was possibly on, or above, the site of Old Orchard, Holy City, where much early medieval pottery has been found. Its land probably included Cleave (cliff) to the south-west. The spring in the garden could be the Holy Well (Halewell) of 1426. Wilmington village is mentioned in 1155 and this may be represented by the grass covered house platforms in the field beyond the lane. "City" was the name given to deserted or shrunken villages and "Holy" means "wooded nook". Old Orchard was called Whitehouse in 1781 and is mentioned in 1646. In 1155, mention is made of both the vill and also of John de Wilmintuna. Wilmington, which included nearby Woonton Farm was, in later times often held with Cotley Manor. Woonton Farm site was possibly moated and it is known to have held a Manorial Court in its Great Hall. The Woonton name appeared in 1677 but the farmhouse later burned down.

Cleeve, Ransom's and Yard Farms
Cleeve Farm was probably just south of Ransom's Farm. It was adjacent to Cleevehill Lane which forms part of the parish boundary. Walter, son of Edward of Clive and his holdings are mentioned in 1155. Edward may, therefore, have been a villein holding 30 acres (1 virgate) at the time of the Domesday Survey. The holdings of Cleevehill in 1781 were Bridge's 16 acres, Chepen's 14 acres, Denning's 28 acres, Pinnney's late Grabham's 18 acres, Ransom's 13 acres, Ransom's late Read's 4 acres and Searl's 15 acres. It can be seen how these are ancient 1 or ½ units of land. Another Chardstock peculiarity is the naming of land blocks after people rather than landmarks. Ransom's late Read's was held by W. Leate in 1781, the name Ransom appeared after 1676. The use of personal names can continue for a long time but eventually, they may change with a change of tenant. Another very early farm is Yarde. In 1332, we find William atte Yzerd and in 1423 Yardlond (land) part of which is in Benetsmede. The year 1552 reveals that this latter is 2 acres, Yard itself is 15 acres and also attached is Yard Moor, Walcroft and part of Goathill. In the original form the 'y' is pronounced 'i' and the 'z' as 'y', and so the name sounded much as is does now. The meaning is more difficult. It can mean poles, a farmyard or a yard land (15 acres).

Bewley Farm
In 1202, Bewley Farm was held by William, son of Robert. Bewley Down itself was called Brelege. In 1332, the farm was called Beilheye which Roger, the tenant, took as his surname. In 1202, the taxable value was 1½ hides for which 30 marks (£20) was paid. In the 15th Century the farm was held by William and consisted of 4 score (80) yardlands on the down, plus Broad Croft. The whole impression is of a very large area, probably including the whole of Bewley Down. The farm was divided in 1582 and a new lane built for access. Further divisions followed and with the two Walker brothers owning a sixteenth each, the matter finally needed resolution in the Chancery Court. The farm buildings are now partly ruined.

Cotley
The sub-manors, most of which appear to have started as Knight's Fees (held of the bishop by Knight service), each had their own home farm (sometimes it was the only farm). By far the most important was Cotley which was long held with Woonton Farm. Roger held it in 1201, and in 1464 the two manors contained 12 dwellings, 400 acres of arable, 60 acres of meadow, 300 acres of pasture, 40 acres of wood and 15 acres of Alder (wet wood). Today the farm has an interesting range of buildings arranged around a barton. On one side of this is a fine medieval barn attached to a part ruined manor house (see Appendix A).

Tytherleigh Farms
Tytherleigh comes next in the 1332 list. In the 13th century, the manor had detached lands in Seaborough, Wambrook and Weston (that in Combe St. Nicholas?). The Manor contained Tytherleigh Moor, Common, Mead, Field and Green. Richard held it in 1201 and Ralph in 1205. The demesne farm was next to the Manor House. Home Farm is now shown on the modern map as being opposite Keates Farm. Although this is an ancient building, it appears to have been known earlier as Lower Tytherleigh Farm and was not directly held by the manor. In 1646, the manor contained 4 dwellings, 2 pigeon cotes, 470 acres, rents and free fishing rights in the Axe.

Coaxdon
Similar in dues was Coaxden. Richard held it in 1155 but little is known of its early days. Its structure resembles Cotley in that there were no tenanted farms in the sub-manor. Even so it had Overland (demesne arable), common meadow (Coaxden Mead) and common pasture (South Common). The mill has no known early origin but Stretford (the meadow beyond the railway bridge) was part of the manor in 1413. In 1622, Thomas Browne, alias Upcott of Cherdstock, was the miller. Coaxdon must not be confused with North Coxdon which was in Crawley.

Axe, Lodge, Burridge and Ridge
The above completes the most ancient documented farms and major farms (as far as the 1332 Lay Subsidy Roll is concerned). Remaining present day farms on this Roll are now considered. Axe, was particularly important because it was a sub-manor and on the King's Highway. Henry held it in 1332. It shared Honeylands Field with Tytherleigh. Axe Mead was very extensive and Colson Common probably extended to the farm. A mill to the north-east of the farm was fed by a leat from the River Kit (known as the Churn at this point). Lodge was apparently similar to Axe, although its structure is little known. The hill behind it, Lodge How, was presumably arable. Rights of common were possibly shared with Wambrook and beside it, on the Kit, was Lodge Mill. The house was termed a mansion in the 16th Century when the Estmonds were there. The manor included an ancient tenement, surrounded by common and in Wambrook parish, called Box (1432). Burridge/Bowditch was another sub-manor like Tytherleigh and Richard held it in 1196. It had its own common fields (divided into strips) and rough pasture. Ridge, nearby, was not a sub-manor but was twice the value of Bowditch in 1332 when William Payde held it. The hilltop arable strips were shared with the tenants at Hook.

Battleford and Farway
Battleford has, throughout most records, been known as Bakelford. It was held by Walter in 1332 and a succession of tenants appear as witnesses to deeds. Its lands were on the hillslope behind the present house. To the northwest was the way to the ford, with part of South Common beside it. A long narrow mead runs down the south-west side. Farway occurs in some of the earliest records and in about 1155 Galfrid held it (his wife Elvefam, holding a nearby tenement). The farm lands project into Farway Marsh on a slight ridge and the farm has its own spring. Lower Farway was possibly separated at a later date.

Crawley Farms
Although Crawley was separated from the main parish when Wambrook was formed (date unclear), it was a sub-manor in 1155 when held by Richard Gulafre. By 1582, it was split into a number of the usual units (30, 15, & 7½ acres). The probable original demesne was held by Widow Bond at Crawlewaye (Crawley Farm). Bond's included the two mill sites (one is now above Crawley Farm and the other at Lower Crawley Farm, Bridge Meadow); North Field, half of Crawley Common Mead, Beers and rights on Crawley Common. Beers was very ancient enclosed woodland, being held by Eliat, in or at about 1155. In 1781, Bond's included Collin's now called Hares Farm and probably connected with the Hares family (Adam le Hare 1362). Crawley Dairy was, until recently, Steven's Farm (Richard Stephene 1330) which in 1781 was combined with Walcrofts (probably an even earlier name). The Walcroft house platform can be seen in Plotts Field. Another Crawley farm is Gilletts (William Gillet in 1741, Late Gillet's in 1781).

Churchill, Millway and Twist Farms
Three old farms in the south of the parish must not be overlooked. Churchill has every sign of age, even traces of possible village earthworks nearby. The name does not occur early and there is no church. The explanation seems to be that the name may be a corruption of Chattoshale (possibly meaning cat's or charter's hill) which occurs as early as 1422. Nearby is Sharkshole, which may be derived from scucca (a goblin's or demon's hollow). They are so close that it may be that they are two corruptions of one original name. So far as the farm is concerned, its name came from an original topographical feature which could make it very old. Another such farm is Millway which was Mulnehale when Stephan Tyrrell held it in 1201. The stated original value was probably based on revenue from the mill but there were lands attached. It is thought unlikely that this was one of the 1086 mills. The third old farm is Twist, the original site is Old Twist which was burnt down and is now a ruin. This is another topographical name referring to the turn in the valley, the farm being listed in 1280.

Recent Farms
The remaining farms are more recent than those detailed above. Many were formed when the commons were enclosed in 1856. They are listed below:-

Name	Date	Origin (also see Appendix C)
Birchill	post 1896	
Catmoor	1781	"Late Steven's into common' Camoore 1648
Chilcots Colston	1781	Colsons Barn
Chilcotts	1933	Tenant Farm
Colston, Higher	1781	Coxton Common House
Greenend		
Greghams	1898	Grubhams, 1781 John Grubham
Homelea	post 1896	probably a corruption of Homely
Hollbrook	1781	Hallbrooks
Hoopers	1781	Hoopers late Rounsevills formerly Gilletts-in-Town
Knights	1842	Farm
Myrtle	1781	a cottage
Sandford	1781	Sandfords, 1569 Samford
Sycamore	1842	a cottage
New House	1933	Tenant Farm
Fosseway	1842	a house
Uphaye	post 1896	source of name not known
Stockstyle	pre 1781	1933, Tenant Farm
Waggs Plot	1781	Wags Plot, 1405 Wagg
Brooms		
Fordwater	1781	Higher Ford, 1537 Ford
Burrows	on 1842 map	
Holly	1781	late Combes or Hills
Alston	not before 1842	
Dummetts	1781	Dometts, 1597 Dummet
Crabbs	1781	Crabbs, 1624 Crabb
Keates	1781	late Turners
Whitehouse	post 1600	see Woonton above.

Source
Henley Estate Map, 1781 Dev. R. O.

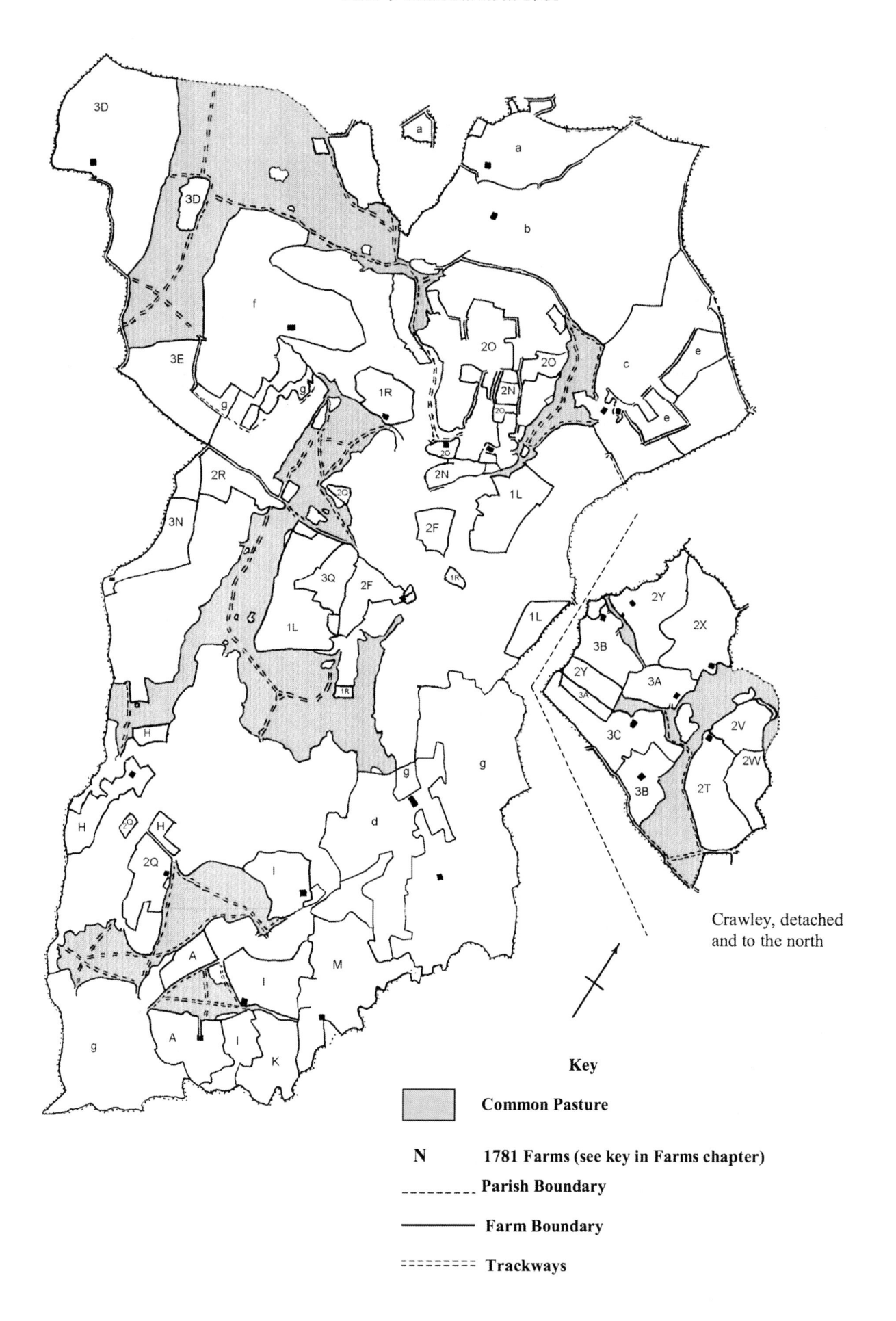

MAP 9 Main Farms in 1781

Crawley, detached and to the north

Key

Common Pasture

N   1781 Farms (see key in Farms chapter)

- - - - -   Parish Boundary

———   Farm Boundary

========   Trackways

Key to Map 9 - Main Farms in 1781

In Chardstock Manor (from Henley Map).

A	Sandfords	60 acres	copyhold	to John Wills
H	Churchill	49	leasehold	?
I	Colsons & Higher Ford	38	copyhold	Mary Godwin
M	Axe	107	copyhold	Margaret Seward (widow)
2F	Court House / Old Parks	45	leasehold	?
2N	Hook	32	copyhold	John Bragg
2O	Late Wyatts & Rudge	91	copyhold	Robert Deane
2Q	?	56	leasehold	Grace Dean nee Wilmot
2R	Cleave Hill	28	copyhold	Samuel Apsey
2T	Crawley	56	copyhold	Robert Deane
2V	Stockmans	?	?	John Bennett
2W	?	36	copyhold	James Wiatt
2X	Collins & Bonds	74	copyhold	Rachel Wills
2Y	Bonds or Labeers	68	copyhold	Betty Marks
3A	Brooms	36	copyhold	Jonathen Wiatt
3B	Walcroft & Stephens	64	copyhold	Samuel Palmer
3C	Gilletts 5	7	copyhold	Eleanor Biggs
3D	Bewley	227	leasehold	
3E	Garnspitts & Eastcombs	65	leasehold	?
3N	Twist	41	copyhold	Mary Coates (widow)

Independent Farms (From 1840 Tithe Apportionment Map)

a	Lodge	Thomas Babb to Joel Evans
b	Cotley	Thomas Putt to Thomas Deane
c	Bowditch	Thomas Deane occupied by himself
d	Tytherleigh	Mr. Pitt (1781) occupied by himself
e	Bowditch	John Marks occupied by himself
f	Woonton	Thomas Putt to Elizabeth Bently
g	Miscellaneous	

PLATE 6

A blocked medieval window at Huntley Barn

Wellhead and mechanism at Bewley Down

Medieval Roof at Cotley Barn

Former Engine House at Cotley Barn

Chalk Rock Window Quoins at Old Twist Farmhouse

Worn Newel Stairtread Stone found at Woonton Farm

Chapter Ten
HOUSES

When considering the dwellings of the past it must be remembered that it is only the houses of the wealthier members of the community that have survived. It is also true to say that very few buildings containing medieval construction remain. Only those considered important and therefore made predominantly of stone have stood the test of time. It is probable that even they have been considerably altered and adapted to meet the needs of succeeding generations. The houses of the ordinary people have long since disappeared and the only evidence of their existence is to be found in the ground and from references in contemporary documents. Many would have been rebuilt several times on the same site, ensuring that some of the present houses stand on the same plots as their predecessors. During the pre-Norman period, houses and communal buildings would have had low stone walls or wooden hurdles kept in place with stakes, the roofs being covered with turves or some form of thatch. They would have been grouped together near water and on hilltops. Depressions in the ground, the colour of the soil and the scatter of stone provide valuable clues. Excavation could provide a plan of the dwelling and from all this evidence a conjectural picture of the settlement can be constructed. Such a settlement may have existed on Bewley Down and indeed in the village of Chardstock itself.

Between the end of the Roman occupation and the coming of the Normans, nothing is known of the living conditions of the inhabitants of Chardstock. No Saxon remains have yet been discovered, although some place names are suggestive and there must have been occupation as by Domesday, there was a flourishing settlement with two mills. The first reference to an actual building is in 1158, when mention is made of the gift of the church to the Cathedral of Sarum by Gilbert de Percy. It is probable that by this time the building would have been of stone. In 1377, a royal licence was granted to Bishop Erghum of Salisbury to crenellate or fortify his mansion at Chardstock, again probably, a stone building.

Local materials would have been used from the earliest times and with the abundance of wood and chert in the area, these are found in most medieval houses in the village. Oak was most commonly used. In the oldest houses a curved timber stretching from a stone or flint base to meet its opposite member at the apex of the roof, provided the main support and is known as a true cruck. In later houses, the timber was in two pieces, the join being made where the slope of the roof begins. These timbers are called jointed crucks and are useful guides to the date of the house. There were often several sets of these crucks thus dividing the house into bays. The walls were thick and in this part of the country, were filled with lime mortar mixed with chert rubble. Cob, a mixture of clay mud and straw and/or cow manure was used mainly for farm buildings but is also found in many medieval houses. The materials were mixed on the ground, placed in layers on the walls, trodden to make them firm and then were lime washed. As long as the walls are built on a stone footing and kept dry, they last for hundreds of years. There are several examples of cob built walls in Chardstock (see Appendix A). Roofs were thatched mostly with reed and long straw. The internal walls were of wattle and daub with wooden stud and panel screens in the more important houses. One unusual building material was chalk rock. An example of its use in Chardstock was at the old farmhouse at Twist, where blocks of this were used on the insides of the window openings, probably to enhance the light reflection.

Most houses were of the open hall variety with the fire on a stone hearth in the middle of the room and a hole in the roof to allow the smoke to escape. This blackened the thatch and the roof timbers, thus giving another valuable clue to the date and former construction of the house. There are a few examples of possible Longhouses remaining in Chardstock. These houses were built on a slope with the rooms arranged in a row. The family would live at the high end and the animals at the lower end, known as the byre. Cottages would consist of perhaps one or two rooms, only one of which would be heated. Very few cottages have survived, those that have being considerably modified. During the 16th Century, many houses were updated, fireplaces were added and upper storeys inserted. Two of the oldest houses are the George Inn and the Tytherleigh Cott (formerly the New Inn) (see Chapter 18 & Appendix A). The old vicarage was rebuilt c.1838/40 and retains brick vaulted cellars probably of Tudor date. In 1669, two skeletons were dug up in the kitchen, in front of the fireplace. They were of an adult and a child.

Details of Chardstock Court, built on the site of one of the summer residences of the Bishops of Salisbury, are taken from the Schedule of Listed Buildings. The fabric of The Court is of early 14th Century origin with 15th and 16th Century alterations. The building fell into disrepair in the 20th Century and has been largely rebuilt around the original features and a new roof added. Various medieval fragments survive. The detached range of buildings which had a 15th Century roof, was destroyed c.1930.

In the Manor Court Books are many interesting references to the property and houses which belonged to the Manor. It is not clear who built these houses, or more correctly cottages, but it seems that the tenants and copyholders were responsible for the maintenance of their accommodation and holding or tenement as it was called. With so many houses roofed with thatch, fire was always a worry, as indeed it is today. There are numerous references to fireplaces, known as mantels, being in decay and needing repair. In 1595, Mary Seward's mantel was in decay. In 1597, John Welsh of

Chardstock and Nicholas Westofer of Alston were ordered to "amend" their mantels. In 1598, Widow Seward, Widow Strong and others were forbidden to make fire before their mantels were amended. In 1599, the mantel of the kitchen of Andrew Parrock was in decay. This may have been at the New Inn (now the Tytherleigh Cott), because in one of the upper rooms is a fireplace dated 1594 and bearing the initials A. P. In May 1604, Widow Waldron's mantel was in decay and "very dangerous". She was instructed to amend it before Christmas and "in the meanwhile not to make a fire in the mantle .... and if she make default the Tything to pluck down the mantle within 3 days. Commandment is given to every of the tenants of the south to attend the tythingman in the doing thereof upon pain of xii d" (12d). Nothing was done and at the next court a day was "given" for the mantel to be made safe. Unfortunately there are no further references and so how the matter was resolved will never be known. The Widow Turner was also causing a fire risk. She was drying malt "in her barn having no mantle there being very dangerous". She was given a day "to make a mantle sufficient for the drying of malt and oats".

A survey of the Manor was carried out in 1671 when at least 12 cottages appeared to be "Roofless". Whether these were actual houses or a term denoting a holding without a house is not known. A number of Roofless pieces of ground were also mentioned, perhaps this meant a tenement without a dwelling house (see Chapter 9). Houses continue to be presented as "out of repair" in the 18th Century, e.g. in 1737, the houses of Dorothy Pines, John Pearce, Widow Bonfield and James Small, all needed attention. In 1778, Elizabeth Amor, wife of Richard Amor, claimed admittance to a piece of ground where a dwelling house called Gillwillsome formerly stood, having been burnt down.

Information on a selection of the medieval houses, which have survived in Chardstock, and on some of the later dwellings are given in Appendix A, Building Surveys.

Sources
Manor Court Rolls - Chardstock, op. cit.
Sarum Charters and Documents, 12-13th Centuries op. cit.
Schedule of Listed Buildings of Historical or Architectural Interest, Dev. C. C.
Survey of the Manor, 1671, op. cit.

Chapter Eleven
EDUCATION

The First Schools
The purpose of this Chapter is to give an outline of education in the village. More detailed information can be found in the book, "A History of Education in Chardstock and All Saints 1712-2009".

In early times, village education was often carried on in the parish church by the priest, but so far there is no evidence of this occurring in Chardstock. However, in the Churchwardens' Presentments made between 1583-1597, it is noted that "John Marker doth Teach within our pishe without Licence of his ordinary the Dean of Sarum" In 1591/3, the following entry occurs, "Item we do present that we have a schoolmaster that doth teach in our parish But wheather he be licensed we know not named Henry Pyckeringe". Private tutors would have been employed by the richer families as in the case of that of Sir Simonds D'Ewes. The Vicar, the Revd. Richard White, must have taken some pupils and the young Simonds D'Ewes was under his care in 1603 but by 1611, Mr. White was no longer teaching and Simonds was sent to the Revd. Christopher Marraker at Wambrook. The first reference to a school in Chardstock is in an Inventory dated 3rd October, 1712 attached to the will of Thomas Guppy, Schoolmaster. The Inventory states:-

    Item   In the School House   Five Forms   0 5 0

The location of the "School House" in the parish is not known.

The next mention of a school in the village occurs in the year 1751 when, at a Parish Meeting held on 25th October, it was agreed to pay Thomas Knight five pounds a year, out of the Holditch Mead Charity, to teach twelve poor children for five years from 29th November 1751. If the children did not attend church services they would be excluded from the school. Exactly where this school was situated is again not known. It was probably in a house and only Reading, Writing and possibly some Arithmetic would have been taught. In 1777, Richard Dening was paid as the schoolmaster, but nothing further is recorded until 1788 when a Mr. Amor received payments amounting to £1 9s 6d "for the Free School". Detailed accounts of payments to Richard Amor survive for the years 1800 and 1801. After this nothing is recorded until 1811 when, at a meeting of the Feoffees (trustees), it was agreed "to pay for the Schooling of 10 poor children at the rate of 3d per week each out of the Rent of Ladymead". Between 1812 and 1815, Miss Toms taught Reading and Mary Turner taught Sewing and Reading. Ann Old and Elizabeth Harris are also mentioned as teachers.

The National School
The first survey of elementary schools undertaken by the State was in 1818 and the return contains the following information. There was "a school instituted on the national system wholly supported by annual subscriptions in which 80 children daily attend and 120 on Sundays" Henry Edwards, the curate who completed the return, noted that, "The parents are not able to spare their children from their labours in the field or many more would be added to the preceding numbers". When the Revd. Charles Woodcock came to Chardstock, he decided to erect a new school for 90 children as near to the church as possible as the existing school, a two storey building, was "at the further extremity of the village". To this end he applied to the National Society for Promoting the Education of the Poor in the Principles of the Established Church, for a grant. He received £80 from the National Society and £100 from the Treasury and in 1839 the schoolroom was erected on Prebendal land opposite the church. Sales and Bazaars were organised to clear the building debt. One Bazaar, held in August 1839, raised £130. In reporting this, the Chard Union Gazette commented that ten years previously, the moral condition of the children of the poor was "truly deplorable". They spent the week "in idleness, rags and filth" and on Sunday descended to "robbery and petty depredation of every kind". This contrasts sharply with the remarks made by Henry Edwards above. The paper continued to praise the efforts made by the vicar and noted that the clean, neatly dressed, happy children were now taught "the rudiments of knowledge" in the week and "the principles of Christian truth" on Sunday. The teacher, who was paid about £60 a year, was possibly William Sumption, mentioned in the Register of Baptisms in 1833 as "schoolmaster" or William Noyes, whose name appears in the 1841 Census as a schoolmaster living in the village. The school was regularly inspected by the Revd. E. D. Tinling whose reports give an insight into its progress. A timetable for 1847 shows that the day began with Prayers and Singing at 9 a.m. and was followed by Religious Instruction, Reading, Spelling, Writing, Arithmetic, Geography or Grammar and Tables. Prayers and Singing completed the day at 5 p.m. There was a two hour break at noon and the timetable was shortened during the winter months. *(National School continued below)*

Industrial School for Servant Girls
During the 1840s, the Vicar extended his project by building a Teacher's Residence and opening an Industrial School for Training Servant Girls. Training was provided for a maximum of ten girls, who were admitted only if their conduct was good and if they regularly attended the day school. After one year's training they would be qualified to apply for posts in domestic service. The matron planned the course, which included dairy work, bread-making, washing, ironing and preparation of fine linen, scouring boards, cleaning furniture, waiting at table and all branches of housework.

Four girls went daily to the vicarage to work under the direction of the Vicar's own staff there and in the evening all assembled for secular and religious instruction given by the Vicar as preparation for Confirmation. The Inspector praised much of the work, but recommended that the Industrial work be limited to the mornings and the rest of the time be devoted to needlework and to improving the general knowledge of the girls.

St. Andrew's College and Orphan School
Mr. Woodcock next turned his attention to providing a Middle Class School in Chardstock. These schools, which did not receive government aid, provided education for "middle-class" children whose parents did not want a Grammar School education which had become unattractive to the more commercially-minded middle class. Therefore, in 1857, the Vicar and Churchwardens, as trustees, bought about half an acre of land from the Ecclesiastical Commissioners and the buildings known as St. Andrew's College were built. The whole project seems to have expanded with the addition of orphans from the Crimean War and the Indian Mutiny and there are references to an Orphans' Asylum in the Poor Law Rate books for the 1860s. According to the Somerset County Herald in 1857, at a National School Anniversary held in Chard, the band of the "Soldiers' and Sailors' School at Chardstock" was one of two bands leading the procession. Another appearance of the band was at the Christmas Party for the Orphan, Industrial and National Day and Sunday Schools in 1860 when they "played some lively tunes". There is a further reference to the band in Nowlen's Weekly Chronicle for 21st July 1860, when the London & South Western Extension Railway was opened. "The Orphan and Industrial School marched with flags flying and drums beating to Huleigh Hill, opposite the Axe, near Tytherleigh." There they planted the flags and "When the special train was passing the drum and fife band struck up the National Anthem". All those assembled cheered "most vigorously", after which games were played. On the approach of a storm "the party marched away with the band playing and all returned to the schools, highly gratified with the day's amusement". By 1859, there were 50 scholars at the Middle School, and after the Midsummer examination in 1860, "the Orphan School fife and drum band playe'".

In 1861, a reporter from the "Illustrated London News" wrote a glowing account of the College Schools. A classical type of education was provided at the Middle School, which became St. Andrew's College, under a University Headmaster and a staff of assistant masters. From the Sarum Almanack and Diocesan Calendar for 1863, we learn that there were courses in Divinity, French, Latin, Greek, English language and composition, Ancient and Modern History, Sacred and Secular Geography, Penmanship, Drawing, Vocal Music, Arithmetic Euclid, Algebra, Mensuration, Land Surveying and Book Keeping. A quarterly report on each boy's conduct and progress was sent to parents and a public examination was held at the end of each half year. There was a gymnasium, cricket field and a bathing pool situated in the river Kitt. The Illustrated London News article noted that "each branch of the establishment, though perfectly distinct, is made to assist and play into the others". This may have been true, though the Post Office Directory for 1867 describes the Industrial children and Orphans as "hewers of wood and drawers of water to the upper school" and "the whole premises including gardens and churchyard are kept in order by the boys". When the National School Log Book begins in 1863, references are made to the orphans attending the National School, a pupil teacher being absent with the band, the master giving drawing lessons to the Upper School and having to be "often absent about the Industrial work", especially when the Industrial Master had bad eyes. There are a number of entries in the log relating to the college until about 1869 when references cease.

As far as is known, the establishment continued on similar lines until about 1874. In that year there is a reference in the log to several children being withdrawn from the National School "as the parents are removing to other parts of the country". This may have been due to a combination of the break up of the College and the decline of the woollen industry in the area. The end of the College came in March when the Sarum Almanack states that since 1858 "the Founder saw reason to introduce into his original plan several changes". His aim was to enable the school "to meet the wants of those Clergymen and laymen who desire their sons to be educated carefully ... with special regard to their training in Church principles". To achieve this, a more permanent footing was needed and, "it being impossible to obtain freehold ground at Chardstock", a house in Salisbury was purchased by the Headmaster, the Revd. G. H. Bourne, author of the hymn "Lord enthroned in heavenly splendour", and the College, together with several members of staff, transferred there to become the College of S.S. Andrew & Edmund.

The College as a Private Boarding School
The College buildings in Chardstock were let to the Revd. H. M. Robinson from Chigwell, who, after altering and extending them, opened a private boarding school which was still to be known as St. Andrew's College. In May 1876, a service was held in the church to celebrate the re-opening and boys continued to come from all parts to Chardstock for their education. The curriculum included Greek, Latin, French, German, Mathematics, Chemistry, Botany, Geology and Land Surveying. The buildings consisted of dormitories, classrooms, studies, lecture hall, dining hall, laboratory, gymnasium, tepid plunge bath, sanatorium, museum, library and so on. For recreation there was a cricket field, fives court, tennis court, bathing pond in the river, bowling green, etc. There was a gas works which had been producing gas for lighting the college, the church and the streets since October 1868. The students attended services in the chapel specially added for the original College use, and an evening service was held nightly in the College itself. There followed

several successful years during which the village enjoyed a series of entertainments given by the College in the hall. The stage, later the dining room of the Primary School, was provided with a proscenium drop scene in 1878, to replace the existing curtain. In the centre was the cross of St. Andrew, surrounded by the college motto, "Per Laborem ad Honorem". The background depicted the college with the tower of the church in the distance. In 1883, the Revd. Robinson assigned the remaining years of his lease to the Revd. A. Evans from Wigan. By 1886 the Revd. Evans found himself in financial difficulties and the College finally closed at Christmas 1886.

The Vicar and Churchwardens were again left with the unenviable responsibility of finding a use for the redundant College, but no one was prepared to take a lease of buildings, the fabric of which was slowly decaying. In 1899, several letters appeared in the "Chard & Ilminster News" supporting an item which advocated the use of the buildings as a home for orphans of the South African war. This suggestion was taken up by the "Daily Mail" and the "Daily Telegraph" and welcomed by the Vicar and Churchwardens. The Parish Council discussed the project but as the necessary funds were not forthcoming, the scheme was never started. Eventually the buildings became dangerous and the blocks to the rear of the present buildings were sold and demolished in or about 1912. The people of Chardstock continued to use the hall and adjoining rooms for dances and a variety of village functions. Amongst these were a Reading Room and the use of the upper floor of the College as a shooting range. St. Andrew's Hall, as it became known, was used until the mid 1970s and when the Community Hall was built, most village activities were transferred there.

The National School (continued)
The National School pursued a completely separate existence under its own master during the period 1876 to 1887. About 1893 the school began to use some of the redundant College premises and the log reports new arrangements for boys and girls. The boys were to use the lobby and front yard and the girls the accommodation at the rear of the school. In 1894 "Drills and Recreation" were taken in the College Hall, and an entry for 1897 notes that classes were taken in the College Hall to avoid overcrowding in the schoolroom. The history of the National School can be traced in some detail from 1863 when John Ash began the Log Book. At that time, there were 84 boys and 75 girls in the school and of those 21 were below six years of age. There were six classes, two of which were Infants under a paid mistress and an assistant. In March 1863, some of the children were kept at home to help in the gardens. Mr. Ash comments this was one of the local circumstances from which Chardstock suffers. Sometimes children were kept at home for hay-making, potato and apple picking and in September to glean the corn harvest.

The older pupils had to help with the teaching and Mr. Ash went over their work for the day before breakfast. The four rules of Arithmetic, fractions and Euclid were taught. The children's spelling and dictation often needed attention, and Singing lessons in the Infant School were "of great advantage in keeping the little ones in order". Grammar and Scripture, which in one examination paper was "indifferently done" also figured in the timetable. The Vicar, his wife, his sisters and his brother seem to have been constant visitors to the school. There are many references to them examining the school, taking church music practice, speaking to the children and requesting half holidays, as in November 1865, when Miss Woodcock requested a holiday "on account of happy news from India" though what this was is not known. Church services were regularly attended and many extra services seem to have been held, as in February 1866, when "all the schools went to a 'fast' service on account of the cattle plague". Throughout the history of the school, children have been absent owing to one illness or another. There have been the usual types of epidemics, measles, whooping-cough, etc., but in 1877 there was a serious outbreak of Scarlatina. The school was closed for a time and one boy died of the illness.

The first record of a Headmistress was in 1869, when Susan Hawkins was appointed. She began by inviting Mr. Woodcock to point out the faults in the school. She writes in the log that, "He thought the teacher talked more than she ought". He also complained at a later date of "bad figures, untidy slates and uncut pencils". The cane appears to have been used fairly frequently. Miss Hawkins notes on 7th. May 1869, "Conducted the school without using the cane - only gave one boy a box on the ear". Some lessons were taken with the children standing and on one occasion a parent threatened to remove her children unless they were allowed to sit at their lessons. Parents were required to make a payment for their children's education. In 1869, Mr. Woodcock increased the fees of farmers' sons from 2d to 6d a week. Several left in consequence. In 1883, the charges were 3d per week for farmers' children, 2d per week for tradespeople's children and for those of labourers, 2d for one child or 3d for two or three children. The hours of attendance in 1883 were from 9 a.m. to noon and from 2 p.m. till 4.15 p.m. Children have been admitted as young as three years and there are several references to pupils coming from Dame Schools in the area. Evening or Night Schools have existed on various occasions. There are references to them in 1864, 1891, 1911 and in several other years. From 1872, there are many references to tea-parties and later to annual treats given by Lady Henley, wife of the Lord of the Manor. By about the late 1890s or early 1900s, these treats assumed carnival like proportions with tea, roundabouts and swings in the College cricket field. Presents, prizes and attendance certificates were given away on these occasions. Lady Henley also visited the school and looked at the needlework etc. Other treats and festivities included Maypole dancing, which was held in 1884 at Edencote, the home of Mr. and Mrs. Rodd. This celebration continued at Chardstock House at least until 1912. The children carried garlands of flowers and danced round the Maypole singing,

> "First of May,
> Garland Day,
> Squire Rodd's Birthday,
> Please to remember the Garland."

after which there would be a tea. Christmas treats have been given at various times, notably by Mr. and Mrs. J. R. Pratt in the 1920s. Half holidays made it possible for the children to attend Club days both in Chardstock and in other villages and they often stayed away to go to Chard Fair. School closure for use as a Polling Station appears to have started in 1885. This is now a thing of the past as voting takes place at the Community Hall.

The heating of the school has always posed a problem, even when hot water pipes were used, complaints about the rooms being cold are still reported in the log. Many coal and coke stoves have been installed and removed but now that the school is heated by gas the temperature can be easily controlled. The original lighting must have been oil lamps and, judging by the presence of gas piping in the ceiling, at one time gas from the College gas works was used. After the closure of the College, oil lamps returned until in 1946, electricity was installed. School meals seem to have existed in one form or another from about 1909, when the Vicar, the Revd. Lewis, and his wife organised 1d dinners in the College Hall. The log for 1944 records that Canteen meals commenced in November. In 1951 the present kitchen and dining room were brought into operation. Cocoa was served in school from around 1932 and the milk scheme was started in 1937.

During the 1939-45 War, children from Bristol, Southampton and the Friern School, Peckham Rye were evacuated to Chardstock. At first a separate school was set up for them in the Parish Room but later, as numbers of evacuees fell, they were absorbed into the village school and the L.C.C. teacher was recalled to London. Before 1902, when County Councils were set up and became responsible for Education, the school had been run by a Committee under the Chairmanship of the Vicar. Only a few records of its meetings have survived in the Minutes of Vestries Book 1864-1959. These include the setting up of a local Committee to carry out the provisions of the Education Act of 1880 and the forming of a School Attendance Committee. The Minutes record that a 2d rate to assist the school was proposed in 1891 and details of the engaging and dismissing of the staff are given. Since records began in 1863 there have been 22 Headteachers, 50 Assistants and 4000 children have passed through the school. The longest serving Headteacher was Mr. Ambrose Shere, who was head from 1921 to 1941 and the longest serving Assistant was Miss Mary Coombes from 1892 to 1923. She had been a pupil before becoming a monitress and finally a teacher.

From about the turn of the Century as well as the "4 Rules and Grammar", subjects taught included Scripture (the Vicar being responsible for a proportion of the lessons), Needlework, Carpentry, Geography and History. There were also Object Lessons (the taking of a particular object and giving a lesson on it) and Gardening, started by Mr. Shere and developed on a large and successful scale. Teaching methods have of course changed significantly during the history of the school, as have punishments and the forms of instilling discipline. Until 1937, the school was an "all age" school, but from that date it catered only for Juniors and Infants, the older children transferring to a new Senior Council School in Axminster or to Colyton Grammar School. In 1989, the 150th Anniversary of the founding of Chardstock school was celebrated with a Service in St. Andrew's Church, a "Victorian Day", during which the pupils and staff attempted to recreate a Victorian teaching situation, an Exhibition and a tea, which was graced by the presence of Lady Henley. At the present time, Chardstock St. Andrew's School continues as a Church of England Voluntary Aided School maintained by Devon County Council and the Exeter Diocesan Education Committee. There is a board of Governors and the Headteacher is responsible for the organisation, teaching and day to day running of the school. There is a Friends of the School Association which includes the parents and anyone interested in the welfare of the children. A playgroup formed in 1978, now called Chardstock Pre-School, is attached to the school.

In 2009 a new school building was completed and the old school was sold. So begins a new chapter in the history of education in Chardstock. "A History of Education in Chardstock 1712-1979" was revised and reprinted to commemorate the fact, and retitled "A History of Education in Chardstock and All Saints 1712 - 2009".

Dame Schools
There were other schools apart from the main school in the centre of the village. To the north was Bewley Down School situated at Cotley Wash, also started by Revd. Woodcock. 29 children were present when a return was made under the Elementary Education Act of 1870, but the Education Department decided that, as the older children could reach the village school, the 10 to 12 infants left unprovided for could be ignored. Bewley Down School was then omitted from the Notice issued under the 1870 Act. These notices set out the various school districts of the country, named the schools to serve them and stated whether or not additional accommodation was required. Chardstock's Notice named two schools, All Saints Church Day and Sunday School in the south of the parish with 118 children and the National and Industrial Church of England School in the village with 196 on roll. The Revd. Woodcock also mentions the existence of "two or three dames' schools" in 1844 and the National School Register of Admissions records children

admitted from Dame Schools in 1869 and every year from 1874 to 1885, the last reference being in 1895, when the following entry appears in the log book, "Admitted 7 children, 5 from Bealey Down (who have attended the Dame School at Cotley Wash.)". This most probably refers to the Bewley Down school mentioned in the 1870 Notice.

All Saints' School
To the south of Chardstock village is All Saints' School (mentioned above) which was opened on 15th January 1872 with about 70 children including 35 Infants. There had been an earlier school erected about 1851, the existence of which was confirmed by the Trustees of the new school in their preliminary statement of application for an Annual Grant from the Education Department. They stated that the school had replaced a private one which had been in existence for twenty years. The Lords of the Committee of Council on Education were informed in 1870 that a number of persons intended to raise money to build a school. The population of All Saints Parish at this time was stated to be about 510, many being employed as farm labourers and quarrymen. Apart from the labouring population, there were about 16 families comprising about 80 persons, including one of the upper class and the clergyman's family. The remainder were tenant farmers who were expected to send their children to the school. It was stated that the nine tenths of the labouring class were Church of England and the remaining one tenth equally divided between Wesleyans and Bible Christians. The population was a very poor one, embracing the outlying portions of the parishes (of Chardstock and Smallridge) in Devon and Dorset and originally, for the most part squatters. The land upon which the new school was built was freehold glebe of the Rectory of Chardstock All Saints, the consolidated chapelry formed in 1839/40 out of the parishes of Chardstock and Axminster Hamlets. There was an enquiry in 1870 to establish whether or not the parish school (the original school) had been erected on consecrated ground. In a letter dated December 1870 the Revd. J. G. Brine, Rector of All Saints' church, complained that he would have to take down the school buildings he had erected 20 years before and re-erect them elsewhere. Canon Woodcock, who was present at the consecration of the ground for All Saints' Church, stated that the ground for the proposed school was unconsecrated. The outcome of the dispute is unclear, but it is certain that the building of the new school and teacher's house went ahead. The cost of the whole project was £726.

A return made to the Government in 1872 showed the weekly payments made for children were, Farmers - 3d for each child but not to exceed 1s for all, Tradesmen - 2d for each but not to exceed 6d a week for all, Labourers - 2d for one child, 3d for two attending together, 2d for four together, 1d for five together and free when five or more attended together. The Headmistress was Elizabeth Brampton and the infants were taught by Hannah Newbery who had been in charge of the original Parish School for the whole 20 years of its existence. Over the years the numbers of children attending the school have dropped, particularly when, in 1937, the 12 to 14 year old pupils transferred to Secondary schools. The school then catered for the 5 to 11 year olds and in about 1965 an extra free-standing classroom was added to the existing two main rooms to accommodate the Infants. Again in the 1980s, for various reasons, numbers dropped to 15. This gave rise, in 1984, to the fear of closure, but with much hard work by the Governors and the active support of the Parent, Teacher and Friends' Association, this was avoided. At present, All Saints is a thriving Voluntary Aided school with an enthusiastic Headteacher and an increasing roll.

Sources
Churchwardens' Presentments D5/28/6/160., Wilts. R.O.
Nowlens Weekly Chronicle, op. cit.
Wood, P. J. & Chardstock Historical Record Group A History of Education in Chardstock 1712-2009.

PLATE 7

INDUSTRIAL SCHOOL FOR TRAINING SERVANT GIRLS,
AT CHARDSTOCK, DORSET.

The Full Range of College Buildings

*The Clock from
St. Andrew's College*

School Class in 1898

Chapter Twelve
THE CHURCH

The church of St. Andrew, as it stands today, was reconstructed in 1863-64 and little of the original building remains, perhaps only the south wall and former porch. Not a great deal is known about this original building but from contemporary newspaper accounts we learn that "the fabric had fallen into a lamentable state of decay, the south wall of the chancel being so bad from damp and age that it was from ten to twelve inches out of the perpendicular, and scarcely safe. The nave arcade was also leaning over at least nine inches and the roof timbers were so decayed and twisted as to be only held together by iron rods and ties in every direction." The only part of the church which was in a sound and decent state was the south aisle and the south transept. The account continues, "It is impossible to conceive anything much worse than the general condition of the old building ..... the walls of the chancel and other parts being perfectly green with damp and mildew for two or three feet high, arising from the ground in the churchyard having risen to that height above the floor of the chancel and to the want of proper drainage." Even the Bishop of Salisbury, who consecrated the new church in 1864, remarked that "this was the first time he had entered the parish with anything like a hearty and cordial feeling. Previously he had sometimes felt that his life was a little imperilled for there were great bars stuck across the chancel which warned him that if he did not move quickly it might come down."

The Old Church

The old church, as described by Pulman in "The Book of The Axe" was also cruciform in plan and consisted of a chancel, a nave with south aisle, north and south transepts, north and south porches and a tower at the west end. The date of its construction is not known but its style was originally Early English. It was lengthened in the fifteenth century when the eastern perpendicular window and a window in the south wall were added. The south aisle was probably built at the same time as the arches, which were perpendicular. The arches of the transepts were in the Decorated style of the 14th century. The windows were generally poor, some having pointed heads but the majority being flat-headed. Some of these pointed window heads have been found in the churchyard under a pile of rubble. Also discovered at the same time were two large stone carved faces and another of poorer quality; these could be gargoyles or figures from a corbel table. They are possibly of Norman origin and were probably from the old church. In the east wall of the chancel there were two large niches decorated with elegant carved work. One of them may have contained a figure of St. Andrew. Under the window were three further niches surmounted by carved stonework and bearing inscriptions. The three lights of the window were filled with plain glass and in front stood a plain Victorian table and communion rail. Also in the chancel were several high wooden backed seats with a row of three lower wooden seats in front of them.

Between the north transept and the chancel, in the angle of the wall, was a mural monument of freestone on the top of which were the figures of a gentleman and lady kneeling opposite each other before a desk. Below them were two similar figures also kneeling and at the back of the lady were three mutilated figures, probably children. Below was a tablet bearing a Latin inscription to the memory of the Simonds family of Cokesden. Under this monument was the Jacobean pulpit which at the time of the re-building was removed but was restored to its original position in 1913. This could have formed part of a three decker, as in 1825, at a Vestry meeting it was agreed "that the pulpit and desk should be removed from its present situation to the North Wall". In 1841 the sum of £10 was allowed towards the erection of a new pulpit and in 1860, T. Parris was paid to remove the pulpit, desk and two seats. There was a gallery in the old church and in the Churchwardens' accounts for 1848-49, Wm. Pearce was paid £2 16s 6d for a door and a partition in the Gallery where, in 1861, four benches were provided for the children.

There is evidence that a Chantry to enable a priest to say Masses for the soul of the benefactor had been founded in the church. A bequest in the will of John Estmonde, made in 1531, gives vjs viijd (6s 8d) to the fraternity of the Blessed Mary of St Andrew's Church. In the Tudor Subsidies list of 1545, "The Brotherede of our Lady ther" is assessed for 10d for its goods. In the Certificates of Colleges and Chantries 1545, it is recorded that a chantry at Chardstock possessed "one chalice, one pyx of silver and twelve spoons". Income to support the priest probably derived from the land at Holditch Mead. It is possible that these references may have been to the same chantry, which could have been situated in the South Transept or in the Tytherleigh aisle. During the re-building in 1864, a stone coffin was discovered when portions of the wall of the aisle were removed. It contained parts of a skeleton and boots which were still on the bones of the legs and feet. Fastened to the boots were spurs which are now thought to be those displayed in the Royal Armoury in Leeds. They are described by the Board of Trustees of the Royal Armouries as prick spurs, unique in form and quality, "Slender necks of diamond section the neck swells into sharply pointed goad. Decorated with dots of gold on a hatched ground." According to Sir Guy Laking in his book, "Record of European Armour and Arms through Seven Centuries", the spurs were, "remarkable examples of their kind and may safely be assigned to the first half of the eleventh Century." Perhaps these relics belonged to the founder of the chantry or possibly to a member of the Tytherleigh family, founders of the aisle. The Tytherleighs were responsible for the maintenance of the aisle, which, at the end of the 17th Century, seemed to be constantly out of repair, as was the chancel. In 1680, it was noted that the "South Ile to be repaired by the churchwardens". There must have been a disagreement about this because in 1693, an entry in the Churchwardens' Presentments states "Tyderleigh Yle out of repair Robert Tyderleigh to repair it". He appears to have done nothing as in 1697, "at a Spiritual Court held at ye sign of the Dolphin" (probably the George Inn) the following entry appears in the presentments, "Imprimis we present the South Isle of the Church comenly called Mr. Tyderleigh's Isle to be out of repair and Mr. Tyderleigh to repair it". In the same year Robert Tyderleigh was presented for "living incontinently with Gertrude Brown". Again nothing was done and the Churchwardens continued to complain. In 1717 Robert Tiderly Esq. was presented "for not repairing the Isle in the Church belonging to him". In 1721, the "Iyle" was still "out of repair" but now it was to be repaired by Henry Codrington. It fared no better under its new owner for in 1726 he was again ordered to repair it. By 1738, the ownership had passed to the Pitts family and the presentments stated "Madam Pitts ile to be out of repair". Mrs. Pitts was mentioned as owner in 1747. Her family sold the Tytherleigh estate to John Stuckey of Branscombe in 1780 and in 1864, Tytherleigh, presumably including responsibility for the aisle, was the property of John Churchill Langton of Parrocks Lodge, Tatworth.

Documentary references to the old church are few. As mentioned in Chapter 13 dealing with the Prebend of Chardstock, when Dean Chandler visited Chardstock in 1405 he found the nave roof, chancel windows and choir stalls were defective. When he came again in 1408 the windows were still broken and the south aisle roof needed repairing, as well as that of the nave. An entry in the Steward's account of the Manor of Chardstock in 1425 for wages of a tiler, "One day above the Lord's chapel" may refer to the church but probably to a private chapel in the nearby Manor House. In 1684, and 1693, the chancel was out of repair and the lay Rector, John Every, was instructed to repair it. Perhaps he neglected to do anything as it was still causing concern three years later! The 1717 and 1718 Churchwardens' accounts show that major repairs were carried out on the old church during those years. One entry reads "paid Mr. Charles Taylor plummar June the 11 Twenty pound in part for work about the church". Another entry states "paid Matthew Noseter four pounds Towards the north side of the Church for work don". Apart from these entries, there were numerous payments for boards, sand and nails etc. One interesting item of expenditure was "paid in liquor to the plomers when the first sheet was cast 0 - 1 - 0 - 1 - 0 the workmen desired that we would make them Drink and we made bold - 01 - 0 - 0" (amounts uncertain).

The New Church

In the year 1834, the Reverend Charles Woodcock came to Chardstock and set about changing the face of the village. He began by demolishing the old vicarage and rebuilding it on the same site. He then built the present school, St. Andrew's College and houses to accommodate the staff and pupils. Finally, in 1864, he demolished most of the old church and rebuilt it as we see it today. While this was being done, the services were held in the school. The whole cost of this project (about £5,000) was borne by the vicar, his brother T. Parry Woodcock and with contributions from friends who remain anonymous. The Architect was Mr. James Mountford Allen, the son of the Revd. John Allen, a former Headmaster of Crewkerne Grammar School. Other examples of his work can be seen in churches and schools around Crewkerne as well as at Cricket Malherbie. The plan of the church, which the architect designed, was substantially that of the former building, a nave, with north and south transepts, the chancel, to which he added a north chapel for the use of the scholars of St. Andrew's College, a south organ chapel, a vestry with a room above and a new north aisle. The foundation stone for the rebuilding was laid in June 1863. The south aisle wall remained as before and the tower containing the ground floor ringing chamber was not rebuilt until 1868. The style of architecture of the new church is that of Victorian Decorated. On the 21st of September 2014 a Service of Celebration, combined with Harvest Festival, was held to mark the 150th Anniversary of the Re-dedication of the New Church on the 29th September 1864.

Chancel

The east window of the chancel is a triplet light in the Early English style and has clustered marble shafts on the interior. The details of the window are identical to the remains of the old one found embedded in the wall during the rebuilding. The stained glass it contains was made by Messrs O'Connor and was the gift of the Revd. Charles Woodcock's nieces. The small two light lancet window on the south of the chancel was given by the architect. Below this window is a two stalled sedilia enriched with Cornish serpentine shafts and carving. The choir stalls are of oak from the roof of the old church. They have carved ends and there is a movable bookboard on iron standards for the front seats. The floor is covered with Minton's encaustic tiles specially designed by Lord Alwyne Compton. The ceiling is panelled with carved bosses at the intersections of the ribs and is richly illuminated. On the north side of the chancel is the College Chapel now known as the Fernie or Lady Chapel. It was furnished by Mrs. Fernie and was dedicated by Bishop Lovett (a former Bishop of Salisbury) in 1950 in memory of her husband Andrew Fernie and of those educated at the College. He was a scholar at the College and a Chorister from 1875 till 1885. One of the frontals used on the altar was part of the hangings from Westminster Abbey displayed at the coronation of Queen Elizabeth II. The east window had stained glass by W. Warrington and was the gift of members of the College but it must have been removed, for in 1911 the present window was inserted. The two windows in the north wall probably had similar stained glass and were given, one by Mrs. King who lived at Burridge and the other by the Revd. R. Hake, a minor canon of Canterbury Cathedral, in memory of his son who died while a pupil at the College.

Nave

Between the Chancel and the Nave is a screen of Bath stone with marble inlays surmounted by wrought iron work. The arcades on each side of the nave consist of four bays the arch stones of which are alternately of Ham and Bath stone and the shafts of Ham stone. A band of purple tinted stone about six inches wide, from Bishop's Lydeard, runs round the arches. Stone corbels consisting of carved angels playing musical instruments are inserted in the walls between the clerestory windows from which spring the curved struts of the nave roof. On the south side, from the east end, the musical instruments are Serpent, Cymbals and Trumpet. On the north side Pipes, Flute, Tambourine, Harp and Violin are shown. Between the angels are shields bearing on the south side, Alpha, the cross of St. Andrew, the letters I.H.S. (Jesus Saviour of men) and Omega. On the north side, Omega, the Greek cross, the cross of Constantine (the Chi Rho) and Alpha. The roof is an opened timbered one with curved and moulded ribs to the principals, purlins and purlin braces and has a richly pierced and carved cornice.

Near the north entrance is the Victorian font and in lettering on the wall is a text from 1 Peter 3, on the subject of baptism. The original Norman font, dating from about 1155, was until recently in the closed Church of St. Francis of Assisi in Hereford, but has now been returned to Chardstock. In the north aisle wall is a stained glass window depicting ministering to the sick, the poor and the needy. The window is in memory of Anna Arabella Sutherland. Masonic symbols are incorporated in the west window of the aisle. A window in the south wall of the Tytherleigh Aisle contains stained glass inserted in 1897 in commemoration of Queen Victoria's Diamond Jubilee. A door in the same wall leads to the original south entrance porch now converted to a lavatory. At the base of this old entrance to the church are two interesting marks, 9 June on the east side and 4 Oct on the west side. The significance of these dates is unknown. Inside the porch on the north wall above the door is a niche possibly once containing a figure of St. Andrew, to whom the Church is dedicated. The earliest known reference to this dedication is in 1405 in the Register of John Chandler.

The music in the old church was probably provided by the musicians, as it was in most churches, but there is no documentary evidence to support this in Chardstock. At some time before the church was rebuilt, an organ was installed and in 1863 the Vicar inserted, in a local newspaper, an advertisement for the sale of this organ, which had two rows of Keys, Pedals and 18 stops. The instrument was to be removed immediately after the sale on account of the Church Restoration. It is not known if the sale was successful or whether a new organ was purchased. A major overhaul of the organ took place in 1882 when the instrument was improved. The work was done by Messrs. Henry Jones of South Kensington at a cost of £150. In 1997, extensive renovation was undertaken at a cost of over £10,000. During this work, a piece of a newspaper dated 1857 was found in one of the older pipes, an indication that part of the instrument predates the rebuilding of the church.

It is not clear what form of heating or lighting there was in the original church or indeed if there was any at all. When the new church was built, an underfloor type of heating must have been installed for ducts and traces of this system were discovered when new small bore hot water pipes were installed in 1984. These pipes were to replace the large cast iron radiators which had become inefficient. Before the advent of electricity, the church was lit by oil lamps and for a short time by gas (some fittings are still to be seen in the building) which was made in the village. Electricity came in the 1920s and in 1983, the church was re-wired and more powerful lamps fitted. In the original church there were 435 seats, 159 of which were free and the remainder allocated. This accommodation was increased in 1864 to 568 seats, of which 267 were free. During 1997, a sound system with loudspeakers and a loop for the hard of hearing was installed.

The Tower, Bells and Clock

The tower was not rebuilt at the same time as the church but four years later in 1868. It was then proposed to add a spire but funds were insufficient and the tower remains at its original level. There are six bells used for ringing in the tower, plus one on which the hour is struck. The ringing six, two of which were broken, were cast or re-cast in 1868 by Mears and Stainbank of Whitechapel. They were re-tuned and re-hung by Arthur Fidler of Bow, Crediton in 1974/75.

The Tenor bell bears the inscription,

> I toll the Funeral Knell
> I ring the Festive Day
> I mark the fleeting hours
> And chime the Church to Pray.

Before 1868 the tower contained five bells, hence the Five Bells Inn which was directly opposite the church. An entry in a manuscript dated 1552, recording bells in Dorset churches during the reign of Edward VI reads, "The Denary of Byrporte - Chardstok Fyve belles in the Tower one lyttyll bell in the Chancell 2 other lyttyl belles". This is the earliest record so far discovered of bells in St. Andrew's Church. According to Canon Raven in his "Church Bells of Dorset" the 1st and 2nd were inscribed "Sit nomen Domini Benedictum" and had two small shields. The first depicted two keys in saltire with a dolphin, emblems of the Fishmonger; the bell and the laver (or jug); and a wheatsheaf. The second included a scourge or whip. There was also an octagonal medallion containing the cross and the words "ihu merci ladi help". These symbols are found on bells in other counties. According to an article by Amherst Daniel-Tyssen published in the Sussex Archaeological Transactions in 1915, they were the marks of William Chamberlain, a London founder circa 1480.

The third bell bore the inscription "Anno Domini 1649 S.K.T.P." and was probably cast by Thomas Purdue, itinerant founder of Lezant and Stoke Climsland near Launceston, Cornwall. The fourth bell was the work of George Purdue, whose three sons were also founders. The family has connections with Salisbury, but the Chardstock bell was cast in Taunton, for written on a paper dated 1599 is a record of an agreement, undated, between the parishioners and George Purdue for the re-casting of the fourth bell. The bell founder was charged "to make her tunable to the third and fyveth bell" and if the new bell proved unsatisfactory "He shall new cast her at his own charge". The bell was inscribed "Drawe neare to God 1618 George Purdy (followed by the stamp of a bell) G S T P I H".

The fifth and heaviest bell was re-cast by Thomas Bilbie junior. He came from the Chewstoke area and the family did much work in Dorset, especially at Beaminster, and in Devon at Cullompton. The bell is the only one of the old five remaining. It is hung without a wheel above the new ring and is used as the bell upon which the clock strikes the hour. It bears the inscription, "I to the church the living call and to the grave do summon all. Mr. William Pryer and John Bragg churchwardens. Thomas Bilbie fecit 1766." The order for the re-casting of this bell is to be found in the Poor Book of 1751. It is dated 31st May 1765 and reads, "At a Vestry Held this Day According to Publique Notice Given in Church for that Purpose to have the Great Bell New Cast in the Parish of Chardstock. So we that are Parishioners that Pays to the Church Rates of the Aforesaid Parish do Hereby Agree to have the said Bell New Cast At the Expence of the Parish As Witness our Hands. Thomas Drayton Hugh Welsh John Wills."

Hutchin's "History of Dorset" 1864, gives the 1766 bell as the third of the ring, the fourth as cast in 1618 and the fifth dated 1646. There is also a small bell in a turret above the chancel arch. This was probably added when the church was re-built in 1864. There is an interesting account in Pulman's "The Book of the Axe" 4th Edn. 1875, of an incident which took place in 1820.

"The 4th bell had its crown broken out in 1820 when the ringers, having been refused permission by the churchwardens to celebrate the abandonment of the Pains and Penalties Bill, broke into the belfry on three successive evenings and rang so vigorously as to commit the damage. The ringers were summoned for the forcible entry, but the grand jury ignored the bill, and the ringers in turn brought an action against the curate, the Revd. Thomas Babb, for a malicious prosecution, but lost their case. The action was tried at Dorchester on March 17, 1821 before Mr. Justice Holroyd." The present church clock is remarkably fine having been made by Benson of Ludgate Hill, London in 1868. The technical details are:

It is a "flat-bed" clock, with Graham dead-beat escapement driving a 40 beats-per-minute pendulum. The Westminster chimes, sounding every quarter and at the hour, and the strike, are rack-operated. There are dials on the West and North sides of the tower, the dials themselves being carved integrally in the faces of the tower, with gilded figures. In the centre of each dial is a quatrefoil opening glazed with very thick clear glass, with the dial rods passing through a hole in the centre. There have been at least two previous clocks for in the Churchwardens' accounts for 1837 are the following entries:

1837		£	s	d
11th March	Journey to Bridport to order new Church clock		5	0
7th April	pd man for taking down old Church Clock		3	0
24th May	Wm Baston for going to Bridport after new Church Clock		7	0
25th Oct	pd for carrying ladder from Tytherleigh to the Church and back for fixing Clock Dial etc.		2	0
23rd Dec	pd Mr T. Farnham for New Church Clock	50	0	0

This clock was removed when the tower was rebuilt in 1868. The "old clock" referred to above may have been the one which, according to the churchwardens' presentments for 1736, was in good repair.

Plate

There is no ancient Communion Plate remaining in the church. The earliest reference is found in the Register of John Chandler, Dean of Salisbury 1404-1417, where mention is made of two silver gilt Chalices and Patens and an ivory pyx in which the reserved sacrament would have been kept. There is also a detailed description of the vestments and books used in the pre-reformation church. In the Wiltshire Record Office is a document, with papers dating from 1558-1603, containing a list of names of those parishioners who, "wolde notte pay to the heyght crosse lyght at ester nor at crestmasse". This was probably the light on the Holy Rood which separated the Nave from the Chancel and to which "John Estmone left xxd" (1s 8d) in his will of 1531. The document also gives details of "Detts owinge to the pishe of chardstocke". These are probably from the early half of this period when church goods were being sold. The sales took place after the Catholic restoration came to an end with the death of Queen Mary in 1558. The entries relate to money owing for "sarteng stoffe of the cherches", for "a crosse of brasse of the cherches" for "a crosse and a panne of brasse" and for "pewter of the cherches". In 1606, the Churchwardens stated in their presentments to the Dean's Visitation Court that, "wee doe want a fayre pewter pott for the comunion wyne". It is hoped that they did not have to wait until 1819 when, in the Churchwardens' accounts, 5s was paid for "Plate for the use of Communion" and £1 12s 6d "for a Flaggon". The present plate consists of a modern gilt chalice and paten inscribed "Panis vivus Agnus Dei", two smaller chalices, one with the cross of St. Andrew stamped on the side and the other inscribed "To the pious memory of Andrew Fernie" There are two patens which match the chalices, a paten and cover in memory of John G. Seward, a ciborium in memory of John Reginald Pratt, a pewter dish and a travelling communion set.

Churchyard and Church Monuments

The Churchyard, the western part of which is terraced, contains a number of table or altar tombs of the 18th Century. As far as is known, the present Lychgate was reconstructed in the first half of the 20th Century by Jack Apsey. The only evidence of a previous gate of this type is from a drawing of the National School, viewed from the churchyard and made about 1850 by Canon Woodcock's sister. The artist has shown the gate on the west side of her drawing. Details of the wall bordering the churchyard can be found in Chapter 13 "The Prebend of Chardstock". In the north porch is one of the earliest tombstones from the churchyard, that of John Bowditch and Joan his wife who died in 1641 and 1611 respectively. There are others to the south of the church in the churchyard. They include that of Thomas Estmond, who died in 1685 and his wife, Elizabeth, who died in 1694. Both these families have monuments inside the church. The Bowditch Hatchment is described in "Hatchments in Britain", Vol. 7, ed. P. Summers & J. E. Titterton, Phillimore.

Dexter and top sinister background, black. Argent a fess wavy between three bows stringed paleways gules (Bowditch) impaling Argent a chevron between three garbs sable (Blake).
     Crest: A sheaf of five arrows points downwards or headed and banded gules.
     Mantling: Gules and argent ending in tassels or.
     Motto: none. Skull and crossbones on frame, unidentified.
Bridget Bowditch, 14th child of Humphrey Blake of Bridgwater and sister of Admiral Robert Blake, married Henry Bowditch on Dec. 8th 1635. Henry was the grandson of John and Joan Bowditch. This hatchment and the Estmond shield are both on the wall of the south aisle. The explanation of the detail on the Estmond shield has been taken from the Somerset and Dorset Notes and Queries Vol. 12 p.347-8.

> The first and last quarterings are those of Estmond of Lodge, Chardstock.
> The second quartering is probably the Bowles family of Wiltshire descended from John Bowles of Bristol living about 1460.
> The third quartering is not known.
> The fourth quartering is lion rampant.
> The fifth quartering is the Lourney family. John de Lourney married Joan daughter of John Attlodge.
> The sixth quartering is lion rampant.
> The seventh quartering is the Agnus Dei.
> The eighth quartering is probably the Kipping family.
> The ninth quartering is most probably the Constantine family.
> The tenth and eleventh quarterings are unknown.

On the south side of the chancel arch is a brass plaque in memory of Canon Charles Woodcock re-builder of the church, Vicar of St. Andrew's 1834-1875 and Rector of All Saints' 1875-1898. Above the Jacobean pulpit is a similar plaque to Thomas Parry Woodcock who provided most of the funds for his brother's re-building scheme. Another plaque, on the north side of the chancel arch, is in memory of the Revd. Francis Parham who was Vicar from 1883 to 1905.

The War Memorial plaque to those who fell in the two world wars is on the east wall of the south transept.

On the north wall of the north aisle is a brass plaque to the memory of Lilian Mary Coombes, a pupil and a teacher at St. Andrew's School for over 30 years. On the west wall is a plaque to John Reginald Pratt, Churchwarden for 36 years. He was a tireless worker for both church and school. On the east wall of the north transept hangs the Royal Coat of Arms of Charles II, bearing the initials C.R. 1660 and the date 1797 with the names of the Churchwardens for that year, William Bently and Thomas Pinny. In the accounts for 1797 is an item, paid William Trott's Bill for painting the Coat of Arms £2 0 0.

Registers

The Registers date from the end of the 16th Century. The heading to the oldest one is "The Register booke of the parish of Chardstocke in the county of Dorset and in the Diocese of Bristowe in the yeare of our Lorde God 1597." Amongst the entries some interesting information can be found of which the following are examples. Under the date July 16 1634, there is a Latin entry to the effect that Archbishop Laud of Canterbury (more likely his officers) visited the church. During the Commonwealth Period, children were not allowed to be baptized in church and so from September 1653 until 1659, only birth dates are registered. Similarly Marriages were published in church but the wedding itself was a civil contract. The first gentleman to perform marriages in Chardstock under the new system was Edward Buttler J.P. In 1632, Richard Turner alias Collins, died excommunicate and was "privately buried without the church bounds" From August 1678 until November 1686, each burial is accompanied by an affidavit that it was done in wool according to the Act of Parliament for burying in woollen (for promoting the trade). There are entries in the Poor Law books for the purchase of wool for burials as late as 1795.

All Saints' Church

In 1840, by the exertions of the Revd. C. Woodcock, the Revd. W. D. Conybeare, Vicar of Axminster and in particular Mr. Arthur Acland of Axminster, a second church was built at South Common on land which was part of the Manor of Chardstock. The Christian Remembrancer of April 1841 states that "there was no public appeal ...... the first laying out and digging of the site was aided by the gratuitous labour of poor persons returning from their day of toil ..... every part of it was occupied by free seats (for 220 persons)". St. Andrew's still charged pew rents for the best seats at this time. The altar and cross are of Portland stone and the font of Beer stone; Ham stone was used for the windows, and plinth and quoins are of blue lias. It has one bell although constructional provision had been made for a tower. Lighting was by oil lamps but was later "improved" by the substitution of candles in the nave! The foundation stone was laid in May 1839 on the site given by the Bishop of Salisbury and Lord Henley, and the new church was consecrated on 23rd April 1840. It had been built by private contributions aided by the funds of the Diocesan Building Societies of Exeter and Salisbury and the liberal assistance of Benjamin Ferrey, the architect, and cost about £1,211. In 1841, "The Consolidated District of All Saints, Chardstock and Axminster" was formed from part of the two parishes of Chardstock and Axminster, and the first incumbent was the Revd. T. A. Walrond, curate of St. Andrew's Chardstock. In 1867, the chapelry was made a rectory and the then incumbent, the Revd. J. G. Brine, became the Rector. To celebrate the Church's Jubilee in 1890, the chancel was extended by 14ft. and a vestry added on the south side. This was made possible by Canon Woodcock, who had retired there as Rector in 1875, and the generosity of his friends. Many other improvements were made and the Salisbury Diocesan Gazette for February 1891 reported that "these apparently small additions have transformed a somewhat mean looking building into one of dignity and good proportions".

Sources

Churchwardens' Presentments, D5/28 Wilts. R. O.
Gerhold. P. K., All Saints - The Early Days.
Church Registers Chardstock, Dev. R. O.
Wood. P. J., 1994 A Short History of the Church of St. Andrew in Chardstock.
Bray. Susan, Bell Founders. New Research.

Chapter Thirteen
THE PREBEND OF CHARDSTOCK

The Parochial system in England may have emerged as early as the 7th Century when Christianity was beginning to spread through the land. Churches were established in the larger centres of population and priests would move out into the nearby villages or settlements to preach. Sometimes they set up a wooden cross to indicate to the people where the preaching place would be. Some of the later stone crosses still remain, e.g. in Whitestaunton Churchyard. It is possible that the priest would be based at a monastery or at an "area" church which came to be known as a minster. Landowners in the settlements visited by the missionary priests may have been persuaded, or be keen, to erect a building for the priest to use. These would have been wooden at first, be later rebuilt of stone and perhaps enlarged at a later date. In some places, the owner might build his personal church or chapel, which was later used by the ordinary people. Landowners also gave land, or its revenues, to the local cathedral for the maintenance of a priest who would be a member of the cathedral chapter. The gift would be known as the Prebend and the recipient as the Prebendary. As early as 690 A.D., donors were permitted to give money, land, or a share of produce to support a resident priest in their neighbourhood. In return, those who supported a resident priest or built a church were given the right, known as the advowson, to choose the chaplain or priest.

It is not known when the first church in Chardstock appeared but as the Bishop of Sarum held the Manor at Domesday, it is possible that some form of ecclesiastical building existed before 1066. In 1158, a confirmation charter of previous endowments of the cathedral of Sarum, together with the bestowal of other estates, gives the information that Gilbert de Percy gave the church of Chardstock to the cathedral, thus exempting it from the jurisdiction of the bishop. From this point it was known as a Peculiar and was controlled by the dean until 1846, when Peculiars were abolished. This gift was the origin of the Prebend or Rectory of Chardstock. The Prebend of Chardstock was originally a Sub-Deacon Prebend of the Cathedral at Salisbury where the whole of the Psalter would have been said daily with certain psalms being assigned to each Prebend or Canon. The Chardstock psalms were 147, 148 and 149. Wambrook, now a parish in Somerset, also appears to have formed part of the grant. In a deed dated 1215-20, the chaplain of Wambroc, Philip of Yarcombe, acknowledged that the chapel belonged to the prebend of Chardstock. In documents dated 1405 and 1535, it was stated that the Prebendary was paid £1 a year by the Rector of Wambrook. As part of the prebend, Wambrook parish had to contribute to the upkeep of Chardstock churchyard wall and the "hatches" (or gateways) into the churchyard. The wall appears to have been a constant source of concern to both the Churchwardens of Chardstock and Wambrook. In 1606, the Chardstock Churchwardens presented, "the church hatch (gate) at the west end of our churchyard to be in decay in the pishers default of wambrooke". A hundred years later in 1714, the presentments include the following item, "the lower part of the church wall which belongs to the Parish of Wambrook that are out of repair a small breach in our wall belonging to this parish which is repaired by the Churchwardens of the Parish of Chardstock". In 1747, the presentments state, "the Churchyard wall out of repair Especially that part that belongs to Wambrook". Payments for this purpose continued until 1811.

A Rector was originally the incumbent of a parish who received the Great Tithes and offerings and was responsible for the upkeep of the rectory and the chancel of the church, while the parish was responsible for the repair of the nave. In 1405, Dean Chandler found that the Rectory walls, the chancel windows and the choir stalls were defective through the Rector's fault. The nave roof was also defective, and the churchwardens were instructed to repair it. The first known Prebendary of Chardstock was Abraham de Winton, whose name appears c.1214. At that time it is not known who was the patron and rector or who would have appointed a deputy to care for the parish. He would be known as the vicar and would receive the Small Tithes. The first known vicar of Chardstock was William Briton, who in 1286 was presented to Netherbury and Beaminster as vicar, by the Abbot of Ford. There were probably other earlier Chardstock vicars whose names have yet to be discovered. On 5th November 1298, Walter de Sideling, the Abbot of Milton Abbey presented the first non-monastic priest, William de Mileburn, to the vicarage of Middleton (in Hampshire) and his institution took place at Chardstock on 17th November 1298. There is a record in the Patent Roll of 1297, of a vicar named William at Chardstock. Whether he was William de Mileburn or William Dave who was vicar in 1318 is not known. There is also a mention in the same Roll of William de Cerdestok, canon of the church of St. Mary, Salisbury.

The Chardstock Rectorial Tithes would have been paid to the Prebendary, who was the Rector, or to a layman who had leased the Rectorial or Prebendal lands. In 1836, the Ecclesiastical Commission for England was set up and from then, the tithes were commuted to a money payment and were collected by the Commissioners. A map of the parish was made c.1840, the land valued and the money payments apportioned. In the 1860's, Joseph Winter of Combe St. Nicholas attended at the Tytherleigh Inn to receive the year's rent charge in lieu of the Rectorial Tithes due to the Commissioners. The prebendal lands were situated to the north of the church where the present Church of England Primary School is built. In 1235, the prebend was worth 12 marks and in 1291, 24 marks (£16). According to an entry in the Patent Rolls of 1348/50 (at the time of the Black Death), William de Compton was farmer of the Prebend. The same Roll states that the King (Edward III) took the Prebend as it was held at that time by an alien, possibly John de Mota.

PLATE 8

Rev. Charles Woodcock M.A.

The Nave and Chancel of Old Chardstock Church

Parish Chest

Oldest Bell, dated 1766

South Porch Doorway

Bellringers

Prebendal seat at Salisbury

In 1405, it included a hall with two rooms, a barn, byre, dovecote and 20 acres of land; in 1447, it was worth £30; but by 1534, the value was £18 16s 8d. In 1564 the Revd Robert Hooper, prebendary of Chardstock, granted a lease to John Hooper. After his death the remainder of the lease passed to his son George Hooper gent. of Downton, Wiltshire. In 1581 he sold the remainder of the term of 80 years to John Every who thus became the lay Rector. The lease consisted of the Prebendary, rectory advowson and manor with all the rights, lands, mansion house, etc. thereto belonging. In 1590, Magdalene Every, widow of John, bought from John Estmond of Oxford University his right (being the remainder of a lease "for many years") in the Prebend of Chardstock for £150. From her, it passed to her son John and through him to his son Sir Simon Every, 1st Baronet of Egginton, Derbyshire. In 1626 he leased the Prebend, except the vicarage, to John Petvin, butcher, of Haselbury Plunckett who then assigned it to Enry Hodges also of Haslebury Plucknett. The property, which had been leased to Simon Every in 1634, was sequestrated in 1645 during the Commonwealth period, when it was valued at £160. In 1649, it consisted of a barn, which had been converted from the mansion house, a stable, cockloft, small yard and about 50 acres of land, though not all conjoined. In 1676 John Every of Egginton appointed Mathew Bragge of Thorncombe his attorney to receive possession of the Prebend etc as leased for the lives of John Every and two sons of Sir Henry Every, John and Simon, from Peter Paine the Prebendary of Chardstock, by indenture dated 1668. In 1694 Thomas Every of Burton on Trent leased the Prebend, but not the advowson, to Nicholas Keate and Thomas Keate, his son, of Chardstock for 7 years at an annual rent of £130. Another Sir Simon Every, born in 1660, received in 1698, by the will of his uncle John Every "a lease of the Prebend of Chardstock". In 1752, he authorised his son the Revd. John Every to let the Prebend to George Warry of Chard and Richard Hese of Chardstock for 7 years. Sir Edward Every succeeded to the estates in 1779 and in 1780 he sold the property for £1978 3s 6d.

At the end of the 16th and during the 17th Century, the Everys were often accused of not repairing the Chancel. In the 1590s and in the year 1600, the roof, ceiling and "glasse windowes" were "in decaye" and the Churchwardens blamed the prebendary or his "farmour Mr John Everie". In 1638, Mr Simon Every was presented for not repairing the Chancel. It would then appear that in May 1780, the Prebendary of Chardstock, the Revd. John Huish of Pembridge in the County of Hereford, granted the lands etc. to George Warry. He paid the poor rate for the property in 1781 and 1782. In 1783 Joshua Harcombe, a tallow chandler of Combe St. Nicholas and a relation of the Warrys, leased the land. William Leate must have been his tenant as he is recorded as paying the poor rate from 1784 till 1795. In 1839, part of the land leased by Joshua Harcombe Cuff was acquired by the Revd. Charles Woodcock, Vicar of Chardstock, from his uncle Canon Henry Woodcock, who was the Prebendary of Chardstock. On this land he built the National School.

Although the Prebendal Lands have long since been sold and Chardstock moved to the Diocese of Exeter, a prebendal stall is still to be found in Salisbury Cathedral. The present Prebendary of Chardstock (now an honorary appointment), is Canon Harold Stephens, Rector of Dorchester Team Ministry. Chardstock benefice has now become part of the Axminster Team Ministry in the newly formed United Benefice of Axminster, Chardstock, Combpyne and Rousdon, and also All Saints, to which Membury has recently been added. The advowson or right of presentation of a vicar to the benifice passed from the prebendaries or rectors to the Bishop of Salisbury. With the move to Exeter Diocese, the vicar became the team vicar and is now chosen jointly by the Bishop of Exeter and the Rector of Axminster and is then licensed by the bishop. The prebendaries, vicars and some curates are listed in Appendix E.

The Vicarage
In the valor of Pope Nicholas IV of the year 1291, the vicarage of Chardstock was worth £5. At the Inquisitio Nonarum of 1341, the value was £5 8s 8d. The Valor of Henry VIII states that in 1534, the discharged living was worth £14 2s 4d in the king's books. This included 8d. a year paid to the Vicar by the Rector of Wambrook. A Parliamentary Survey made in 1650, during the Commonwealth, assesses the value of the vicarage house as £3 and the tithes of wool, lamb, cow-white (milk), hay, orchards with fruit, as £40. By 1826, the total value had risen to £300.

Sources
Calendar of Papal Registers and Letters, Som. Local Studies Lib.
Churchwardens' Presentments, D5/28 Wilt. R. O.
Commonwealth Records, Reel 29 Comm XIIa v15 p160/161, City of Birmingham Public Lib.
Every, Mrs. M., correspondence.
Fasti Ecclesiae Sarisberiensis, Wilts. R. O.
Fasti Anglicanae 1300-1541, Salisbury Diocese, Wilts R. O.
Hutchins, 1864 History of Dorset p86.
Overseers of the Poor Accounts, Dev. R. O.
Patent Rolls, Som. Local Studies Lib.
Prebend of Chardstock, D/14 Wilts R. O.
Sarum Charters and Documents in the 12th & 13th Centuries, op. cit.
The Register of Dean John Chandler 1405, Dor. Local History Library.
Every family deeds, D5236, Derbyshire Record Office.

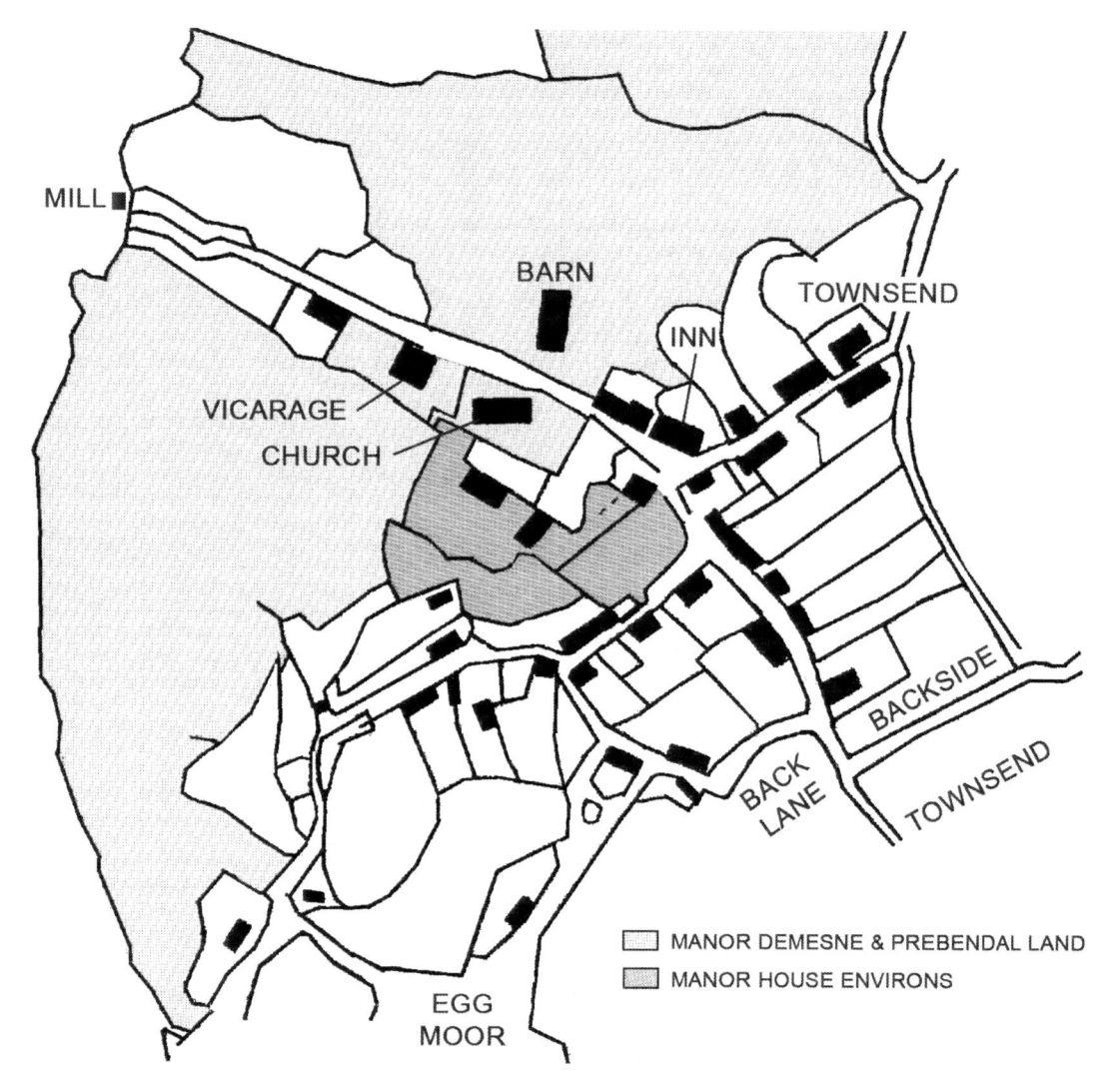

MAP 10 Chardstock in 1781

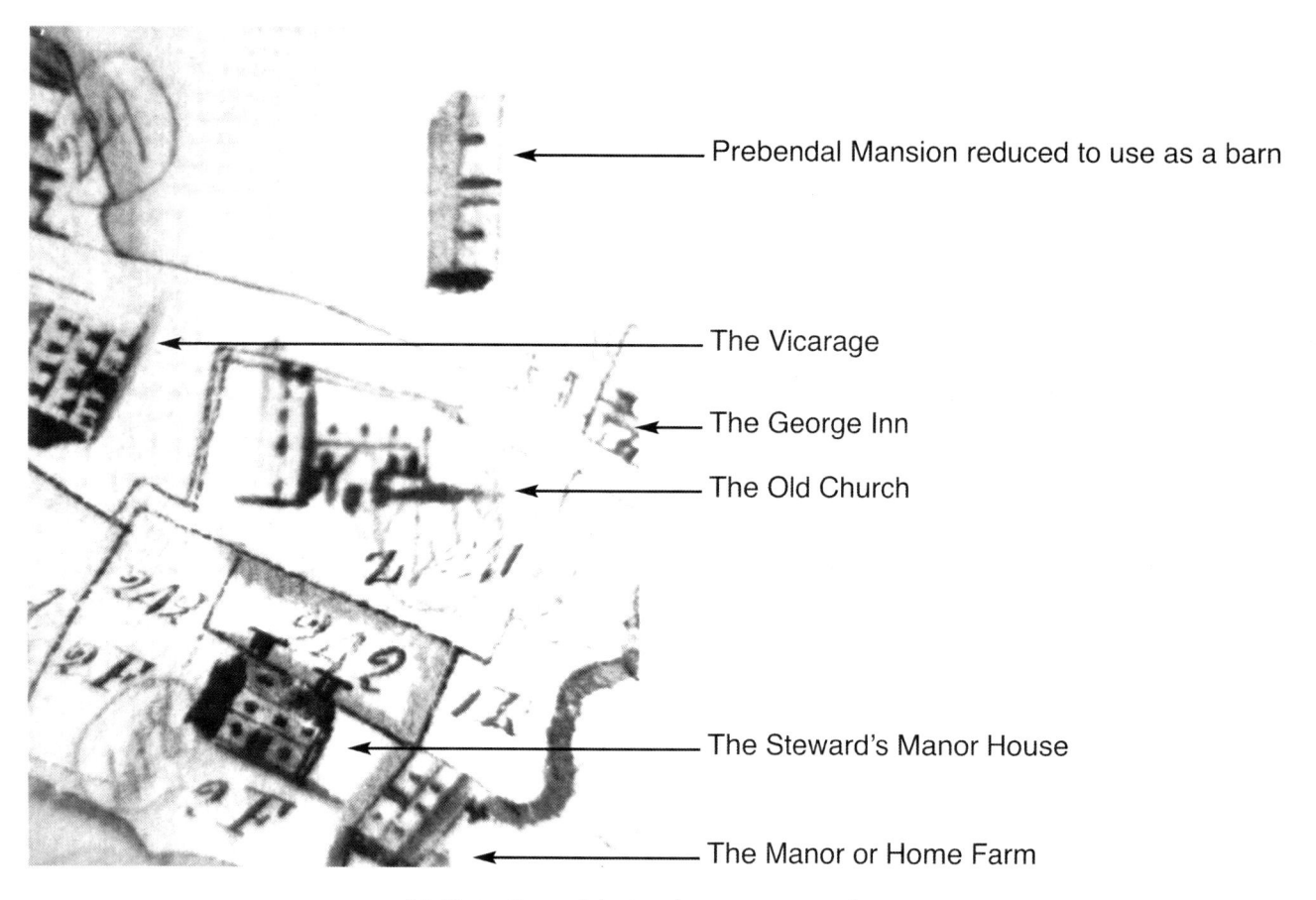

MAP 11 Part of the Henley Estate Map of 1781

Chapter Fourteen
ECCLESIASTICAL AND CIVIL COURTS

The Church, in the widest meaning of the word, that is the people and not the building, has always had a profound influence on the life of Chardstock. From Domesday, and probably before, the clergy were important landholders. The Bishop held the Manor, while the Prebendal Estate, formed from the gift of land by Gilbert de Percy, the glebe and tithe system, which supported the vicar, and the school, were all connected with the Church. The Churchwardens, who, with the Overseers of the Poor, were responsible for the relief of the Poor, often had civil as well as parochial duties. They had, for example, to maintain the parish arms, to pay local soldiers and to control and exterminate vermin within the parish.

Parish Arms and Soldiers
An entry in the Inventory to the will of Thomas Parys dated June 1557 reads "It .... a harnes bows and arrowes a sheffe ... viijd" (8d) (a harnes was armour and a sheffe was a sheaf of arrows). There is in the back of the oldest surviving Poor Law Book, "A list of those who are to maintain ye armor and Souldiers imposed on ye parish of Chardstock". The list is not dated but was probably made about 1676/8 when James Keate was Vicar. It records 95 names of parishioners who, between them, were responsible for 23 "Armour". Unfortunately there is no indication of exactly what the "Armour" was.

Vermin
The statutory destruction of vermin dates from 1532-33 when every parish was required to kill certain types of birds. Later Acts extended this to predatory mammals and further species of birds. Chardstock records of this requirement do not go back as far as the 16th Century. Only those for the years between 1797 and 1831 give details of the various creatures destroyed and the payments made to the parishioners. The number of small birds destroyed seem to indicate that they were deemed to be an agricultural nuisance. The following statistics give some idea of the scale of the operation in the first part of the 19th Century.

    Birds   Sparrows - 8555, Hoops (Bullfinches) - 948, Crows - 522, Jays - 290.
    Mammals   Hedgehogs - 541, Badgers - 39, Foxes - 25, Polecats - 3.

Most of the birds were killed during the years 1825 to 1831, when 5677 Sparrows and 522 Crows were destroyed. In addition, for many years, an entry "Birds" appears, but the number and species are unspecified. The payments made vary, e.g. Sparrows in 1797 were 2s 6d for 10 dozen, Hedgehogs 4d each, Foxes 1s, Badgers (sometimes referred to as grays) and Polecats 1s 4d each.

Visitations
Some of the earliest records of courts in Chardstock, are those connected with the church and the Visitations of Dean Chandler in the 15th Century. The Visitations dealt with the state of the church building, its contents and the obligations of parishioners. Most of the complaints, other than those connected with the building, contained in the Dean's Register, are related to non-attendance at church, or immorality. In 1405, it was noted that "Walter Peytesyne customarily goes to fairs and markets on Sundays and festivals, absenting himself from church to the grave peril of his soul". He confessed as much on 26th November and was sentenced to be beaten twice through the church. This penance was later remitted in the hope that he would reform. William Budde, Edward Bouchere, William Webbe and Walter Martyn, apparently did the same but their sentence, to be beaten thrice through the church, was more severe. This also was remitted. Edward Boucher, William or Walter Martyn and William Budde purged themselves of defaming the Vicar, of accusing certain of the Bishop of Salisbury's tenants at the visitation, of going to markets and fairs on Sundays and not attending church. The Vicar requested this should be dismissed because peace had been made. William Wagge was accused of defaming the Vicar, Roger Berewyk, of making accusations against parishioners at a visitation, "by which Vicar's reputation is enormously harmed and diminished". Walter Pole heard Mass elsewhere and did not attend the parish church. His penance was a double beating which again was remitted.

In 1412, at the Dean's Visitation, it was stated that John atte Mulle's wife, Katherine, had left her husband and wasted his goods. She denied this and was sworn to stay and look after him, otherwise she would be liable for a fine of 100 shillings and six beatings through the market and church. She was also accused of being a common prostitute, which she denied. William Pas, a married man, Richard Jambe, John Bere, William Pady, Thomas Shawe and John Cokeswell were named as her customers. They all denied it and John Cokeswell threatened to cut off the horse's tail of any servant of prebendal jurisdiction who cited him.

In 1758, the churchwardens had to answer a questionaire. In answer to the question, "Are there any in your Parish notorious for profane Swearing or Common Drunkenness?", the Churchwardens replied, "No more than usual". The same answer was given to the inquiry, "Are there any in your Parish who lie under a common Fame or violent Suspicion of Adultery, Fornication or Incest?". At this time, the parish priest was only obliged to administer the sacrament of Holy Communion three times in the year. According to the Churchwardens presentments in 1758 and 1785, the Vicar only celebrated Communion four times a year in Chardstock!

PLATE 9

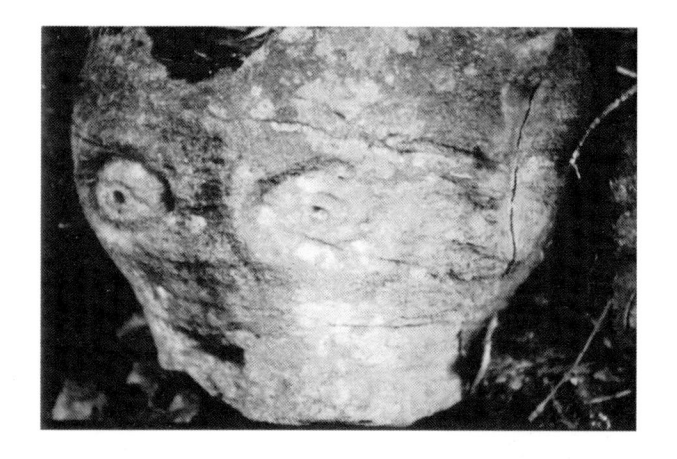

Gargoyles from the old church

Carved Capital depicting the fox and grapes fable

South Porch (part of old church)

Lych Gate and St. Andrew's Church

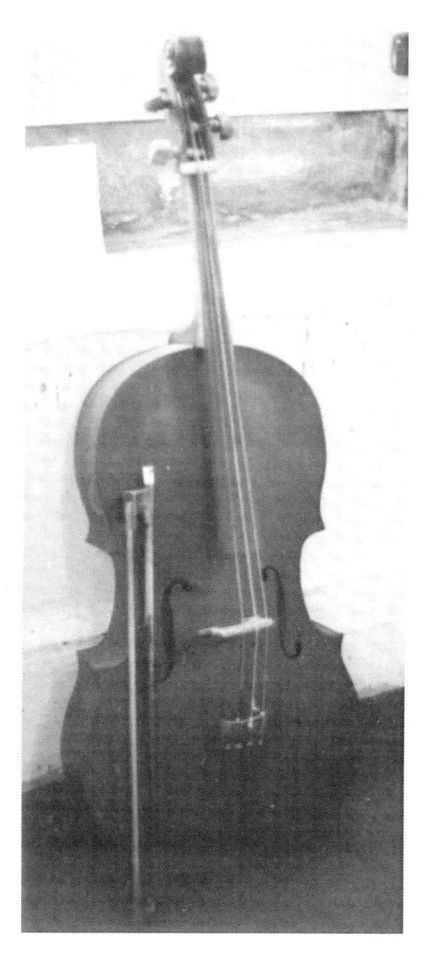

Iron Base Cello made by blacksmith John Bonfield and used before the organ was installed

Manor Court

The earliest Manor Court Records date from the end of the 16th Century and deal with the holding and transfer of land, tenements and cottages. Entries of repairs which the tenants were obliged to make also appear in the books. Minor offences and punishments were recorded in the earlier ones. These records only refer to the customs of the Manor of Chardstock and are not concerned with either the people or the land which, although in the parish, lay outside the manor boundaries, e.g. land at Cotley belonging to Lord Cobham. The manorial court consisted of a Jury or Homage formed by the principal landholders and copyholders. The lord of the manor would not be present, although his steward probably was. The various officials of the manor would be appointed by the court which met in April and October with meetings in other months as necessary. Matters not connected with the tenure of land include the following entries.

1597 Esme Martyne was to be punished for "upholding her children in pickering and that her son Thomas shall be whipped in some open assembly before Sunday night next for his pickinge". This was probably pilfering, though it may be robbing hedges for firewood as the next entry mentions several persons, including Esme Martyne, as "hedge teares".

"Joan Staple wid. has received into her house one Symone Haydon a stranger not there born and has forfeited 20s and is to put him out of her house by Whitsuntide on pain of 30s (pain here meaning a fine). Welsh received Anne Denman into his house as under tenant which Anne doth keep in the said house a man child not born within this parish but was born at Littleham (near Exmouth) and must put the said Anne out of his house before 1st May".

1598 Richard Parroke ought to make his hedge between him and Margery Woodlands backside before Christmas.

1599 The ducks of Nicholas Westofer annoy the potte water of Christopher Sandford Gent.

The Cookinge Stool is in decay. (This was probably a Cucking Stool, an instrument of degradation, consisting of a chair on which a woman offender was fastened and exposed to the abuse and missiles of passers-by. It may have been fitted for ducking or have been in the form of a close stool, carved with devils flying away with scolds. There are several references to it being in decay, e.g. in 1602, it was mentioned, together with the pillory, as being "insufficient". The same year Johane Bull, a widow, is stated to be "a scold of her tongue". Perhaps she was a candidate for the "Cookinge Stool"!).

There are noe butts (? for archery practice) by the space of three months (apparently no one bothered to remedy this for there were still "no butts within the parish" in 1603.)

William Hellard, William Wyate, John Wyate, John Lyne, Thomas Vyoncombe do use typplinge (brew ale) but it is not known whether they have licence or not.

William Hellard and William Wyate do keep unlawful games at the time of divine service.

The bridge lying at Kitbridge is in decay and the South Tithing must place a new bridge there before All Saints' Day.

1600 Mary Seward supports leawde persons in her house and is a woman of leawde behaviour in divers ways.

John Ferris is a common hedge tearer and steals rails and other wood and absents himself from the church very often.

John Parrocke the son of Richard Parrocke is a fellow of leawde life and evil behaviour and also is Timothy Seward and William Abbotte and do live only by filching and stealing and the neighbours greatly fear of them for burning of their houses and stealing of their goods.

1601 Mary Abbott did take and carrie away fagots of Nicholas Chubb's out of Stonycroft to the valeue of 1d.

The dunghill that John Wyate doth make at the personauge style doth anoye the pott water of the inhabitants belowe toward Mill Bridge. Day given him to take away the same (he did not do this and in 1602 he was fined xii d. (12d)).

1602 John Marsh doth keep a dog noisome to his neighbours. Day given him to put away the dog.

1603 And that there was an assault between Robt Wilking ixd (9d) and George Staple ixd and blood drawn in both parties".

One entry records that, "The stock, pillory and coucking stool is insufficient" and another "A fyne for speaking of contemptius words against the Steward ...... and Jury in open court.

1604 Day is given to the South Homage to view ...... whether that Robt Atkings do annoy the widdow Parrocke in setting a prevye or other noisome or hurtful thing in the said Atking's ditch ...... and whether the widdow Parocke do annoy Robt Atkings in her ditch or hedge."

Prebendal Court

Presentments were made by the Churchwardens at the Prebendal Court or Visitation by the Dean of Sarum. They consisted of reports on the fabric and ornaments of the church and gave the names of the retiring and newly appointed churchwardens. Early records give a wealth of information but gradually this diminishes. The modern presentments are made to the Archdeacon of the Diocese at his annual Visitation Court and still deal with the fabric and general life of the church. In 1583-5, the churchwardens complained, "we have not our quarter sermons, we have not had any Sunday an homily but we had them formerly" and "in the absence of our vicar & his curatt our clarke Thomas Dorben did burie one Marjorie Wyatt". They also presented, "divers of our pishe do not recyve the Communion thrice in the yeare but we cannot gete their names". During the same years Thomas Poole of Axminster was accused of calling Christopher Sampford "knave" in the church and Robert Woolmington similarly insulted Robert Trivett, also in the church. In the 1591-3 presentments the following complaint was made, "Christopher Wylles and Nicholas Dawlinge did chide and brawle in the church whearupon the sayed Wylles did geeve Dawlinge a blowe". "Our vestre is fallen downe the tymber sould unto Robert Wyatt by Mr. Burrage and Mr. Quintyn churchwardens and Mr. Quintyn did confess that he cared away a seeme (a cartload) or two of the stones and sayed wheras he caryed one seame others caryed away loades." In April 1600, the churchwardens presented that "one John Pynney of our said pishe called John Pynney the carryer hath of late and doth live verey suspiciously and is suspected to have done a notorious cryme with one Joane Mudforde his kinswoman and now a servant". And in July, "We present Joane the wife of George Wolmenton for her slack and necligent Cominge to the Church Lunatice and vocale". The only reference to witchcraft so far found appears in 1609/10 when a presentment states, "that Elizabeth Hoop was suspected for a witch and was by the Judges comitted to the Gaill".

There are several complaints that Sunday laws were flouted, as in the 1590s, "Item we present that our myller John Lange doth grinde on the Sabath Dayes but uppon greate necessety. Item we do present that John Seller did use a cariadge with plowe upon the Sabboth Daye." In 1606, everyone was in trouble according to the churchwardens, "we present the slacknes of the whole pish in not sending of their young children & young servents to be cathechized according to the law cannon in that case provided". Also in 1616, "Item wee present Marie Welshman for keeping and mainteyning of dancing & drincking upon the Sabath Dayes in her house". As in many parishes, games, especially fives, were played in the Churchyard. In 1722, it was noted that "several windows of the said Church are broken and was so by young people playing at fives".

Various parishioners were accused of causing trouble in the church. In 1622, Danniel Lake was presented "for disorder in casting a stone at Wm Savory the younger his head in time of Divine Service in the Chancel." In 1626, Peter Fowler was in trouble "for desturbinge of Thomas Soper of our parsh of Chardstock In the Church with Railinge to himm in time of saurmon sayinge when the mynister denounsed a Judgement againste notoures lyers, Soper look thou to that". 1663 was a particularly trying year illustrated by two presentments, "Item we doe present Richard Pearce for wearing his hat constantly in the time of sermon which he doth meerly in contempt for that he hath promised amendment but still persists & we doe present him for very frequent neglecting of divine service, he very seldom or never coming to the church till ye divine service be neer ended. Item we doe present James Dawberey Gent for putting up of a board upon his seat to ye hindrance of theye that sit behinde him from the sight & convenient audience of the auditory (the pulpit)".

In 1638, there was what appears to have been a marriage of convenience, possibly to gain or preserve the inheritance of an estate. The presentment was, "Item we the sayde Vycar wardens and sydemen (Robert Cogen excepted) doe present that by the generall fame (gossip) of our pishe and by the confesson of one Marye Marshall & others of the same house that she the said Marye was married to one Thomas Parris the elder, without banes asked or any lycence; A man of about 80 yeares & upwards lyinge in his bedd, not able to stand, or goe wholye decayed in bodye & mynde, who dyed as tis reported the day followinge but by what mynyster or by what Authorytye they were married; or whether by any mynyster at all; or whoe was present wee know nott, more than by common fame. The marryage, as wee are informed was at an unreasonable tyme. Secretly in a pryvate Chamber, with a companye of unfytt & unworthye people". Robert Cogen disclaimed the accusation that "Thomas Parris was wholy decayed in body & mynd at the tyme of his mariage & of the rumor there of the people there present". The Church Register records the burial of Thomas Parris, gent. on 24th June 1638.

In September 1670, Francis Sandford was presented for refusing to come to the sacrament and for not coming to the church. In 1680, Thomas and Elizabeth Estmond, his daughter Elizabeth, Mary the wife of John Estmond and Anthony Penquait's wife Joane were also presented for the same offence. Other complaints concerned unmarried couples living together and births of bastard children, whose upkeep might fall upon the parish. A rather unusual case occurred in 1626, when the Churchwardens presented "Magdalin Michell the wife of Salathiell Michell beinge her husband at sea & taken by the Turkees & was not in England this foure years & more to any mans knowledge but he hath written home also many times where he is & now at Michaellmas last shee had a child borne".

Another interesting case was recorded in the examination of Elizabeth Marsh on 20th April 1626 "Affirmation of Elizabeth Marsh of Chardstock that upon Sunday was six weekes since (crossed out) she was delivered of a mayde childe begotten by a stranger upon Bealy Downe in the Countie of Dorset by a stranger who beate her with a kudgell from her horse and saith she being in the extremitie of forgefulness never required his name her occasion as affirmeth was to buy oates of one Cicely Gardner of Whitestaunton in the sd Countie which was upon S. Peeters day laste and the said day shee procured the hue and cry to be made and sent forth by Mr. Freeke of Chardstock and she being demanded what was the complainte that made the sd Mr. Freeke to send forth his hue and cry she replieth because she had xvijs and xd (17s 10d) taken from her in the said place and by the said man and she saith she complayned not unto him that she was ravished but only unto her owne father mother brother and sister the said night and further she saith that neither her father or mother upon the present occasion sent for midwife and being interr whether she was not inforced about x or xi days before St James his day of the scandal notified but saith upon midsumers day laste att Exminster Fayre and saith she returned home in the company of Peeter Fowler her brother in lawe to his house in Chardstock pish but denieth she wente into his Chamber and was tumbled on the bed by him."

All was not doom and gloom, for in 1624, the officers petitioned the authorities to show compassion: "Wee whose names are subscribed doe certifie in the behalf of Margery Waldron of Chardstocke in the said Diosses that the said Margory (being excommunicate by order of your Court) is a very poore woman and very olde not able to travell by any meanes doe therefore in her behalfe intreate your worshipp to be pleased that she may be restored to the Church agayne of which we thought good to certifie your worshipps in the poore womans behalf".

In 1668, the then churchwardens presented James Harris, "for defaseing of the churchyard by cutting downe severall timber trees there, who being questioned for it, replyed, that hee would cut them downe all for hee had bought them of the vicar Mr Luce". Seating was also a source of trouble from 1634 to 1638 when the presentments record that the seats, many of which belonged to private houses, needed to be repaired. There was great opposition from the holders and in 1636 the churchwardens complained "Wee fynde most of these challengers so obstynate that wee dare not overmeddle with them without spetiall authorytye from your Courte". In a separate letter, the vicar, John Pytt, appealed to the Dean "to appoint two discreet ministers Mr Geere & Mr Chase" to view and give advice about the placing of the seats "which now stand disorderly". He goes on to say that there would be no agreement between the parisioners especially about the positioning of his seat and the pulpit unless the Dean prescribed how they should be set out. Apparently the dispute was still going on in 1638.

A public penance was imposed on Jane Cooke for committing the sin of fornication in 1672. The unfortunate girl was made to stand in the church during the Service and Sermon "and being covered all over from the Necke to the Feete with a White sheete & holding up in her hand a White Wan (wand) about an El long (about 4ft.) to make this confession following,

"I Jane Cooke doe here before Almighty God & you my good neighbours assembled humbly confesse & acknowledge that I being a grievous sinner have highly offended his divine Majesty through my manifold transgressions & particularly the dreadfull sin of fornication or incontinency with Richard Gollop of this pish gent & by him begotten with a base child lately borne of my body for which my wickednesse I am heartily sorry & doe unfeinedly repent of the same from the bottome of my heart humbly beseeching god to forgive me all my sinnes that I may the better obtaine pardon for the same & pray ye all here present to joyn with me in prayer saying Our Father who art in Heaven etc."

The case was also brought before the Quarter Sessions where Richard Gollop charged Edward Cload with being the father of the child. It was said that Jane Cooke pretended that Richard Gollop was the father because Edward Cload had promised to give her £5 to do that. It was also said that it was common knowledge that "Cload did usually lye with her". As Cload did not appear before the Court or make any defence it was ruled that he should be charged as the reputed father of the child. Did Jane Cooke make her confession in church knowing it was a lie? We shall never know!

Quarter Sessions
In the Somerset Quarter Session records for 1679, at the Examination of Mary Phelps of Chardstock, William Moore and John Browne, both of Chard, were stated to have been with her at a house in Chard in May. They insisted on her paying 1s for the beer they had drunk and when she refused they took, by force, her sleeves (probably ornate and detachable) and lace handkerchief "which she woore about her necke". They gave them to the landlady to keep until she paid the shilling, after which they accompanied her part of the way to Chardstock. She then accused them both of having "carnall knowledge of her body by force" after they had gone about a mile, and she was now "with Child by the aforesaid John Browne and William Moore". According to the Chardstock records Joan, the bastard daughter of Mary Phelps, was baptized the following February.

Dorset Quarter Session records begin in 1625 and for the most part deal with settlement and removal claims. The court also settled disputes between individuals and the parish relating to the maintenance of bastard children. Occasionally more serious matters found their way to the Sessions. An example of this occurs in 1704, when Joan Damp, who had been apprenticed by the Churchwardens to Samuel Bowditch, was brought before the court. She was accused of stealing £8 worth of goods and money from Bridget Bowditch and as a result, her apprenticeship was terminated. The court sometimes recorded gamekeeper appointments, mostly by Lord Henley for his estate, e.g. in 1772, Robert Summers of Chard was appointed, in 1779, John Amor of Chardstock, in 1783, John Seward of Membury and in 1789, George Smith of Axminster. An interesting case in 1792 was an appeal made by Thomas Palmer, a Chandler of Chardstock, against his conviction for making candles without first delivering a written notice to the Excise office as the Law demanded. He also appealed against his conviction for opening his dipping mould after it had been sealed by the Excise Office. Both appeals were dismissed.

One of the most serious offences was sheep stealing and two Chardstock men were among 9 hanged, for various offences, at Stonegallows in Taunton on 15th April 1801. It was recorded that sheep stealers William Warry and Edward Jeffery, both aged 49, acknowledged their guilt. An Edward Jeffery from Chard married Elizabeth Daw of Chardstock in 1785 and he may have been one of the men hanged. The Chardstock Church Records show a William Marks Warry, the bastard son of Elizabeth Warry, baptised in May 1757, making him aged about 44 in 1801. Could this have been the other man hanged for sheep stealing?

In the late 18th and early 19th centuries newspapers began to report court cases and legal proceedings.

April 1824 The Taunton Courier reported that Robert Pinney stole an ass called Tim from Ann Goff. He was sentenced to 12 months imprisonment.

The following examples are taken from The Chard and Ilminster News.

August 1874 After an inquest, the verdict on Joel Honnyboon, found dead in his garden was, "Died by the Visitation of God".

January 1877 Mary Davey was remanded at Beaminster charged with concealing the birth of her daughter who had been found dead on Wotton Farm. She had been caught at Cullumpton and was committed for trial at the Assizes.

March 1878 John Newton, a tailor, was charged at Beaminster with setting fire to James Willey's cottage at Crawley. He had been seen running away after the alarm had been raised by two lads, Sidney Hussey and John Bonfield.

June 1878 At Beaminster Petty Sessions, John Enticott, "a miserable looking fellow with one arm", was charged with being "drunk and riotous" Apparently this was a habit of his as was "ill using" his wife. He was fined 13s and 7s costs or 14 days hard labour. Thomas Porcey, a Chardstock butcher, was also charged with the same offence but as it was said that "he appeared to be suffering from some sort of hallucination", he was "let off on promise to keep sober".

November 1886 A long and expensive right of way dispute was amicably settled at a special court in Axminster before Judge Paterson. Mrs. Pryor had claimed £50 damages from Mr. R. Wale whom, she said, had made a roadway for his horses and carts in her field called Baker's Meadow to Stockstyle field belonging to him. She thought that "she was a very ill-used woman" and that "It was a question of a woman's rights against men's wrongs".

January 1889 At Beaminster Petty Sessions. there were proceedings against drunks, such as George Hounsell, a labourer of Tytherleigh, who was found lying drunk in the road. P.C. Elliott picked him up and took him home. Hounsell was fined 2s plus 8s costs. In a more serious case reported in the same month, Thomas Genge and Eli and Selina Larcombe were involved in a dispute over the possession of a cottage. Furniture was thrown over a wall and a fight took place during which hair was pulled, ribs broken and a pair of tongs wielded. The case ended with the Larcombes being sent to gaol for two months with hard labour.

December 1889 At Axminster County Court before Judge Paterson, Richard Isaac and Thomas Culverwell Dean claimed a cottage from James Denning. It had formerly belonged to Richard Denning, who had left it to William Bentley, who had left it to his sister and her husband for life. In 1885, a deed conveying the property to the Deans only mentioned one "moiety" (i.e. part) of the property. The Judge ruled that the cottage should be sold and the proceeds divided equally between James Denning and the Deans. In April of the following year the half acre property, which was at Holy City, was bought by James Denning for £52.

October 1890 George Taylor, a travelling tinker, was charged with assaulting William Toms, the landlord of the Tytherleigh Arms. This was dismissed but he was fined 10s for breaking a window. He also had to pay 7s 6d costs and 10s 5d damages. As he had no money he was "removed in custody" to a month's hard labour.

Village Police

In the 19th Century, the responsibility for law and order passed from the manorial constable to the newly formed County Police Force. The village police station was once at St. Andrew's Cottage, then at Wayside and finally at the purpose built police house opposite (now privately owned). The last village constable, PC Bater, was withdrawn in the 1960s.

Sources
Chard and Ilminster News, op. cit.
Churchwardens" Presentations, Wilts. R. O.
Manor Court Books - Chardstock, Dor. R. O.
Poor Law Books - Chardstock, Dev. R. O.
Quarter Session Records, Dor. R. O.
Quarter Session Records, Som. R. O.
Register of Dean Chandler, op. cit.

Chapter Fifteen
NONCONFORMITY

Very few records exist of the origins of Nonconformity in Chardstock. Dr. Edmund Calamy noted in his 17th Century record of incumbents ejected, that the vicar, Benjamin Mills, was ejected from Chardstock in 1662. He goes on to say that while Mills was in the village he had a full congregation in church and that the parish was more civilized than it had been before or since! Mills was a Presbyterian and went on to preach in Chard. In 1663, the Chardstock Churchwardens complained at the Prebendal Visitation that Thomas Crandon entertained Benjamin Mills to preach at his house on Palm Sunday. Mills was also accused of preaching at or near to Crandon's house "contrary to the Cannons Ecclesiasticall and contrary to ye late Act of Uniformity". By 1758, there were three dissenting families in Chardstock and in 1785, some Protestant dissenters were Presbyterians, some were Anabaptists and some Methodists.

Quakers
In April 1665, Elizabeth Clothier, wife of John Clothier of Montacute, was living apart from her husband in Chardstock with Elizabeth Harris. She was accused by Richard Luce, the vicar, of trying to persuade her husband, and others, to join the Quakers. He stated that he had burnt the books she had given him. In June 1665, the Churchwardens presented Elizabeth Clothier and Grace the wife of Christopher Collins, to be Quakers. They also stated that Thomas, John and William Crandon did not attend the parish church but "follow conventicly as we have been credibly informed". However, it was reported in the Episcopal Returns of 1669 that there was no conventicle (i.e. a clandestine religious meeting) in Chardstock. Meetings were held at Weycroft in the 1670's but in the 1680s the congregation was persecuted, causing it to resort to secret meetings in the woods and occasionally in the house of one of the members. The Sherborne Quarter Session minutes for 1692/3 note that the house of Richard Baker's at Chardstock was used for the "Worship of God by a Congregation of dissenting Protestants" After many alarms and raids by the authorities, peace descended on the land and in 1698 a new meeting house was built in Axminster.

Methodists
In Wambrook Wesleyan Methodists met in the kitchen of Loomcroft Farmhouse at the turn of the 19th century and, no doubt, some of the inhabitants of Chardstock would have attended. The first Methodists in Chardstock were reported in 1823, when there were 23 members, but it is not known where they met. A Wesleyan Methodist Hall was opened in 1891, services previously being held in the open air. The Mission Hall, as it was called, was situated in Back Lane and is now a private house. There is a very full account of its opening in the Chard and Ilminster News for 30th May 1891. The Revd. C. Harrison, Superintendent of the Devon and Dorset Mission, preached at the opening service. After tea, a large crowd assembled on the village green (probably what is now the beginning of Eggmore Lane) to listen to a concert given by the Honiton Mission Brass Band. In the evening another service took place, with so large a congregation that the adjoining cottage was used to accommodate the overflow. By 1928, the Mission Room, at the east end of the building, was in ruins. This was possibly due to a fire started by a spark from a traction engine belonging to Thomas Pratt, who bought the property from Albert Beasley. The deeds stated that the premises could not be used for the manufacturing or sale of intoxicating liquors or as a theatre, dance hall, music hall or club. Thomas Pratt built the present house and converted the Mission Room into a garage.

Churchill Methodist Church, to the south of the parish, was a Bible Christian meeting place usually known as an Ebenezer chapel. Built in 1840, and part of the Crewkerne circuit, it was linked with another meeting place (site unknown) at Holy City. In 1889, a legacy enabled the chapel to be renovated and improved. In October, a special harvest service was held in thanksgiving for the improvements. The chapel was chosen in 1924 to celebrate the centenary of Methodism in Chardstock, when the Revd. M. Hoare of Hayle and the Revd. J. Dobson of Barnstaple were the special speakers. A Sunday School Souvenir Booklet of 1911 includes recipes and quotations, one of which is concerned with Women's Rights. It also indicates that chapel life included a Young People's Group, a Band of Hope, a Clothing Club and a Lending Library.

Sources
Axminster Ecclesiastica, West Country Studies Lib.
Chard and Ilminster News, op. cit.
Churchwardens' Presentments - Chardstock, op. cit.
Quarter Session Minutes, County R. O.
The Mighty Oak, private library.

Chapter Sixteen
THE POOR IN CHARDSTOCK

"The Poor are always with us" is a well known statement and this was certainly true in Chardstock in the 17th-19th Centuries. The Parish is fortunate in possessing an excellent and almost continuous record of collections and payments of money to those less fortunate members of the village from 1645 to 1835. The record of parishioners receiving benefits begins in 1692. This was to comply with a Parliamentary Act of 1691 which required a register of beneficiaries to be kept. The accounts record that the Overseers of the Poor "Laid out for an Act for the poor...6d."

Vagrants

Apart from the establishment of certain Charities (Chapter 17), we do not know how the poor in Chardstock were cared for in the years before the 17th Century. Nationally an attempt to control vagrancy was made in 1388, when, if a parish could not maintain a beggar who was not able to work, he was sent back to the parish of his birth. At that time a labourer was not allowed to leave his parish unless he had authority from a Justice of the Peace. This is an ancient office. Justices had been appointed as early as 1277 and 1287 when they were known as Keepers of the Peace. They became Justices in 1361 and by an Act of 1388, six were appointed for each county. In 1391 the Statute of Mortmain stated that in parishes where the Great or Rectorial Tithes were received by the church or a monastery, part of the money was to be used for the relief of the poor. A hundred years later conditions had not improved. Vagrants were made to work and penalties for disobeying included whipping, loss of ears and, for persistent offenders, hanging. From 1530 vagrants, incapable of working, were obliged to obtain a begging licence from a magistrate. Five years later, parishes were made responsible for the poor and after the reformation, priests and churchwardens were empowered to ask for donations on Sundays. In 1547, vagrants who refused to work, could be branded with the letter "V" for Vagabond and made a slave for two years. Should they be caught running away, they could be branded with an "S" on the cheek. They would thus become slaves for life.

From 1563, each parish had to appoint men to collect money for the poor. The collectors were often the Churchwardens and in 1572 they were joined by Overseers of the Poor, elected by the Vestry meeting and approved by the J.P. Begging licences were abolished and compulsory rates introduced. Other officers were also appointed from the parishioners and were mostly unpaid. They would have been a constable, a waywarden, to make sure the parish kept the roads in repair, and a hayward, whose duties included supervision of the repair of fences and impounding stray animals. In 1702, William Warry was Constable, Richard Coggen was Waywarden. Samuel Wiatt was to be Constable in 1703. In 1737 John Hoar was Waywarden, in 1748 John Burch was paid 11s 6d for his "Waywardening Bill", in 1749 Mr Wiat received 15s and in 1750 John Amor claimed £1 2s 6d. Apart from these no other records of the appointments have been found in Chardstock.

Law and Order

Law and order was the responsibility of the Parish Officers and there are numerous payments for expenses incurred. In 1759, one shilling was paid "for the Guard that kept John Leaves when drunk in Church". One of the duties of the Parish Officers was to search out and deal with fathers of "base born children". One case in 1743 concerned Thomas Deane who was probably the father of an illegitimate child. He was possibly married to Mary Dean who died in 1742, after receiving money from the Poor Rate since 1736. Her coffin cost 7s and 1s 9d was paid for "strachen out of Mary Dean and woll (for a shroud)". Earlier poor rate entries about him were:-

pd ye Expense at Axminster when we Apprehended Thomas Deane 7s 6d
pd for Thomas Deane's mittimes .... 2s (a Mittimus was a warrant committing a person to Bridewell i.e. prison.)
pd ye Gard for carring him to Bridwell £1 5s 0d
pd ye Expenses at Axminster concerning Thos Deane 4s
pd to Mr Welch for Horse hire and my own horse hire to carry Thomas Deane to ye Justice 1s 6d
pd ye Expenses at ye George Concerning Thomas Deane 1s 6d
pd att ye meeting about going to Exeter Sessions about Thomas Deane 1s 0d
for horse hire caring Mary Pearce to Exeter 7s 0d
pd ye Bridewell Keeper concerning Thomas Deane £3 1s 0d
pd for a coppy of ye Register for Tom Deane 2s 6d
pd for a deliveration for Thos Deane 3s 0d
pd ye Expenses at Exeter at ye weding .... 10s (Thomas Dean was married to Mary Pierce at St. Leonards Church in Exeter on 22nd January 1743/4.)
pd ye Turnkey .... 1s (The Turnkey would have been one of the under-jailers.)
for going to Esq Williams .... 4s (Esq Williams would have been the magistrate.)
for carring the Warrent to the hundred Constable 1s 6d
pd att Exeter Sessions to the Council against Thomas Deane 10s 6d
pd Mr Gow for Drawing a briffet 3s 6d

pd for ye Examination of Tom Deane about his parish 1s 6d
for my Expenses at Exeter and horse hire 7s 6d
Spent concerning Thomas Deane at ye George 1s 6d
for Expenses about Thos Deane at ye George and at Axminster when he was carried to Bridewell 1s 6d
for horse hire and Expenses taking Thos Deane 1s 6d

In the middle of the 18th Century, those who broke the law must have been treated far too leniently for at the "Regular Parish Meeting" in April 1748, the following resolution was passed, "if any person is catch'd in any Fellonious Crime is to Suffer what ye Law Directs by the Expence of ye Parish" To assist the Churchwardens, two Overseers of the Poor were appointed from the more substantial landowners of the parish, one for the North Tithing and one for the South Tithing. This seems to have proceeded fairly amicably, usually no one having to serve for more than one year at a time. Sometimes the estate owner chose a deputy to act for him, as in 1694 when Robert Cooke acted for his father. In 1706, William Warry acted for Hezekiah Summers and in 1716, Henry Turner deputised for his brother. Women were sometimes chosen, although they did not always serve themselves. In 1678, Henry Stevens served for Mrs. Butler and in 1788, Giles Apsey was Overseer for Mrs. Marks's Estate at Bowditch. These were probably widows who had inherited their husband's copyhold or leasehold property. In 1794, however, a memorandum stated that, "Widow Paris for Higher Ridge ought to have done the Office of Overseer but her circumstance was such as the Parish did not approve off". What her "circumstance" was is not stated but Richard Dening had to serve for two years instead of one, presumably in the place of Widow Paris.

Under the Great Poor Act of 1601, a Poor Rate was levied on the landowners, the occupiers of their property and the better off parishioners. Everyone with property had to pay and the voluntary principle of poor relief was finally abandoned. This was really the beginning of the modern system of taxation. At first the rate was paid once a year, but in the 19th Century it was collected more often, usually twice a year. The Parish Officers endeavoured to keep as much money as possible within the parish. A great deal of energy, and indeed money, was expended in removing people from Chardstock who were not native and contesting claims for relief from those considered ineligible. In 1751, it was agreed "that no money given to Strolers of any Denomination shall be allowed", i.e. vagrants. Some poorhouses were built, though there is no record of such a house in Chardstock until the middle of the 18th Century. There were, however, two houses called "poore" houses listed in the 1671 Survey of the Manor. They were both copyhold, one being occupied by Sarah Sorry, a widow, and the other, which had an orchard and 4 acres of arable ground, by Thomas Colman. There is no reference to either of the people or the houses in the Poor Book. Perhaps they were "Houses of Correction", which began to appear from 1609/10, to accommodate vagrants.

Paupers
Children of paupers were to be apprenticed to the wealthier members of the community. A pauper was deemed to be a person who was destitute and had to be supported by the parish or some charity set up for that purpose. The term continued in use throughout the centuries and was not abolished until 1929. The charities established for the relief of the poor in Chardstock include the Ladymeade and Holditch Meade Charities and these are discussed in the Charities chapter. By 1601, the poor had been divided into three categories, the able-bodied who could be found work, those who were physically unable to work and finally those unwilling to work.

The first record of a Poor Rate collection in Chardstock appears in 1645. It totalled £2 10s 7d and was collected from 143 occupiers of land, landowners, leaseholders and copyhold tenants. Payments ranged from 1d to 2s 11d which was collected from Mr. Evory and his tenants of the Parsonage or Prebendal lands. The collectors were Edward Denning and William Wyatt the Churchwardens, and Nicholas Pinny and Henry Alford the Overseers. The money could be spent on, (a) setting to work all able-bodied paupers, (b) setting to work children of parents who could not maintain them, (c) providing flax, hemp, wool thread, iron, etc. to enable the poor to work and (d) for the relief of the lame, impotent old, the blind and others not able to work. Clothing, shoes and payments of money were given to those in need and in sickness while shrouds, coffins and graves were provided for those who died. In Chardstock totals of money spent each month were kept but it was not until April 1692 that lists of paupers names appear. These show those who were receiving money and the amounts each was paid. The lists provide a record of many of the inhabitants of Chardstock right down to 1832. This was probably in compliance of an order to keep a register of recipients of poor relief.

The following entries show how many forms of relief were carried out and noted in the accounts.

1692	Laid out to Thomas Knight in the bad weather 2s 0d	
	Laid out to Elizabeth Wills when John Larcombe turned out of door 2s 0d	
1693	Item paid to John Damp towards the building of his house £2 0s 0d	
	Item to Joane Mettford in Sickness 3s 0d	
	Item to Mary Dunster for to buy her a pare of shoes 2s 0d	
	Item paid for a shirt for Charles Savory 3s 0d	
	Item Paid for a bed for Richard Manning and for a pott of ointment 5s 2d	
	Item Paid for a bed and a bedstead for Kathleen Parris 6s 4d	
1695	paid for the repairing of Mary Chards house which William Deane pulled down £2 2s 0d	
	and for William Deanes house rent and Richard Mannings 16s	
1696	paid for taking down of Henry Pollards house and carring it away 2s 6d	
	paid for reed & tymber which Dorothy Deane burnd in Chards house 4s 0d	

In 1662 the Act of Settlement was passed, under which a stranger in a parish could be removed by the Overseers. There are many references in the Chardstock Poor Law books to the removal of men, women and children, not native to the parish, to other places, mainly to avoid having to pay for their upkeep from the Poor Rate. A man could be removed if he did not rent a property worth £10 per annum, but if he was resident in the parish for 40 days, he could obtain poor relief and could not be removed. This led, in 1685, to an amendment to the Act under which a written notice of arrival had to be given to the Overseers to prevent strangers hiding from the authorities until the time limit expired. A temporary worker had to obtain a certificate from his home parish guaranteeing to take him back if he became chargeable to the Poor Rate. From 1697, all Settlement Certificates had to meet this condition. The following examples are from the Poor Book:-

1692	Laid out when the masterless persons were taken up 6s 2d
	Laid out to Edward Savory for going forth with the masterless persons 1s 0d
	Laid out for 4 horses to carry forth the masterless persons to the Justice 5s 0d
	for two warrents for the masterless persons 3s 0d
	for the Mittmas to carry them to Bridwell 2s 0d
	Laid out for taking up of a vagabond & for carrying of her to the Justice 2s 6d
1693	Item paid for the order of removall of the Widdow Bovett to Stockland & about ye wench att Esqr Tytherleigh 4s 0d

The Case of Mary Nott

Children born out of wedlock became the responsibility of the parish and the Overseers often found themselves involved in considerable trouble and expense. The case of Mary Nott is a good example of what happened when the reputed father became difficult.

July 1745
pd ye Midwife for Delivering Mary not 2s 6d
pd Mrs Tederleigh for attendance and House roome for Mary Not 5s (the child, a girl, was baptized at Chardstock on 16th. June 1745 as Betty base born daughter of Mary Knott).
pd Mary Not 4s
pd at the George when we meet to consult about Mary Nots Bastard & to take up ye fellow 1s 1½d
pd for Hors Hier when we took him 5s
pd Expenses when we took Carrel & layd out two nights 15s
pd for his Examination Before Maigger Waldron 1s
pd the Expences of Carring Downe Mary Not to be Exammoned before Magger Waldron 7s 6d
pd Mary Knot 1s

September 1745
pd for Hors Hire & Exspences for going to Kinsbeare & Collumpton in order to take up ye constable of Collumpton for Letting Goe of Elixander Carrel & for Lying out Three Days & two nights £1 13s 6d
pd Mrs Tyderlidge for two months House Rent For Mary Knot 2s 8d
pd for a pare of Shoes for Mary Knot 3s
pd Mary Knot 2s

This payment was made in September 1745 and it is not until July 1747 that the next references to Mary Knot appear. It is not known what happened to Mary and her daughter during these years but they must have been in Chardstock in 1747.

pd Mary Knot for a pair of Shoos 2s 6d
Pd att ye George about Mary Nott 1s
pd for keeping Mary Nots Child 6s

August 1747
pd for keep Mary Nots Child 4s 6d
pd Wm Dening for Gard over Mary Nott 4s
pd Mr Heale for Marring Mary Not .... 6s (the Revd. Richard Hele was the Vicar)
pd for a Lissions for Mary Not £1 6s 6d
pd John Green when he was Married 5s
pd for Going Wrombrook for ye Lishens 1s
pd ye Exspences when Mary Not was married 12s 6d

In the Church Registers it is recorded that on 30th July 1747, John Green of Uffcombe married Mary Knott. Why William Dening stood "Gard" over Mary is not clear, perhaps it was a "shot-gun" wedding! Many payments of 4s 6d for keeping Mary Nott's child, perhaps in the Parish House, are recorded. The payments cease in October 1753 when Elizabeth Knott was apprenticed to John Bishop, the occupier of John Cornish's Estate. The Indenture was dated 27th September 1753 and stated that Elizabeth had to be taught "Good Housewifry Work" until she either reached the age of 21 or was married. What became of Alexander Carrel is not known as there are no more references to him - perhaps he was not the father after all.

The Case of Martha Bovett
Another case was that of Martha Bovett, who was a recipient of poor relief. The Officers travelled to an inn near Beaminster to resolve the parentage of the child.

for going to ye Bottle with Martha Buffit to sware to ye Father of ye Child .... 1s 6d.
pd for her Examination & Warrant 2s 0d
pd for horse Ire for Thom Knight & his Exspence at ye Bottle ...... 6d.
pd Mr. Heal Lishance for Marrying Mary Buffet .... £1 12s 6d.
Gave Hockey to Marry her .... 5s 0d.
pd Page for keeping ye night before they were Marryed & for a Quart of Ale .... 1s 9d.
pd at ye George for Ale & Eating .... 8d.

An entry in the Church Registers states that John Hockey of Chard married Martha Bovett on 18th September 1752. No doubt the Chardstock Officers were pleased to have completed a successful operation in removing the responsibility of mother and child from their parish.

Settlement
As mentioned above, to obtain any form of poor relief, a person had to be born in the parish or to have lived there for at least 40 days. In 1748, Dorothy Holliwell's husband died and burial costs were paid by the parish poor rate. Dorothy was not a native of Chardstock and so she applied for a settlement order. She was examined before two Justices of the Peace and according to the following report, it was found that she had been married five times!

The examination of Dorothy Holliwell now residing in the parish of Chardstock taken on oath before us, two of His Majesty's Justices of the Peace for the said County on Tuesday the 6th. day of December 1748. Who on her oath saith that she was born in the parish of West Buckland in the County of Somerset and from there she came to Shute in the County of Devon when she was about eighteen or nineteen years of age and agreed with one Richard Warry for a year, with whom she lived about half a year, and then she was married with one Charles Turner of Chardstock in the County of Dorset with whom she lived about the space of twenty years at which time her husband died, after which time she married twice with two men of Chardstock aforesaid, Namely Bernard Welch and John Bennett, and she survived them both after which this Examinant saith that she was Married to one John Pyne of the Parish of Trull in the County of Somerset with whom she lived about the space of six months in the said Parish of Trull, and from thence she came to Chardstock again and was married to one William Holiwell of the parish of Offhill labourer with whom she lived about the space of a year and a half, and rented a Cottage House in the parish of Chardstock at yearly rent of Twenty Shillings and that she had done no other act whereby to gain a settlement than what is written.
Sworn before us the day and year above written.   The mark of Dorothy Holiwell
Raymond Putt and John Tucker

Apprentices
Payments were made in respect of bastard children from an early date though it is not until 1826 that the names are actually entered under the heading of Bastardy. The Parish supported these children until they were seven years old when they were hired out to local estate owners as apprentices. It was the duty of all owners of large estates to take in these children and train them. The girls were taught housewifery and the boys husbandry, i.e. farming work. Some boys would be apprenticed to craftsmen. Amongst those mentioned in the apprenticeship records are a papermaker, clothier, twine spinner, blacksmith, mason, miller and a cordwainer.

From the collection of Apprentice Indentures the story of base born John Seward can be followed. He was apprenticed in 1757, when seven years old, to Ann Keate and Hugh Welsh. There was insufficient work and so he was sent to Thomas Patch of Kingston, a weaver. He moved about the county with his employer until his master was bankrupted or as the Examination Paper describes it "his Master broke". James was returned to Ann Keate who gave him a shilling and "told him to go about his business". After that he worked as a day labourer and in 1789, after being married for 17 years, he applied for a settlement order in Chardstock.

A letter written on 2nd December 1780 by a Mrs. Godwin of Crewkerne to the Parish Officers of Chardstock, tells of another, less well behaved apprentice.

Sir, I received a letter Thursday last from one Eliz Dalie at Chard, which is from my a Prentice maid are her mother where she inform me that Chard People will not let her bide their. She was bound out by the Parish of Chardstock to me. I took to her and cloath'd her, in the first seting out she behaved so bad that I cou'd not keep her. Her mother came to me and told me if I would find her in cloathes, she would take care and keep her for what she could get. She told me she could earn two shillings and sixpence a week and so she remain till about twelve month ago. Her mother came to me and said she cou'd keep her no longer upon that condition. I then took her here and new cloath'd her, and intend to have made a servant of her, as soon as she was cloath'd she ran away from me back to her mother. The Monday following I send to know the reason of her going back to her mother, her answer was that the divil shou'd have Crewkerne and me boath before she would ever see it again, if she come chargeable send her to me, and I have a horse and man which she shall immediately be sent to bridewell. She have got about five weeks before her time is up. Please to acquaint the Gentlemen of the Parish with this, if she come their. My Compliments to Mrs Pryer. I should be glad if you will go to the Clerk at Chardstock and get her age, as I am inform'd she is in her 22 year of her age, a line by the return of Post will oblige your humble servant. M. Godwin.

According to the apprentice records, an Elizabeth Bovet, who was aged 10 in 1769, was bound to Mary Godwin. It is possible that this was the same girl of the letter. Unfortunately there is no further information and the conclusion of the incident remains a mystery.

The First Parish Poorhouse
From 1697, paupers had to wear a "P" and the initial letter of the parish on their clothing. No badges have survived in Chardstock, though the accounts for 1735 when John Pook was paid 2s for badges show they were purchased. In July 1762, "two Dozen of Badges for ye Poor People" cost 4s 0d. Later at a Vestry Meeting in October 1773, the Overseers were "forthwith to get Badges for all the Poor belonging to the sd Parish that receive monthly pay"

The General Workhouse Act of 1723 gave parishes power to erect a workhouse or to join with other parishes to form a Union. Most of the poor in Chardstock were paid in cash and provided with tools and clothes to enable them to live in their own homes. Sometimes rent payments were made, as for example in 1693, "Item house rentt for William Deane and Thomas Knight to Nicholas Speed .... £1 8s 8d" and in 1758, "Sarah Gregory to pay house Rent ...... 3s 0d". In April 1720, eight house rents of £1 each were paid. Some of the poor were housed in a rented house. The first record of such a house appears in 1758. In that year, it was agreed at a Parish Meeting held on 22nd June "to take a house of Mr. Robert Guppy, late Gears, the Garden behind the House, the Stable and the Orchard (excepting the little garden plot next the Barn for a Mow Barton and a plot in the Orchard inner Garden with Gribbles) at the yearly rent of six Pounds and ten shillings a year from Lady Day next" (a gribble was an apple stock upon which apple trees were grafted). It was also agreed "to rent the said house and at a rent of four Pounds from Midsummer to Lady Day (the apples excepted) and if the Poor who are to be put into the said House shall commit any wilful Damage then the Parish shall make it good". This was signed by the Curate William Palmer, the Churchwardens and Overseers and four other gentlemen. Other entries concerning the first poorhouse include:-

1758 July	Spent when ye Parish House we took 2s 6d
August	The boath Overseers and Churchwardens Attend to have poor into ye house ... 3s 0d
October	Martha Damp came into ye house 1s 0d
	Tending Mary Bovet in the house 1s 0d
1759 April	The rent for Mr. Guppy's House £4 0s 0d

The house and its inmates feature again in the accounts for 1760 when the following intriguing entries appear:-

January	G. Vincent & M. Follet for tending S. Gregory 2s 0d
	Geo. Bond for chaining her 6d Staple & Nail 6d 1s 0d
	To her in money 7s 2d Spent with the Dr. 1s 1d 8s 3d
	A Jump for her .... 2s 6d (a "Jump" was a short coat).
April	Spent when Sarah Gregory was confined 1s 6d

We are not told if Sarah Gregory was chained to restrain her as a violent person, or during childbirth. Chains fixed to the foot of a bed were sometimes used for a mother to pull on during labour (perhaps this is one reason why childbirth was referred to as confinement!). Sarah Gregory's name is included in a list of women and children living in the Parish House in June 1760.

Money was spent in purchases for the house:-

1760 January	Furse ½hd for the Parish House 1s 3d
February	Straw for Parish House sick 1s 3d
	Sheet and 2 blankets 2s 2d
June	Straw 5 Bundles for the Parish House 7½d
	Potters Ware for the Parish House 1s 4d
July	Beding for the Parish House 9s 6d
August	Staple and Hasp for Parish House 4d
October	Rugg for the Parish House 6s 0d

There must have been considerable trouble in the house in February 1761 when this entry appears:-

Mr. Guppy in full for wilful Damage £2 6s 0d

Health

The health of the poor was not neglected, for in 1764, a subscription of one guinea was sent to the hospital in Exeter and a doctor employed in the village. An agreement was made with Robert Gammes in May 1764, "to take care of the Poor of this Parish from last Easter for three years in Physick etc. for the Sum of Four Guineas and half yearly". In 1780, Dr. Gammes was still looking after the poor "with Medicines and Attendance in all cases except Midwifery," his payment was now "seven pounds for one year". Various women, who helped in childbirth, were the Midwives of the Parish. They usually remain anonymous, though in April 1767, Mrs. Pinney was paid 5s "for Delivering of Sam Seward's wife and John Hutchin's Wife". The previous February, William Tucker had been paid 2s 6d for "Makeing of a Timber leg for Sam Seward's Wife". In 1787, a new doctor, Mr. William Spicer was appointed, his terms being identical to those of his predecessor. At a Vestry meeting held on 27th April 1788, the agreement was more specific. "Mr. William Spicer Surgeon and Apothecary of Chard in the County of Somerset do agree with the Churchwardens and Overseers of the Parish of Chardstock to find Medicene for the poor of the said Parish from the above date till Easter 1789, Midwifery excepted as well also all Compound Fractures and extraordinary cases of Surgery the aforesaid performance I do agree to Execute and fulfil for the sum of seven pound for the year as Witness my hand the above date". This agreement was renewed for the following year. Examples of Medicines and treatment include the following:-

1693	Item paid for a bed for Richard Manning & for a pott of ointment .... 5s 2d.
1695	paid Nathaniel Pyney with Petter Cox and for curing his head 3s 6d
1716	paid to Dr. Stoodly for what he did for John Seward 4s 6d
1725	pd Doctor Bowdich Curing the old damps 15s
1726/27	To Doctor Bowdich for a cure 8s 6d

In 1736, Doctors Tomkings, Wadden and Pattridge are mentioned as receiving payments. In 1743, 4s was paid "for Curing Tuckers boy of ye Itch" and in 1745, William Cox was given "one shilling wch he pd to Doctor Whity for his father".

1745	pd Dockter Hounsel for a jurney and medisens for Cristian Grigory 5s 0d
1786 March	James French allowed towards curing of the King's Evel .... 15s 0d (the King's Evil was an unpleasant skin disease supposed to be curable by the touch of the King).
1791 May	Payd for Gin at the George for S. Gregory sickness 1s
1793 March	Daniel Seward had an Ague 6s 0d
May	To Stuff for the Itch 1s 0d

In 1791, there was a serious outbreak of smallpox with several deaths recorded in the Church Burial Register. In April, 2s 3d was spent in buying apples on the Doctor's orders, "to make Dumplings for the Inoculated Persons" and in May, 5s 4d "By Mr. Spicer's Order for Port wine for them that had the Small Pox Fevers To prevent he said if possible a Putrid." It was shortly after this that Edward Jenner carried out his experiments with vaccination. His results began to be published in 1798, when they were severely criticized. As prejudice against being injected with Cow Pox was overcome, outbreaks of the disease became increasingly less severe and in 1853, vaccination of babies was made compulsory.

Death

The money collected from the Poor Law ratepayers was also used to pay the expenses incurred when a pauper or a pauper's child died. There are many entries for shrouds (burial clothes) which in 1692 cost 4s 2d and in 1832, 2s 8d. The reason for the difference in cost was possibly due to the Burial in Wool Acts of 1667 and 1678 which ordered shrouds to be made of "sheep's wool only" A fine of £5 for a breach of the law was levied, not only on the estate of the deceased, but also on anyone connected with the burial. From 1792 to 1795, wool for burials varied between 2s and 1s for each burial. The Acts, which were originally passed to help the wool trade, were repealed in 1814 but they had by then fallen into disuse. In 1695, a coffin cost 6s and by 1735 it had risen to 7s with 2s 6d for that of a child. In 1831/32, it varied between 15s and 16s and for a child 7s. Other costs included payment in 1755 of 1s 6d to the Sexton, William Cox, "for making ..... Grave & ringing bell 1s 6d", Wool and Stretching out and Liquor 2s. In 1726, there is an entry, "pd to 5 men for carring Geo Harris to Church and for drink .... 5s". Another entry, in 1751, states "Gave ye Singers for Singing Grace Freak to Church when She was Buried ...... 1s."

The Second Poorhouse

It is not known why the original Poor House was abandoned. Perhaps it was the result of damage similar to that which occurred in 1761 or perhaps the lease of the house could not be renewed for some other reason. An entry in December 1765 states that 17s 9d was paid for "A Bedd and Beding for the use of the Poor at Grace Vincents". In 1766, the second Poor House was rented at £3 a year for three years from Thomas Drayton. The agreement stated that all necessary repairs were to be done by Thomas Drayton, except for glazing the windows after they were put in order. The Overseers agreed to provide "Beding and other necessary things" and to appoint a "Proper Person" to look after the poor. The house was situated at Mill Bridge and became known as "the house at the water" (Waterloo Cottage?).

Militia

Rates for the relief of the poor continued to be collected and lists of persons receiving benefit were written by the Overseers each year. Payments which were made to the dependants of men serving in the Militia were also included in the Poor Book accounts. The Militia, to which these men belonged, was probably the County Militia and was similar to the modern Territorial Army. Men would be liable to serve either in their own county or adjacent counties as well as outside these limits. The money was paid to the Overseers for distribution to the families. They claimed their expenses e.g. "Expenses to Birdsmoore Gate to get the Militia Money ...... 1s 11d" In 1793, Tim Mooring's wife was paid 12s, William Seward and Joseph Dunster's wives 8s, while Daniel Seward's wife only received 2s. The annual accounts were inspected by the Vicar, Churchwardens and members of the Vestry, before being taken to the local magistrates' Sessions for signing.

The Workhouse

In 1786, it was decided to erect a purpose built Workhouse. The previous parish houses were known as Poor Houses but their function was the same as that of the last parish house, which was called a Workhouse. In February, a Committee was set up to find a suitable site. It reported back to the Vestry Meeting in April, a majority of the members having "agreed and fixed to Build the said Workhouse on Symes late enclosure adjoining late Hawkins Orchard in Farmyards" Whether there were objections or whether it was considered the site was too far from the centre of the village is not known but the project appears to have been abandoned. Two years later, in April 1788, it was agreed by the "Principle Inhabitants of the Parish" that a Workhouse should be built on "the ground lately Bought of Samuel Apsey" The house, which was built by George Bond for £150, still stands and today is known as Victoria Place. £200 was borrowed from Charles Bull of Thorncombe to furnish and complete the Workhouse. John Winsor was appointed Governor and his daughter, Mary, Governess, at a combined salary of £20 for the first year. He was to be paid expenses and "for attending any Justice Meeting"

Detailed accounts of the cost of building and furnishing the Workhouse survive in the Poor Book from which the following extracts are taken.

Mr. George Bond for Bakers Plan for the Work House £1 11s 6d
James French for taking away the earth from the Work House 14s
For Drawing away the Earth from the Work House £1 10s 0d
Pd Thos. Pearce for Digging a Well at the Workhouse 10s 6d
Pd Mr Abraham Pages Bill for a new Pump £6 2s 4½d
Pd Thos. Bonfield for Bars for the Guard Chamber & Iron for the Racks 7s 8d
(this room might have been used as the village lock-up).

It is not known how many residents there then were in the house, but the Committee responsible for furnishing the Workhouse ordered ten beds to be made by Isaac Tucker of Axminster. Other items listed in the accounts include 12 brooms 2s 0d, 2 candlesticks 3d, tubs and pails 66s 8d, a brewing tub 42s 10d, 6 chairs 9s 0d, and a 27lb brass kettle 20s 3d. Only the Churchwardens and Overseers were empowered to authorize the purchase of goods for the Workhouse and at a Vestry meeting on 10th. May 1793, the following rules were laid down:-

Also .... That no poor person shall be suffered to go out of the poor House without leave from the aforesaid Officers.
Also .... It was ordered that the Governor is not to be sent out on any Journey whatever.
Also .... No Clothing nor Tools of any kind whatever to be allowed out of the Poor House.
          And only six pence per week to any person out of the house except in case of sickness.
Also .... The work done in and out of the poor house shall be made out separate from other amounts once a month and the poor to be kept Close to Work.
Also .... It was ordered and agreed that the whole quantity of Coal shall be bought in in the Summer for the ensuing year.
Also .... An Inventry to be taken Immediately of all the Furniture in the Poor House.

This was signed by the Vicar, the Revd. Robert Stephens and nine other gentlemen.

The work, which the poor of the parish had to do was mainly connected with the cloth trade. This is confirmed by the many entries in the accounts for wool, thread, lincy, worsted, yarn, tape and other materials. Payments in 1792 for "A Spinning Turn", "Spills & Whurrows" and "Bottoming & Baskets" were possibly for this trade or for other employment within the Workhouse. Payments were made for journeys to Merriot for "work" and for "work to Dowlish". There was, however, a small concession to one form of pleasure, that of smoking. In June 1790, Mrs. Dare was paid 3s 6d for "Coarse Cloam Pipes & Tobacco" (cloam being another word for clay).

A weekly menu for the inmates of the Workhouse was agreed by a Vestry meeting in 1796.

Sundays	Broth Breakfast. Pudden for Dinner. Bread and Chees for Supper.
Monday	Flesh Dinner Bread Chees.
Tuesday	Broth Dinner Bread Chees.
Wednesday	Flesh Dinner Bread Chees.
Thursday	Broth Dinner Bread Chees.
Fridday	Flesh Dinner Bread Chees.
Saturday's	Pease if not Pease Broth in lieu.

also Liquour one Pint of Table Beer each to grown up people Children water.
also it is farther agreed that Cyder is to be used in the House.
Malt in lieu of Cyder to the Dis................ of the officers.
The officers to purchase Wheat and Barley for the use of the .... at the best Markets.

Also that the governor is not .... be allowed neither Butter, Tea, Sugar but to his own expen....... and the said Governor is str.......... to adhere and follow the orde.......... of Vestery dated May 10th. 179.. should the said Governor su.......... from the order of Vestery of 10th. .... 1793, than the present off......re authorised and directed to gi... .the said Governor three Months Not....... in writing to quit the Possession of the said House." (many of the words in the above entry are incomplete owing to the page having been torn from the book). The name of the Governor, who may still have been John Winsor, is not given. James Pering is the next person mentioned as holding the office of Governor. This was in 1818 when his name appears in Church Registers as Workhouse Governor. In 1830 the then Governor was given three months notice, though not all those present at the Vestry meeting agreed. A list was recorded of 11 names, including one of the Overseers, of "those who wished the Governor to remain in his present situation". He was, however, dismissed and an advertisement was placed in the "Sherbourne Mercury" for three weeks for a Workhouse Governor and Governess. The result of this was the appointment of John Staple and his wife Mary at a salary of £15 and two hogsheads of Cider. He was not to be allowed any tea, butter or sugar at the expense of the parish. He didn't stay long for in April 1832, Thomas Perren and his wife became Governor and Governess. They were paid a salary of £20 per annum, two hogsheads of cider and £10 for attending to the parish business. Thomas Perren only stayed a year. It is not known if he was also dismissed but he was given "one week to carry his goods from the house". There is no more information concerning the next Governor or indeed the story of the Workhouse as the account books finish in 1833. This may be because of the implementation of the Poor Law Amendment Act of 1834, under which parishes were grouped into unions.

Axminster Union Workhouse

Chardstock became part of the Axminster Union of parishes administered by a Board of Guardians. The parish was entitled to send two representatives known as Guardians to this Board. Valuation and Rate lists continued to be produced and Overseers appointed. The first meeting of the Axminster Union Board of Guardians was held on 18th April 1836 with Mr. Loveridge and Mr. Pryer attending as the Chardstock members. In May of that year, it was resolved that the Chardstock Workhouse should be used as a temporary Asylum for Able Bodied Paupers. 22 iron bedsteads were bought from a Bristol manufacturer named Poole and the Chardstock Guardians also obtained other necessary articles for the house. The situation of Master was offered to Robert Bonfield, the assistant overseer of Chardstock. His salary was to be £15 a year, paid from 1st August 1836 until the new Union House at Axminster was ready. At the meeting on 21st July 1836, the Parish Officers of Chardstock were ordered "to bring all Paupers who shall be inmates of the Chardstock Workhouse to the Axminster Workhouse on the first day of August next" This was later changed to the 8th August. The "old and imfirm inmates" were to be allowed to remain in the parish, if they wished, and receive "such Relief as the Board might direct."

In November 1836, the future of the Chardstock Workhouse was discussed and it was decided to continue the tenancy of the building and use it as a Pest House, i.e. for infectious diseases, until 25th March 1837. The rent was fixed at £20 and the Parish Officers were to keep the premises in repair, being allowed 10s to pay for the repair of windows broken since 20th August. After March 1837, the Board discontinued the tenancy and all remaining Chardstock paupers who needed housing were sent to the Axminster Union House. Elizabeth Hoare was one who went to Axminster. She was brought before the Magistrate in 1838 for absconding from the Workhouse, "taking away with her sundry articles of wearing apparel belonging to the Union". As for the Chardstock Workhouse, it probably became the building called the Barracks or Orphans' Asylum. This was used to house some of the orphans of the Crimean War and the Indian Mutiny, brought to the village by Canon Woodcock. These children attended the National School and almost certainly were the "skivvies" of the College. The workhouse also acted as the laundry for the College inmates and possibly continued in that role for the private boarding school, opened in 1876 in the College premises. Eventually the building was divided into separate housing accommodation, as it remains today.

Various forms of relief appear to have been granted to the poor who remained in the village. A loan of money was one of these. John Turner, a pauper of Chardstock, was given a loan of 10s in 1839. In other cases a grant of bread was made to poor families. Malachi Apsey, who had a wife and six children, four of whom were under ten, had his allowance of bread cut from 16lbs a week to 8lbs. The reason given by the Guardians was that, "this mode of relief was more to the advantage of the Parish than that afforded in the Workhouse and more desirable to the pauper". Charles Chick, with a wife and seven children all under ten, was allowed 24lbs of bread a week. Sometimes the Guardians offered to take the children of a pauper into the Workhouse, as a form of relief.

The "Union" was never very popular, either with the ratepayers or the paupers. Chardstock was one of the parishes that always seemed to be in arrears with contributions to the Axminster Board. The Overseers were regularly summoned and threatened with a fine of £5 for non-payment. In 1883, according to the "Chard and Ilminster" newspaper, a "Remarkable Disclosure" was made. It appeared that John Baker, the Assistant Overseer, had been "collecting rates on sums in excess of those to which properties were assessed" thus prompting many ratepayers to complain that they had been robbed. A meeting was called which this Assistant Overseer, who was 87 years of age and very deaf, did not attend. As no one could understand the accounts it was proposed to fetch him, but this was abandoned after a comment from a member of the public to the effect that, "He would not be any good if he was present. He would not hear anything that he did not want to hear!" It was agreed that the Overseers should ask the Axminster Board of Guardians "to help them out of the mess" The Chairman of the Guardians, together with one of the Overseers, examined the rate book and "found it in such a muddle that it was impossible to make anything of it". It was agreed that the Overseers should make a new rate which they would collect before another assistant was appointed. The newspaper then reported, "It is stated that the late assistant overseer has taken his departure from the parish and that he will not be interfered with". All appears to have gone well until the 1890s. In June 1891, the "Chard and Ilminster" reported under the headline, "An Obstinate Overseer" that Joseph Miller, the Assistant Overseer at Chardstock, had failed to attend the audit of the Poor Law accounts for the fourth time in succession. At the Axminster Petty Sessions it was stated that when the books were sent to Honiton they were found to be in a disgraceful state. Apparently Joseph Miller had previously been fined 40s and was in very poor circumstances. He was again fined 40s with £3 17s 4d costs, but as all he had would not realise £5, the magistrates ordered a distress warrant to be issued if he did not pay within a week.

Clubs and Social Insurance

At this time, the poor also benefited from the great energy of the Vicar, the Revd. Charles Woodcock, who was instrumental in setting up clubs which included a Boot Club for the children of the school, a Coal Club, a Clothing Club and a Lending Library. Friendly Societies also flourished. One such was the Rational Society which helped members in sickness. In 1913, the Workhouse was officially retitled a "Poor Law Institution" and in 1911 the National Insurance Act began the provision of social insurance. Finally the modern system of benefits began in 1946.

Boot Club

The boot club was open to all children attending Chardstock or Bewley Down Schools. Three pence in the shilling (interest) was given to all members.

Clothing Club

The clothes club began on the first Monday in December. Members could only join in December or June. Payments were made in any sum from 1d. to 1s. per week regularly on the first Monday in the month, at the parish room at 11.00a.m. 2s. 6d would be added at the end of the year, unless the member had joined in June when only 1s. 3d. was paid.

Coal Club

The coal club began in the first Monday in June and members could join up to the first week in August. A minimum of five shillings had to be deposited in the fund by the first of December or members would have their money returned.

Rational Society

The Chardstock branch of The Manchester Sick & Burial Club was set up in October 1891 and held Club Days when the members paraded with a band through the village.

Sources

Axminster Union Minute Books 1-5, Dev. R.O.
Chard and Ilminster News, op. cit.
Overseers Accounts - Chardstock, 2590A/PO1-7, Dev. R.O.
Poor Law Books, Dev. R. O.

Chapter Seventeen
CHARITIES

The Poor in Chardstock, as in many other parishes, benefited from various charities. The proceeds of these bequests are still distributed today although their value has fallen and the necessity which prompted the benefactors has largely disappeared. Originally the charities drew their income from the rents accruing from land bought with the bequests or with money raised from within the parish. In modern times all the land was sold and the proceeds invested. It is the income from these investments which the trustees now distribute.

There are two main charities, The Thorncombe Lands charity dating from 1548, and that set up by the will of the Revd. Richard White in 1621. These charities were amalgamated in 1910 and are now known as the United Charities. Two other small charities (details of which appear below) have disappeared and a modern bequest known as The Ethel Langdon Charity has come into being. Ethel Langdon was connected with the Tytherleigh Aisle (see Chapter 12) and was a nun of the Order of the Anglican Society of Our Lady of Nazareth. The term, "Thorncombe Lands" appears in 1833/35 in a Report of the Commissioners for Inquiring Concerning Charities and in 1910 when the United Charities were formed from Holditch Mead and Ladymead. The first mention of Holditch Mead is in the "Augmentation Office Certificates of Colleges and Chantries". The Act of 1545, confiscating the Chantries, had never been fully implemented and it was not until 1547 that the majority were suppressed. In Chardstock, the income from endowments for "the mayntenance or fynding" of a chantry priest came from land, and was recorded, together with other Dorset chantry details, in January 1549. The list includes "lands yn Wolmyngton," "lands calld Garnetts pytte," and "Certeine landes callid holdyche meade and Avense in the pisshe of Chardestock, of the yerelye value of xli." (£10). Rent "out of the land callid holdiche meade," was paid "to the lorde Cobhm vili. xiiis. iiiid." (£6 13s 4d).

Thorncombe Lands Charity

An indenture dated 1548 between George Brooke Lord Cobham and John Colman, John Pynney and John Parris, parishioners of Chardstock, gave them a grant for their lives of certain lands in Holditch in the Parish of Thorncombe. These lands consisted of two meadows, one called Holditch Mead and the other Avenersmede, together with some smaller pieces of adjoining pasture, possibly the property of the Knights Hospitallers. A yearly rent of £3 6s 8d was to be paid to Lord Cobham. When John Pynney died, Lord Cobham's son William made a new agreement in 1560 with Thomas Estmond, Edward Wilshire, William Colman, William Parris Sr., William Parris Jn., William Weston Jn., Robert ...., William Wilmington and John Bently. This was for the term of 90 years after the deaths of John Colman and John Parris or on the surrender of their agreement. The rent continued to be the same as before.

In 1624, Richard Bragg of Thorncombe acquired the lands from Lord Mountjoy who had been given the Holditch Estate by King James I into whose hands it came after the Brooke family (Lords Cobham) had fallen into disgrace. In 1628, Richard Bragg granted them to Sir Simon D'Ewes and others of Chardstock for the sum of £400 paid to him by the parishioners. The rent charge of £3 6s 8d was to be paid to the King. In 1631, Sir Simon D'Ewes granted another quarter of an acre to Henry Bowditch and two other feoffees for £4, for the use of the parish. This land, part of the Manor of Coaxdon, was in Avernas in Chardstock and Holditch Mead in Thorncombe. In 1716/17 the estate was conveyed to Robert Tytherleigh, Samuel Bowditch and other feoffees or trustees. At this time, conditions for the disposal of the income were set out. It could be used for the relief of the poor, for placing out poor children as apprentices and towards the repair of the church.

An entry in the Poor Law Book for 3rd February 1752, shows a payment of £4 4s 0d to George Warry "for new Deeds for Holditch Mead". These are probably the deeds referred to in the 1910 Scheme. During May 1752, another small piece of ground situated by Holditch Mead was purchased from John Pitts for £10 10s, "out of the monies arising from the Parish Stock". The first agreements do not specify any trust or purpose but it appears that the lands were let by the parishioners and the income spent in various forms of relief. A collection of papers for the years 1598 and 1599, now in the Devon Record Office, give details of how some of the money was disbursed.

In 1598, Thomas Estmond, who lived at Lodge in Chardstock, was the collector or receiver of the rent and a number of other men of the parish authorised him to pay out various sums. In January Stephen Merymonth and his father were allowed 3s 4d towards the thatching of their house. In March, "Chubbe" was paid for shoes "he hath delivered to poore folks". In July, 6s 6d was paid "to the relief of the maimed soldiers untill the feast of midsummer last past". Nothing is known about these soldiers but as English ships were once more on the high seas to intercept or destroy in port a second Spanish Armada, perhaps they were part of that force. It would appear that parishes were forced to provide for these unfortunate men and that this was not popular. In December, a petition was sent to Thomas Estmond complaining, "that there is nowe another sudayne charge of forty shillings or to be leavyed in this parishe for these soldiers and that such a some is not soe quickly collected amonge us". It was requested that the sum should be paid to the Constable out of the Holditch rent "and if you and the rest shal think good hereafter this be supplied any other waye we for our parte shal be readye to be burdened Quarterly wee Comend us to you this xiiii th of December 1598".

The petition bore 10 signatures. Again, in May 1599, it was stated "shortly there must be layd out more towarde the releef of maymed soldyers". It is of course possible that the soldiers were the men of the local Militia who had been injured.

During the Tudor period the lord lieutenants of the counties had the responsibility of mustering the local militia. Each Hundred was expected to provide a number of militia men and every parish had to make its contribution of men and weapons to the Hundred. In 1569, Beaminster Hundred, to which Chardstock and Wambrook belonged, had to raise 222 "able men". The Chardstock Muster Roll lists 69 from the two parishes. There were 24 Pikemen, 22 Billmen who each carried a weapon similar to an agricultural bill hook, 14 Archers and 9 Harquebusiers. An Harquebus was an early type of firearm about 3 feet long and weighing about 10lbs. The Roll for 1539 is even more detailed itemising the type of armour and the number of arrows each archer must provide. In 1599, it was agreed that 16s should be paid to William Vyncent from the rent of Holditch Mead. This was Chardstock's contribution to compensation of 20s which was demanded for the loss of "an amor" he had "sent away in the service of her majestie". The remainder of the 20s had to be paid by Wambrook.

In October, William Larcombe gent., described as "late Constable" of Chardstock, was given 4 marks (£2 13s 8d) to reimburse him for "relief of the poor he hath disbursed of his own purse more than he hath received". These years were obviously a time of hardship for the document speaks of "in that extreame time of dearth". During the same month the churchwardens were paid 6s 6d which they had "layd out for the maymed Soldiers" and 4s 4d "towarde the relief of the hospitall". During the year it was thought that the Poor Rate then charged was insufficient and so it was agreed that 2s a month, back dated to the previous June, should be paid to the Overseers. In addition they were to receive 4 nobles (£1 6s 8d) to buy "apparell & shoes" for Christopher Gill, William Merymonth, Jane Christmas, George Abbot and …… Greenslade.

The documents for 1599 begin by authorising the payment of 26s 8d to the churchwardens for their "necessary uses" Apparently this was insufficient, for in May another payment was made. The Wardens obviously found it difficult to obtain this money as not all those authorised to approve the actual expenditure seem to have been present when the accounts were submitted. Finally in November 1599, Thomas Estmond, still the receiver of the rent of Holditch Mead, was instructed to pay them. He had earlier been warned that more money would be needed "for repairs about the church & especyally the glasse of the wyndowes which being omytted will bring the said wardens farther troble besyde father expese to the parish". In December 1599, the churchwardens were again "out of hand to disburse more aboute business belonging to their office" and they were given an extra "four nobles" from the Holditch Mead Charity. Also in the same month, the Vicar, the Revd. Richard White, was given 40s to distribute to the poor at Christmas. An interesting note attached to Thomas Estmond's authorisation reads, "I know you see the great necessitie of our poore and nowe the more by reason of this last great wynd".

Not only was money granted towards the repair of the church but also for the building of bridges. In December 1599, a sum was paid for "makinge a new bridge callyd Kite bridge". In the accounts for 1743, an item "pd for putting up of Axe Bridge …… 12s 2d." indicates that money was still being spent on bridges. Grants were given for the maintenance of apprentices. In 1688, £6 was paid "toowards the quitting out of the apprentices" and in 1752, "Paid for a Waistcoat for the Boy Bound to Holditch Mead & Holditch Bridge …… 5s 6d". In 1827, one apprentice was placed at a premium of £10. As noted in the "History of Education in Chardstock and All Saints", by Peter Wood and CHRG and published by CHRG in 2009, money was given to assist the Charity School and to help pay the salary of the schoolmaster.

In 1711, it was agreed to let Holditch Mead and Hill to a tenant on 26th December every three years. Later this must have been changed, as on 13th April 1747, 6s was paid "for Crying Holage Meade three times at Chard, Axminster, Thorncomb, HayChurch and Winsome". This was probably the Town Crier's fee. £1 8 0 was allowed as "the Exspences att Thytherly Inn when Lady Meade was sale up twice". In the accounts for 1724, the amount of rent received was £21 8s 10d from Lady Mead (possibly this should read Holditch Mead). The rent received in 1738 for the land, this time called Holditch Mead again, was £26 and by 1730 it had risen to £30. In 1741, however, the rent is quoted as £28 10s from which Mr. Pryor gave £26 15s 1d to the poor. In 1746/7 the rent reverted to £28 10s but it is for Lady Mead. As Holditch Mead is not mentioned it is possible that these two places are the same. Lady Mead and Holditch Hill are named in 1749 and 1750 but Holditch Mead is missing. From 1808 until 1818 the rent was £109. It was then progressively reduced until in 1832 it was let to Richard Dean, who was connected with the clothing industry, for £60. The lands were now three closes of pasture of 36 acres called Holditch Hill and Lady Mead. Fieldwalking evidence suggests that flax-retting, i.e. the soaking of flax to soften it, may have taken place nearby. There were no buildings to maintain, although a linhay was erected by the feoffees at a cost of £63 in 1832/3. In the middle of the 19th Century part of the land was sold to the London and South Western Railway Co. to build the Exeter Extension.

As might be expected, not all the income could be given away because there were other expenses. In 1743 John Backeler was paid 5s "for 5 days dicking" (cleaning or digging a ditch), 9d was paid "for a hook for the gate and nails" while 6d was allowed "for mending the gate". In 1747, the gate was again causing trouble for Mathew Noster was paid 9d "for putting in ye Post & Mending ye Gate". The post cost 2s, nails 1d and "a head (or lead) & stuf to mend ye Gate" 6d. The same man was paid 1s 6d for putting up 30 fencing rails, which cost 3d each, "against Chard Mead". More rails were placed "alhurt ye River against Chard Meade & above Tyhtherly Brigh" now known as Broom Bridge. The Henley Estate Map of 1781, shows that fencing was used in areas where banks would be washed away. In 1752, "a Swinging Flood Gate" cost 5s, "Diging the Hedges" 3s, "Stopping the Gaps" 2s and "Cutting Up Emmett Hills" £2, or ant hills, of which there must have been a great many! In September 1740, there are entries in the Poor Book regarding the movement of stock kept in Holditch Mead e.g. "Pd when ye Stock of Holidge medow was Driven at Axminster 1s 6d".

The number of persons benefiting from the income during the first decades of the 19th Century varied between 120 and 150 and the amount given away was about £59 a year (a considerable sum). In 1832, owing to a failure of a tenant, probably Richard Dean, only £4 was distributed and nothing in the year when the linhay was built.

White's Charity

The most important of the other Chardstock Charities was that of the Revd. Richard White, Vicar of the parish from 1597 until his death in 1626. In his will dated 24th May 1621, he left £100 to the Churchwardens and Overseers of the Poor to buy land and use the income for the relief of the poor. It appears that the Churchwardens did not receive the bequest until February 1628. They then bought about 7 acres of land, consisting of 5 small fields, at Holway in the parish of St. Mary Magdalene in Taunton. The Poor Book accounts usually show that the income from this investment was received and distributed, but in 1719 the entry is more explicit, stating, "Recd of Mr Whitts money ...... £6 and distributed".

In October 1751, a petition was made to the Steward of the Manor of Taunton Dene by William Burridge, James Pinkard and Henry Rowsell, who described themselves as tenants of the Manor. They asserted that footpaths in Holway leading from Jaspers Acre to a house belonging to the Poor of Chardstock and from a farm house belonging to Thomas Exon to the end of a causeway from Taunton, had been blocked by Thomas Exon. As a result of the petition, Thomas Exon was ordered to remove the obstructions, which were "several large High Gates", within three months or incur a penalty of £5. In May 1786, 12s 6d was paid out of the general funds for "Expences of Three Officers Going unto Holway to visit the Parish Land" and in February 1794, £1 "To Mr. Geo. Bonds Bill respecting an Acre of Ground that was like to be lost at Holway". In 1872, with the agreement of the Charity Commissioners, it was decided to sell the land in Taunton. The sale was completed in November and the proceeds of £1070, invested in 3% Consols (Government securities).

Sampson's and Turner's Charities

Of the remaining Charities, little is known. Entries in the Poor Books only state that Long's (Samson's) and Turner's money was received and distributed. An amount of £1 for each is recorded in 1719. A Charity Commissioner's Report, dated 1912, gives a few details of the Charities of William Turner and John Sampson. The will of John Sampson, dated 6th January 1618, gave to his nephew, J. Long, his tenement at Bathcote in Membury. From this, the churchwardens and overseers of the poor of Chardstock were to be paid an annual sum of £1 to be distributed each Good Friday to the poor. In 1631, William Turner, on the instructions of his father Henry Turner of Alstone, granted to John Pitt the Vicar of Chardstock, and several others, £1 each year to be distributed to the poor. This was from lands called New Close at Wyke in Axminster. It would appear that payments from both charities were somewhat erratic. Nothing was done until 1895, when the Parish Council of Chardstock applied to the Axminster Trustees of the Parish Lands, for payment of Turner's Charity, which had not been made for several years. It was considered that the Council should apply to the owner of the Sampson's Charity land for his payment, which had also lapsed, but he declined as no payment had been made for more than 20 years. The Axminster Trustees then resolved not to resume payment of Turner's Charity and the whole matter was referred to the Attorney-General. He agreed that under the Statute of Limitations, recovery of the rentcharges of both Charities were barred and therefore all payments ceased.

All the charity capital was invested and the income, after the deduction of the portion allocated to church repairs, was distributed by the trustees to parishioners at Christmas each year. Now these investments have been sold by the Charity Commissioners and only a small sum remains as cash in the bank.

Briefs

Not only was money received and distributed in the parish during the 17th Century but it was also collected and sent to other places in need. The first Poor Law Book records two collections, one of 13s 9½d made on 15th May 1686 by the Churchwardens for the "French Briefe" and the second on 27th May of 2s 8½d for the "London Briefe". Briefs were started at the Reformation to give help to those in distress. Permission was given for a collection to be taken in every church and chapel in the country on a certain day. These Briefs were very unpopular because as time went by they became more and more frequent. Samuel Pepys notes in his Diary for June 1661, "To church where we observe the trade of Briefs to come up to so constant a course every Sunday, that we resolve to give no more to them". Two collections are recorded in the parish register, one by James Keate, Vicar 1669-1705, and the other by an unknown hand.

In October 1680, £2 18s was collected "for the redemption of slaves from Turkey" and in October 1700, 16s 1d was collected for the same purpose. Before the foundation of Fire Insurance Companies and during their early years, Briefs were often issued to pay for damage caused by fire, which was an ever present hazard in thatched buildings principally constructed of timber. In June 1690, there was a house to house collection of 8s 10½d for the benefit of Southwarke. Two other collections raised 10s 2½d for Bishops Lavington, Wiltshire and 10s 3¾d for East Smithfields.

Sources
Augmentation Office Certificates of Colleges and Chantries, P.R.O., E 301/16 certs 16 53 72.
Dorset Tudor Muster Rolls, Dor. R. O.
Feoffees Accounts, 2590A/PF 1-11 18 19 Dev. R.O.
Overseers of the Poor Accounts 2590A/PO 1-7 Dev. R. O.
Manor of Taunton Dene DD/SP/23/61 Som. R. O.
Proceedings, Dor.NH&AFC XXVII p227.
Report of the Commissioners for Inquiring Concerning Charities (Dor.), 1833/4 Som. Local Studies Lib.

Chapter Eighteen
INNS AND ALE HOUSES

The earliest Chardstock victualler so far found is John Bag, whose will was proved in 1597. In October 1599, it was recorded at the Manor Court that William Hellard, William Wyate, John Wyate, John Lyne and Thomas Vyoncombe "do use typplinge but it is not known whether they have licence or not". Perhaps they were the Chardstock innkeepers or they just brewed their own ale. In a case before an Ecclesiastical Court in 1667, the house of Robert Zelwood was mentioned as being a Chardstock alehouse in the year 1665. Unfortunately it is not known where this house was situated. There have been at least four inns or beer houses in Chardstock Village with two more at Tytherleigh. Those at the village were Travellers' Rest, a beer house half way up the hill towards Holy City; The Five Bells Inn, almost opposite the church; The George Inn, in the centre of the village; and The New Inn, a beer house now known as Tytherleigh Cot. The two at Tytherleigh were The Tytherleigh Arms and Bonds Inn, which was almost opposite Tthe Tytherleigh Arms on the east of the main Chard to Axminster Road. Bonds Inn, kept as an Alehouse by Anne Bond in 1667, was never licensed in the same way as the others were and it has long since disappeared.

Tytherleigh Inn
For many centuries there has almost certainly been an Inn on the site of The Tytherleigh Arms, which was sometimes known as plain Tytherleigh Inn. Probably it originally belonged to the Tytherleigh family who would have let it to various innkeepers. The present building has been much altered making it difficult, if not impossible, to date it accurately. The earliest mention of the property, thought to be the inn, so far found is in the Poor Rate Book for 1676 when Nicholas Cate or Keate paid a halfpenny rate. He was an Innholder who, in his will of 1709, left the residue of his estate to his son Thomas. The will of Thomas, proved in 1740, left Tyderleigh Inn to his son Nicholas. From this, it can be inferred that the Nicholas paying the Poor Rate in 1676 was at the Tytherleigh Inn. Thomas also left Bonds Inn and Orchard to his daughter Susannah who paid the Poor Rate for Bonds Inn and Orchard until she died in 1763. Thomas Drayton then held Bonds Inn and Tytherleigh Inn until he died in 1782. From 1782 till 1784 it is presumed that his widow ran the inn. Then John Northcut was the innkeeper until 1790 and from 1791 to 1795 Richard Amor was the occupier. Another Thomas Drayton appears in 1802 and from 1820 to 1848, when Tytherleigh Inn is called the King's Arms, the innkeeper was John Miller. From 1851, Abraham Follett was the licensee and he was followed in 1862 by Patience Follett. She held the Inn until 1871 when Robert Dare was the publican for 10 years. In 1881, William Toms was at the Tytherleigh Inn and in 1897, the inn is first mentioned as the Tytherleigh Arms.

It was reported in "The Chard and Ilminster" in October 1890, that George Taylor a travelling tinker, was charged with assaulting William Toms and maliciously damaging a window to the value of 15s. He denied the charge of assault which was dismissed but pleaded guilty to the other charge and was fined 10s with costs of 7s 6d and 10s 5d damages. Having no money to pay he was removed in custody to serve one month's hard labour (for another "incident" see Chapter 19 - Rev. Richard Luce). In 1903, when Mitchell Toms & Co. were Lessees, Francis Charles a Dairyman, occupied the inn as a fully Licensed Public House. Sam Coles was there in 1910, Walt Grabham in 1919, Joseph Honey in 1923, Percy William Ripley in 1926 and Patrick Murphy in 1930 and 1939.

Travellers' Rest
At the opposite end of the village, near Holy City, was the Travellers' Rest, once called "Henry Ally". Very little is known about this inn. It does not appear in the Poor Rate books as an inn except for one entry. That was in 1751, when Robert Seward was paid "for Returning an amount of money collected for the use of the poor to Travelers Rest .... 4s 0d". In the 19th and 20th Centuries it was kept by the Deem family. Robert Isaac Deem was also a grocer, seedsman, nurseryman and cordwainer, as well as a beer retailer. In May 1882, a report of a "Destructive Fire" at the Travellers' Rest appeared in "The Chard and Ilminster" newspaper. Apparently a chimney caught fire after the occupants of the inn had retired to bed. The flames spread so rapidly that it proved impossible to save the house and a large proportion of its contents. However, Mrs. E. M. Deem, whose husband and his father were both born there, doubted the truth of the report. In May 1982, she wrote to the newspaper saying that her husband had never heard of the fire taking place. Perhaps the inn was rebuilt on a different site, for it certainly continued as a beer house and in July 1884, an inquest was held there. This was on Mr. Shute of Holy City who had fallen into a well at his cottage and drowned. The inn was held in 1897 by Cedric Deem, who is mentioned in Kelly's Directory, until at least 1924, as a beer retailer. Travellers' has now passed from the Deem family and is a private house.

The Five Bells Inn
The Five Bells Inn, near the church, is mentioned in the Manor Court in 1751 as belonging to Robert Guppy. The entry deals with the reversion of a messuage of a Tenement of 2 acres lying in Chardstock town, formerly belonging to John Gare. George Turner paid a rent of 3s 6d and Fine of £16. The property was known as Five Bells Inn. In 1769, Richard Amor of the Five Bells was recorded as the innkeeper at the Victuallers Recognizances in Bridport. In the Poor Law accounts for 1773, the Occupier of Five Bells Inn paid a 1d rate. In 1775, the Overseers of the Poor recorded in their accounts that 2s had been spent on the expenses of Samuel Seward's family while at the Five Bells. The inn again

features in the Poor Book when, at a Vestry Meeting in 1784, it was agreed to pay out the Charity money at the Five Bells on 23rd January. At the Manor Survey of 1781, Thomas Guppy held the Five Bells Inn. He also held the garden and the stables, which were mentioned in 1739, with a garden opposite the inn as belonging to Mr. Gare, (probably Dare). Thomas Guppy or the occupier continued to pay the 1d Poor Rate till 1795 and in 1825, Henry Parris paid the Rate which had risen to 8d. The Five Bells is no longer an inn, although it has retained its old name as four 19th Century houses.

The New Inn
The New Inn is one of the oldest surviving buildings in Chardstock. After a fire in 1992, the outstanding and unusual medieval roof of the building was revealed. There is in the roof an example of a rare type of cruck, cusped windbraces not commonly seen in this area, and heavily smoke blackened infill. This and other evidence suggests an open hall house of high status dating from perhaps about 1400. It was possibly constructed by craftsmen working away from their home territory and adapting details of a framed tradition to the massive walls of the Dorset area. The first floor and chimney stack of the hall were added at the end of the 16th Century. The fine upper storey fireplace with carved lintel bears the date 1594 and the initials A P. These are probably the initials of Andrew Parrock (see also Chapter 3) whose daughter Agnes was baptised in 1601. Perhaps the Parrocks were park keepers, for their name is derived from the old English, pearruc, which can mean park. There is a wing at the west end of the house and this has the remains of a timber framed chimney with vertical posts and rods between them to support the mud filling. There seem to have been no major improvements to the house in either the 18th or 19th Centuries.

The New Inn property does not appear on the 1781 Manor Estate Map, nor is it referred to in the schedule. The plot where it stands is merely labelled "Land". Obviously, this house was not held in the same way as other properties in Chardstock. However, on the 1840 tithe map and apportionment, Lord Henley is shown as the landowner and the 22 acre holding is occupied by John Forsey. It was transferred to Mitchell Toms, the brewers, and by 1867 was licensed as a beer house. It was run by Dinah Fowler, a widow, whose unmarried brother was living with her. His occupation was described in the census as "Historical Reader". In 1914, James Hutchings, described in Kelly's Directory as a beer retailer, was at the inn. His speciality was cider and in one autumn over 100 hogsheads (approximately 6,300 gallons) were made. The property was not included in the sale of the manor by the Henleys in 1915 and James Hutchings continued there until at least 1930. His son-in-law, Ernest Hawkins, was the next retailer followed in 1953 by Anthony and Gladys Apsey, who were to be the last to sell beer and cider at the New Inn. They were offered the Tytherleigh Arms where they remained until Lionel and Joan Featherstone took over the licence. The New Inn continued as a beer and cider house until the end of 1953, after which it was sold by Mitchell Toms and became a private dwelling known as New Inn House. It became the Tytherleigh Cott Hotel in 1984 and is known in 2004 as Tytherleigh Cot, part of Tytherleigh Court Apartments.

The George Inn
The George Inn is perhaps the third most important building in the village after the church and the Court. Its history can be fairly accurately traced back to the late 15th Century. It is thought that The George was once known and served as the Church House where meetings were held and food prepared and eaten at social gatherings. In all probability, ale was brewed there and the Church or Churchwardens' Ales, occasions when the proceeds of the entertainment assisted in the upkeep of the church, would take place there. Church House buildings were usually sited near or adjoining a church or churchyard. They varied in size and status and it is possible that the Chardstock Church House was not The George but a separate building which has long since disappeared. However, the evidence seems to point to the premises being those of The George Inn, although it was not as large or a particularly high status building as some Church Houses were. The Chardstock Manor Account Roll for 1537/8 contains the following entry, "8d yearly rent from Frances Farnham for one parcel of the lord's demesne farm lying in the north of the same grange for one house built above in the same measuring in length 24 feet and in width 22 feet a perquisite to the use of the village church, which he (i.e. F. Farnham) holds for the term of his life at Ovyrlond" Overland was a term used in the west-country for a holding which had no common rights. From the Reeve's Account of 1545, the entry for the same property is, "8d in ninth rent from Francis Farnham for one parcel of newly reclaimed land lying in the north part of the grange and for one house built thereon at the back containing in length 24 feet and in width 22 feet provided for the use of the parish church". Francis Farnam appears in the Tudor Subsidy Roll of 1523 as having goods worth 7d for taxation. He is Francis Fernam in the 1545 Roll having goods worth 10d. The name Fran Farneham, is listed in the 1542 Tudor Muster Roll when he was expected to provide a bow and a sheaf of arrows. It is not known if he lived in the house or merely paid the rent. In 1646, during the Commonwealth period, the Manor was sequestrated and the building was sold as "All that house commonly called by the name of Church House and halfe an acre of land by estimation there unto belonging with all their appertenances".

When The George was surveyed by Ron Gilson in 1981, heavily smoke-blackened thatch and jointed crucks were found. He came to the conclusion that the building was a medieval open hall house, modified in the 16th Century, extended in the early 17th Century and changed in the later half of that century. The measurements of the oldest bays are 24 feet in length and 20 feet in width almost exactly the same as those noted in the 1537 and 1545 Accounts. The area of the land associated with the inn always appears to have been about half an acre, as in the Survey of the Manor dated 1781.

In 1625, the Constable, Churchwardens, Overseers of the Poor and several other parishioners of Chardstock applied to the Dorset Quarter Sessions for a brewing licence to be granted to John Clode. The following extract, taken from the application, indicates that the Church House was indeed an inn: "This corte ..... be pleased to give licence unto him to Brew and Bake for the poore of the said pish (parish) as other persons living in the house wherein he now dwelleth anciently have done the same being the Town house or Churchouse of the said pish" The name given to the inn was probably that of Saint George, although in tax assessment records it is often referred to as "the Inn"". In the Churchwardens' Presentments for the year 1697, reference is made to a "Spiritual Court held then at ye sign of the Dolphin in Chardstock". Perhaps this name was given to the Church House as, in the Middle Ages, a Dolphin was believed to be the first living creature created by God. However in 1636, a deposition, made in a court case between John Chubb and John Clode, mentions "ye sign of ye George in Chardstock". Was the Dolphin another Chardstock inn or was the name of the George changed to the Dolphin and back again? Manor courts and meetings were certainly held at the inn right down to modern times.

The Clode family paid the Poor Rate for the inn from about 1645 until 1708, when payment passed to the Wills family. Mrs. Ruth Pryer nee Wills, whose first husband was John Bentley, was the ratepayer for some years. Then in 1795, after her death, payments were made by the Bentleys and others. When the Manor was sold in 1873, Lord Henley became the owner. The rate payers and owners were not necessarily the innkeepers, though it is probable that Edward Clode, whose name appears in the list of Monmouth rebel suspects, kept the inn in the late 17th Century. Other innkeepers were Charles Beer, John Solway, John Apsey, Robert Parris and William Whiscomb. From 1859 to the 1950s, with one short break, the Parris family held the inn. They were also carpenters, coffin makers and undertakers, as was Jack Apsey who had his workshop behind the inn during the first part of the 20th Century.

Sources
Reeve's Accounts of the Manor, op. cit.
Poor Law Books, op. cit.
Quarter Session Records, op. cit.
Commonwealth Records, op. cit.
Style, Colin & O-lan, 1997 "The George Inn" and "Tytherleigh Inn".
Chard and Ilminster News, op. cit.

Chapter Nineteen
THE PEOPLE OF CHARDSTOCK

This Chapter is concerned with some of the more notable inhabitants of Chardstock. Sir Simonds D'Ewes born at Coaxden in 1602, the Revd. John Pitt, Vicar in 1627, his protégé James Strong, and Sir Edward Marshall Hall who attended St. Andrew's College in the 1870's, are but some of the few from the past whose lives have had an influence on events outside the village.

The Estmond Family
The Estmond family, whose large shield of arms hangs in the church, lived, in the 16th and 17th Centuries, at Lodge on the Wambrook border. Thomas Estmond was receiver of the rents of Holditch Mead in 1598/99 and several documents connected with his duties have survived. In 1590, John Estmond sold his rights in the Prebend to Magdalene Every. The members of the family were staunch catholics in a time of persecution and on several occasions were presented by the Churchwardens for non-attendance at the parish church. In 1609, Martha Estmond, the daughter of Thomas Estmond "doth not come to this church to our knowledge nor doth to our knowledge receive the communion". Again in 1613, Nicholas Estmond, his wife Mary and his sister Martha were presented as "obstinant Recusants" and in 1616, they were stated to be "excomunicate for Recusante". Another sister, "Dorothie the nowe wife of one Mr Fursdon" was presented for "not comunicatinge and cominge to Church". In 1620, Nicholas died and the Vicar and Churchwardens made the following presentment:-

"To the Right Worshipfull the Deane of Sarum or his Surrogate.
Wee the Vicar and Churchwardens, doe Present that the bodye of Nicholas Estmonde gent, an Excommunicate recusant, was buryed, as is supposed, in the Church of Chardstock aforesaid, in the nyght secretlye, unknown to eyther of us, on the feast of St Thomas last past, Notwithstanding, by the advice of the Justices and Cheefest Divines of our Cuntrye neere adjoynyng, wee have removed his said Coffyne out of our said Church, and have placed it in a remote place of our Churchyard, without the bounds of our Christian buryall. In witnesse of the truth heerof wee doe heereunto put our hands the xxviij th instant December 1620."

In 1625, Mary, the widow of Nicholas Estmond and daughter of George Fursdon, whose family lived at Cadbury, north of Exeter, and who was also catholic, was visited by two Dorset Justices. After a search they found "divers copes, altars, chalices etc." in her house. She refused to take the oath of allegiance and supremacy, escaped from the custody of the constable and failed to appear at the assizes. Unfortunately, a letter from the Secretary of State, Lord Conway, allowing her to return home peacefully was read to Parliament but not approved. As a result she was mentioned every year from 1627 to 1638 in the records of the Receiver of Revenues from Recusants and by 1637, had to pay £21 per annum. At this time, a Benedictine monk Nicholas Fitzjames resided at Lodge, or nearby, no doubt acting as a priest, though this would not be admitted. As Lodge was on the borders of three counties, he found it easy to escape but after the search by the justices, he did not resume his duties. By 1628, the estate was in financial difficulties and Mary arranged that she should marry John Coffin of Parkham (in Devon) and her daughter should marry his son Humphrey. Dom Nicholas was to officiate at the double wedding but when he discovered the true state of the finances and that his annuity was invalid, he became very angry. He kidnapped Mary, Mrs Estmond's daughter and heiress, who apparently did not want to marry Humphrey Coffin, and made several demands. A distressed Mrs. Estmond agreed to the conditions, the weddings took place and Dom Nicholas escaped abroad carrying with him the fruits of his actions. During the Civil War, Lodge, now much impoverished, was sequestrated from John and Humphrey Coffin and in 1658, Humphrey's son was leasing the property. By the 1662-4 Hearth Tax, however, Christopher Eastmond was listed as possessing two hearths.

Sir Simonds D'Ewes
Simonds D'Ewes was born at Coaxden in December 1602 and was baptized in the open gallery there, because of the cold weather, by the Revd. Richard White. His father was Paul D'Ewes, of Milding, Suffolk who was one of the Six Clerks of The Chancery, and his mother was Cecilia daughter of Richard Symonds (sometimes spelt Simonds) of Weycroft and Coaxdon. He remained in Coaxdon for about a year. His parents then returned to Suffolk but Simonds became ill on the journey and was left in the care of a nurse at Dorchester. When he had recovered, his grandfather, Richard Simonds, took him back to Coaxdon where he stayed till he was about 7¾ years old. During this period he fell into the stream at Coaxdon and was almost drowned. He narrowly escaped being kicked by a horse and suffered from various illnesses, one of which was brought about by over indulgence in his grandfather's cider and wine cellar. He received his education from the Revd. Richard White, the Vicar of Chardstock. He again fell victim to a fever from which he was cured by Mr. John Marwood, "a very skilful physician" who lived at Colyton. Shortly after this, Simonds was reunited with his parents in Suffolk and went to school in Lavenham and was admitted a member of the Middle Temple. His grandparents both died at Coaxdon and Simonds returned there in 1611 to his grandfather's funeral. He decided to remain at Coaxdon which his grandfather had left to him in his will, to be administered by his father until he came of age.

PLATE 10

The George Inn

The New Inn

Heraldry on the Symonds Monument

The Tytherleigh Helmet

Estmond Achievement

Bowditch Hatchment

Tytherleigh Achievement

87

The Revd. White had by then given up teaching and so Simonds was sent by his mother to school at Wambrook where he was taught, for three years, by Christopher Marraker (Rector there from 1591-1621).

In 1614, Simonds left Coaxdon never to return and the house and land were let by his father to a tenant. The household goods were taken by sea from Lyme to Suffolk but the documents and family papers were sent to Paul D'Ewes' office in London where they were destroyed by fire in 1621. Simonds went first to school in London and then to Bury St. Edmunds, near where his father had bought a house. From there he went up to St. John's College, Cambridge, in 1618. He became a barrister in the Middle Temple in 1623, was knighted in 1626 and became High Sheriff for Suffolk in 1639. He was Member of Parliament for Sudbury in 1640 and was created a baronet in 1641. He was one of the 140 M.P.s turned out of the House of Commons in 1648, by Col. Pride, after which the remaining 50 to 60 members passed an ordinance creating a court of 135 commissioners to try King Charles I. He wrote an autobiography, from which much of the foregoing information is taken, and was a noted parliamentary diarist for which he is now best known. He also made many transcripts of which the most valuable are those of monastic cartularies and registers. He died in 1650 leaving, amongst other bequests, £10 to the poor of Chardstock, "to be paid within two months after my decease".

Rev. John Pitt and Rev. James Strong
Richard White died in 1621 and it is not known who, if anyone, was vicar until 1627 when John Pitt had a dispensation, confirmed by King Charles I, to hold the vicarage of Chardstock (worth £50 a year). Pitt had been Vicar of Timberscombe, Somerset, in 1619, but resigned when he was made Rector of the sinecure parish of South Braydon which had no church and a small population. He was one of four sons of Robert Pitt of Isle Abbotts who leased land from Nicholas Wadham of Merrifield. In 1603, at the age of 19, he went up to Magdalen Hall, Oxford but nothing is known of his career there. He had been named to one of the foundation fellowships of Wadham College, Oxford, by Dorothy, wife of Nicholas Wadham, when she founded the College in 1613. He held various offices there between 1613 and 1626, including that of Greek Reader, Bursar, Dean and Sub-Warden. As he would be obliged to give up the fellowship in 1629, he acquired the living of Lewcombe in Dorset as well as that of Chardstock in 1627. He befriended James Strong, son of Thomas Strong, a poor tailor of Chardstock, who "wrought for a groat a day, his pottage and bread and cheese". Pitt sent James Strong to New Inn Hall, Oxford, in 1636 and lived to regret it. He returned to Wadham College as Warden in 1644 during the Civil War, when Oxford was the headquarters of the Royalists. As well as being Warden, Pitt became the leader of the dissident heads of houses who denied the authority of the Parliamentary Commissioners. In 1648, he was dispossessed of the Wardenship, having previously, in 1645, been turned out of the Vicarage of Chardstock because he was a Royalist, by no less a person than James Strong, who carried off his books and goods, presumably for his own use, to his living at Bettiscombe. James Strong's name appears in the Chardstock Registers for 1645, when he was probably minister. Pitt went to live at Ilton, according to his Will which was proved in 1654. He was buried at Isle Abbotts where in the 1970s a fragment of his tombstone was found.

The first reference we have to the Strong family in Chardstock appears in the Division of the Manor dated 1582. This was a document from the Court of Chancery, giving details of the holdings of the lessees and tenants. Emme Strong is mentioned as holding a 1 acre tenement, which probably would have been in Alston. There is no doubt that the property in Chardstock village, now called Strongs, was once occupied by them and structurally dates from when one George and his son Thomas were alive. Other sites that over the years have also been called Strongs, include two farms in Alston, a hamlet on the south-west of the parish, and a cottage nearly opposite the present Strongs, all of which have been rebuilt. From the Manor Court Rolls for 1596, George Strong appears at the homage for the south, i.e. the tenants of the Manor coming to the court. He was probably a serge maker from Chard and may or may not have been related to Emme. In the same year, Margaret Strong, a widow, is mentioned when she surrendered half an acre in one of the "open fields". These were fields where strips of land were allocated to copyholders, not leaseholders. She was probably the Margaret Strong, widow, who in 1598, was forbidden to make a fire in her "mantle" (the canopy over the open fireplace) until it was repaired. In 1600, she received William Denman into her house as an under-tenant without the permission of the Court. William Denman married Honora Strong in 1600. Unfortunately, the relationships between Margaret and Honora cannot be worked out and it is not known if Margaret was related to George. In 1601, a widow Strong was again in trouble for not maintaining her hedges and in 1602, her "mantle" was again in decay. Did she survive to become Margaret, widow, buried 1621, twenty-four years after the death of her husband or have we another Margaret here? Her property reverted to the Lord of the Manor in that year and in 1625, Alexander Stevens took a cottage "late of George Strong". George continued to appear at the court held twice a year, till 1618 and again from 1626 to 1629 he was among the homage. He probably lived in the house we know today as Strongs, as in 1636, the following entry appears. "George Strong tenant since the last court to a cottage in Chardstock town and doth happen to the lord for a death duty, and that Thomas Strong is the next tenant." This Thomas is much more likely to be George's brother than his son; he would be the last life on the original copyhold. George Strong was also the tenant of Purdys Hay, a field at the end of Chardstock town, now part of a housing estate in Green Lane.

George seems to have been in trouble with the court on many occasions. In 1597, the court ordered that "the fylthy faulte" beween John Welch and George Strong to be amended. Several times he is told to clean his ditch at Purdys Hays and another "against his meadow and orchard in Chardstocke Streete". On another occasion he "hath made a diche which is noisome". In 1629, he is accused of selling "fuell furres in the Commons and carry them into another parish and burn them contrary to the customs of our manor, therefore, he is fined ten shillings". At one court it was reported that "George Strong hath pulled downe a Barne builded upon posts upon his cottage and carryed the tymber into another mannor and hath also rooted upp certayne apple trees growing uppon his said cottage and carryed the same out of this manor". His son, Thomas seems to have fared little better. In 1608, he was accused with William Tyatt for "lyeing of soyle at the Shamells end in the high way". He was again presented before the Court in 1620, with "divers persons" for "laying of soyle in the streets of Chardstocke being the King's highway ..... severally fyned at 4 pence a piece". The Shambles was the slaughterhouse and the soyle was manure. In 1614, the South Homage was instructed at the Manor Court, to view Thomas Strong's oven and yeast. Whether this was his own family oven or one used as a bakery is not known. He married Joanna Bagge and had one son, James, born in 1618, and possibly six daughters, and is included in the Chardstock Protestation Return of 1641. We know little more than this about him except that he died in May 1663 and James preached illegally in his father's house at his funeral. Thomas was buried in Chardstock but not according to the rites of the Church of England.

In 1654, James Strong came to the sequestrated vicarage at Ilminster being appointed "public preacher" nominated by Oliver Cromwell. According to "The Mynster of the Ile" by James Street, several of Strong's sermons still exist, including one preached at the Assizes at Chard in 1657. His reputation in Ilminster was, it seems, no better than in Chardstock. On one occasion when, after three women had gone to his house to object to his conduct, he swore that he was "in fear of his life from them" and they were fined and sent to prison in Ilchester. In the 1671 survey of Chardstock Manor, James is listed as a copyholder of one cottage containing one dwelling house, orchard and garden and 3 acres and pasture, at a rent of 8s. He also appears in the Chardstock Hearth Tax Return for 1662/4 and as a rate payer in the Poor Book for 1676 and 1678, when he pays 3d for his tenement. He is included in a list of "those who are to maintain ye armor and souldiers imposed on ye Parish of Chardstock". This list is undated but is probably for the year 1676 or 1678. James, with three others had to provide one armour. James Strong was the author of a poem, promoted by his Royalist enemies in 1674, entitled "Joanereidos, or Feminine Valor" about the bravery of the women at the siege of Lyme Regis. According to Pulman's "Book of the Axe" this was a miserable work of over two hundred lines. The poem and the author were ridiculed in another ballad which precedes it and describes how Strong ill-treated his first wife, Katherine Minterne, how he took the font out of the church at Bettiscombe and made a pig's trough of it and how he preached a sermon to justify the sequestrator, a man named Raw who had hanged himself. Even his personal habits were held against him.

"For James doth breathe so foul an Air,
That he can Spiders slay
At three yards distance, and Few dare
I'th Room, where he is, stay.

This is the Cause that near his house
No Rose Or Flower blows,
Nor on his Body will a Louse
Come, nor within his clothes."

James Strong was appointed "Rector" of Earnshill in 1686 and "Vicar" of Curry Rivall, livings which he held at his death in 1694. Perhaps the last word on James may be left with the following verses from the ballad.

"And being now a Widower,
He would a Wooing ride,
To get a Rich Wife, far or near,
His Palfrie he'd bestride.

In order whereunto he goes
The Rich Black Velvet Coat,
(Which worn is, Every Body knows,
Onely by Men of Note.)

In This he swagger'd up and down
Ilmister, Taunton, Chard,
On market-daies; scarce any Town
Near him, but saw, or heard

How Brave a Gallant Jimmy was
Become. But though the Skin
Without was Lion, yet the Ass
Enclosed was within."

Cousins of the Chardstock Strong family sailed to America on the "Mary and John" in the 1630s where they settled in New England. Their decendants have been much involved in the renovation of Strongs Cottage.

Rev. Richard Luce

According to the Commonwealth Records for 1654, Richard Luce was presented by the patron Richard Osborn, to the living and Vicarage of Chardstock, but in the margin is written by another hand and possibly at another time "the pson scandalous and never admitted papers not drawn". This assessment of the character of Richard Luce was probably not far from the truth as he managed to cause so much bad feeling in the parish. He was inducted as vicar in 1661 by Gamaliel Chase, the Rector of Wambrook. The Churchwarden's Presentments for the year 1667/8, show how relations between vicar and parishioners had deteriorated: "... we present that by reason of the vicious and uncivill behaviour of our Minister Mr Richard Luce divers of our pishoners have neglected to receive the holy Sacrament this last yeare at his hands. wee present our vicar Mr Richard Luce for that hee hath a long time neglected his cure and more, esspetially for these six weekes who hath left us alltogether without makinge provision for our supply in his absence as hee ought to have done which hath caused great distractions & much disorder in our pish as I have heard on the Sundayes. And on the 29th of January last hee spent but little time in the Church, & redd but very few prayers onley for hee spent the moste parte of that day in the Alehouse. And for his life & conversation it hath bynn too notorious debawcht much given to drunckennes cursing & swareing quarellinge & stirring up discord amongst his neigbors with many other vicious & rude deportments."

The Vicar responded with his own presentments, accusing various members of the congregation of "refusing to receive the sacrament of ye Lords Supper these last seven yeares". He presented John Knight and Phillip Palmer, churchwardens, "for not washing the surplyse & for not seing due reverence in ye time of divine service but have suffered divers persons to stand talking in ye churchyard during ye time of divine service on ye Lords daies & other daies appointed to be kept holy be ye constitution of the church of England". He complained that several children had not been baptised in church but in their homes by a minister from another parish. He presented Nicholas Cate for entertaining "several persons in his house being an Alehouse on the Lords daye tipling in the time of divine service". By 1667, his behaviour had become the subject of an Ecclesiastical Court case and many witnesses testified to the drunken behaviour of the Vicar. A testimonial in his support was presented by his fellow clergy and Mr. Luce charged "Phillip Palmer and John Knight the late churchwardens Robert Tyderlegh Esq William Warry Henry Bowdich Gent for taking the pish stocke which should be employed in the reparation of the church & maintenance of ye poor to maintaine a lawsuite at ye instance of Nicholas Cate against myselfe which ye said Cate promoted in ye Ecclesiastical Court of ye worshipfull Deane of Sarum. And the summe so ordered by ye said Robert Tyderlegh etc was ten pounds which they by warrent under their owne handes and others to George Bowdich Gent treasurer for the said stocke ordered to be delivered to ye said Cate".

We are not sure of the outcome of the court case but in 1669, James Keate was Vicar of Chardstock and in 1671, the Revd. Richard Luce is recorded as Curate of Chideok.

Revd. William Liddon

From St. Andrew's Registers we learn that:-
"On ye 21 day of March in ye year of our Lord 1807 Thomas Carter clerk A M was inducted into the Parish Church of Chardstock by me Wm Liddon Rector of Sandringham with Babingley in the County of Norfolk.
George Bond Wm Pickering of Axminster Churchwardens."

William Liddon, son of William Liddon of Rackenford, Devon, was Rector of Sandringham from 1797 to 1812/13 where the Patron was Henry Hoste Henley. He was Curate of Chard from 1781 to 1806 and Curate of Chardstock from 1806 to 1812. It is known that from 1801 to 1806 he resided in Chard. Being Curate of Chardstock he was able to induct Thomas Carter into the Parish Church of Chardstock in 1807.

Henry Hoste Henley's ancestor was Henry Henley of Taunton, brother of Andrew Henley, Mayor of Taunton 1627 and from whom the present Lord Henley is descended. The marriage of Henry Cornish Henley to Susan daughter of James Hoste of Sandringham led to the acquisition of the Sandringham Estate and the patronage of the living. It remained in the family until its sale to Spencer Cowper circa 1836 before being sold to Queen Victoria in the mid 1840s. Henry Hoste Henry was the son of Henry and Susan Cornish Henley.

The Revd. Thomas Carter was Assistant Master at Eton College 1801 to 1814, Lower Master from 1814 to 1829 and at the same time Vicar of Chardstock until 1830 when he became Rector of Southmere in Norfolk.

Tytherleigh Family

Many generations of the Tytherleigh family were associated with Chardstock, living at the Sub-Manor from which their name comes. Richard de Tuderlege (Tytherleigh) was a witness to a deed in or about the year 1201. Ralph de Tyderling, with others, held land at Tyderly in 1235/6. It was warranted to him for one pair of gloves and one penny at Michaelmas. A Richard de Tyderlegh appears in the Lay Subsidy Roll of 1332 and in 1379, William Tyderleigh is recorded as holding land in the Manor of Chardstock. Another Richard Tyderle is mentioned in Dean Chandler's Register of 1405. He may be the same Richard who held land at Kittemor in 1422/27. William Tyderly de Tydemore, had land in Tyderley in 1431 and in 1497 Richard Tiderley was listed in the Perkin Warbeck rebel returns. In the 1525 Tudor Subsidies, William Tetherley appears and in 1545 Joan Tyderley is mentioned. William's name is included in the Tudor Muster Rolls for 1539, when he had to provide a harness (a general term for armour), a bow and a sheaf of arrows. In 1594, Robert Tidderleige, gent., paid subsidy on his land and in 1598 and 1599 signed Robert Tyderleigh on several documents, which until recently, were preserved in the Parish Chest and are now in the Devon Record Office. Richarde Tytherleigh appears in the 1641 Protestation Returns and in 1645, Mrs. Tyderleigh, widow, paid a 6d Poor Rate. Robert Tiderleigh Esq. was included in the Hearth Tax of 1662-4 as having 7 hearths. From 1684 till 1718, Robert Tyderleigh paid the Rate, but was possibly not the Robert who paid the Hearth Tax. Robert Tyderleigh died in 1744 and Marjory Tytherly, gentlewoman, was buried in 1759.

Rev. Charles Woodcock M.A.

Charles Woodcock was born in 1809 in Madras, the son of Charles and Anne Woodcock. His father was a Judge and Magistrate of Combaconum district in Madras. About 1820, the family returned to England and settled in London. Charles went to Haileybury and up to Christ Church, Oxford to study for his M.A. in 1829. He was made deacon in 1832 and a year later priested, becoming curate of Ealing. In 1834, he came to Chardstock as Vicar on the resignation of Elborough Woodcock, his cousin. He was presented to the living by the patron, who was his uncle, Canon Henry Woodcock D.D. of Christ Church, Oxford and Prebendary of Chardstock. He remained as vicar for 41 years, becoming an honorary Canon of Salisbury Cathedral and Prebendary of Grantham Boreal in 1869. During his time at Chardstock he rebuilt the vicarage, reconstructed the Church and built the schools and college, using much of the family capital, including a large amount from his brother Parry Woodcock. He also organised clubs and societies, as in 1843, when he set up a Farmers' Club for circulating magazines and ideas.

In 1875, the Canon retired to All Saints which he had helped to set up in 1840 and where he lived as Rector until his death in 1898. From his obituary in the "Salisbury Diocesan Gazette" for April 1898 we can gain an insight into his character. "He was a man when once seen not easily forgotten. His tall and commanding figure, fine features, powerful voice, physical and mental energy, genial manners, bright humour, originality and quaintness of expression, together with a certain indefinable charm of personal attractiveness, made him, even to those who were but slightly acquainted with him, a person full of interest."

Eliezar Denning

Eliezar Denning was born in Chardstock in 1828. He enlisted in the Metropolitan Police and rose to the rank of Inspector in charge of the police at the House of Commons. In 1885, he was promoted to Chief Inspector of the Palace of Westminster, responsible for policing both Houses of Parliament. On the 40th anniversary of his enlistment he was presented with an autographed picture collection of all the Members and staff of the Commons. On his retirement, after 21 years at Westminster, W. H. Smith, the First Lord of the Treasury, said that Chief Inspector Denning's influence had been of the highest value to the police at the House of Commons. Mr. Gladstone echoed this and said that the Inspector's qualities and conduct had been reflected in the fidelity and courtesy of the force. Chief Inspector Denning was then presented with a number of gifts in appreciation of his loyal service.

John Jones (see Chapter 1).

John Wills

John Wills was born at Tytherleigh in 1832. After studying horticulture at Cricket St. Thomas, he became head gardener at Abbey Farm Lodge, St. John's Wood. In 1860 he was in charge of the garden at Oulton Park in Cheshire and by 1868 he was manager of a London nursery. Two years later he had his own business at South Kensington. He was appointed florist to the Prince of Wales in charge of the gardens at Marlborough House and other royal residences. In 1880, John Wills opened, in the words of the "Chard and Ilminster" newspaper, "new and handsome premises" in Regent Street, London. The ceremony was performed by Lord Skelmersdale, Chairman of the Company. John Wills won several Gold Medals, including one for Bronze Leaved Pelargoniums. In 1879, he was presented with the Sevres Cup by the French Government for "elegant and artistic representations" The following year he was awarded the French Cross of the Legion of Honour for his services to horticulture.

Sir Edward Marshall Hall K.C.

Edward Marshall Hall was born in Brighton in 1858 and was the son of Dr. Alfred Hall. He came to Chardstock as a pupil at St. Andrew's College about 1866 or 1867 and is listed in the 1871 Census. Nothing is known of his career at St. Andrew's apart from a reference in the "Dorset County Chronicle" to his appearance in the College Cricket Team in 1873. He left Chardstock in 1874 and spent two years at Rugby, after which he went up to Cambridge to read law. He was called to the bar in 1882, became a barrister in 1888, took silk in 1898 and was knighted in 1917. He became Member of Parliament for Southport in 1900, but lost his seat in the General Election of 1906. He was returned to Parliament in 1910 as one of the members for Liverpool. Sir Edward Marshall Hall K.C. was eventually to become one of England's outstanding advocates making a brilliant reputation as counsel in criminal cases, appearing in many outstanding trials, including that of Thompson and Bywaters. He died in 1927.

Constant Permeke

Constant Permeke was an artist of international renown. He was born in Antwerp in 1886, moving to Ostend the following year when his father became the first curator of Ostend Museum. He studied art in Bruges and Ghent and, in 1912, married Maria Delaere, a lace worker from Bruges. On the outbreak of war in 1914, he joined the army, was badly wounded and was evacuated to England. After demobilisation he moved to Chardstock, living at Dunsters, Holy City. Francis King, the headmaster of St. Andrew's School offered him a room to use as a studio. There he painted some of his masterpieces, "The Butcher" and the "Ciderdrinker", now in private collections, and "The Stranger" now in the Royal Museum of Art in Brussels. He moved to Sidmouth in 1919 and returned to Belgium two years later, where he continued his work until his death in 1952. In 1980, a Belgian film crew arrived in Chardstock to shoot scenes for inclusion in a film celebrating his life.

Old Chardstock Families

Some of the surnames which appear in early documents and registers can still be found in the village in the early 21st Century. Among them are Apsey, Baker, Bond, Bowditch, Chubb, Churchill, Fowler, Harris, Holland, Hutchings, Jefford, Keate, Larcombe, Long, Loveridge, Marks, Newbery, Parris, Pierce, Searle, Spiller, Stoodley, Talbot, Turner, Waldron, Willmington. It must be admitted, however, that some of those with the same surnames living in the village today may not belong to the original Chardstock families. The names of some important families of the past are not represented in the present day village although their descendants may still live in the Chardstock area. These include the Bentleys, Deanes, Estmonds, Everys, Tytherleighs and the Wales. Many representatives of the families listed above appear in the chapters of this book together with others not mentioned here. They have all played their parts in the long history of the village as their decendants and namesakes do today.

Sources

Bickwell, Mrs. E. M. and Davies, C. S. L., The Revds. J. Pitt & J. Strong Som. & Dor. Notes & Queries.
Chard & Ilminster News, op. cit.
Churchwarden's Presentments, op. cit.
Constant Permeke, Catalogue, Provincial Museum Jabbeke Belgium.
East, Mrs. C., correspondence re. Sir Edward Marshall Hall.
Halliwell, James Orchard, 1845 The Autobiography and Correspondence of Sir Simonds D'Ewes.
Somerset and Dorset Notes and Queries, Various refs. Chard Lib.
Street, Jas., 1904 The Mynster of the Ile.
Wood, P. J., The History of Education in Chardstock Revd. C. Woodcock.

Chapter Twenty
THE INFLUENCE OF NATIONAL EVENTS

Every period of history must have had an effect on the village and on the lives of the inhabitants. Some events would have exerted a profound influence while others may have been ignored. It is very difficult to assess the exact impact of what was happening in the country on the local community before the advent of mass communication and we can only guess at the effect of events beyond the immediate surroundings of the parish. More details of many of the following references to events will be found elsewhere in this book.

Early Times
In Bronze and Iron Age times, settlements, which undoubtedly existed and which were probably on the higher ground, must have held some allegiance to the tribe that dominated the area. This tribe may have been the Durotriges who were established in modern Dorset and South Somerset, or possibly the area could have been under the Dumnonii of Devon. Boundaries were being formed and Chardstock was probably on the frontier between, what is now Dorset and Devon. There is, of course, no record of this. Whether the people living in this area were left in peace or whether the land was being fought over or even if it was only a "no-mans land", is not known. There were hill forts in the vicinity, those at Bounds Lane and Membury being the closest but not necessarily in use at all times. The inhabitants left no written records nor do we have any details of the extent of the population or how it lived. No burials, which would provide clues to the life style of the people, have so far been found although it is known that there were probable burial mounds on Bewley Down (see Chapter 2).

During the Roman advance and occupation, no documentary evidence of an individual or the existence of a settlement has been discovered. Indeed it would be most surprising if such material were to be found. It has to be assumed that the standard of living for local folk improved with their absorption into the Roman Empire, as elsewhere in the area. Similarly, we do not know exactly when the West Saxons reached Chardstock although place name evidence in the area suggests that a language change from Old Welsh to Old English was happening at about 680 A.D. Probably the Saxons demanded a change of loyalty to a local king. It is possible that they took over the existing settlements, establishing the manorial system which, in its turn, was adopted by the Normans and became the Manor. It can be assumed that Christianity come to Chardstock before Saxon times, perhaps from the monastery at Sherborne, and that maybe the site of the later church was being used for preaching and burials.

Medieval
The general area remained very unsettled for some time after the Norman Conquest in 1066. We know that the teams of assessors must have visited Chardstock to carry out the great Domesday Survey. Instability again may have reached Chardstock during the quarrel between Stephen and Matilda when the Manor was taken from the Bishop by the King and then returned to the Bishop. How this affected the lives of the inhabitants can only be surmised. Nothing is known of the effect of the Crusades or even if their existence was known to those living here, although there is an area in Wambrook called Spittle and a field at Crawley called Dotte. These may have been the property of the Knights Hospitalers, Dotte possibly being a donation because they had rights in the area. We also know that their Preceptory of Buckland (near Durston) held lands as close as Holditch. Then, as now, the taxes levied by central government, be it the King or Parliament, made their impact on the people. The Lay Subsidies of 1327 and 1333, in addition to the manorial and church dues, must have caused much comment.

We hear nothing of the Black Death, which allegedly began in Melcombe Regis (at Weymouth, not that far from Chardstock) in 1348. The only clue to the disease reaching the parish is contained in the list of Vicars. Two priests were inducted in 1348 perhaps as a result of sudden death. There is no mention of the French Wars, of the battle of Crecy in 1346 and that of Agincourt in 1415, but the effects of the Perkin Warbeck Rebellion of the 1490s were certainly felt in Chardstock. From 1497, there survives a list giving the names of the village men associated with the attempt of Warbeck to gain the crown. They were heavily fined.

Later Times
The dissolution of the monasteries and the consequent upheavals in the church must have had an effect on Chardstock but we have no evidence of how people reacted to these momentous events. We have lists of the Tudor Muster Rolls to provide arms, armour and soldiers when needed by the monarch but no clue as to the state of mind of those men who were listed. Catholics were persecuted, as presentments by the Churchwardens to the Visitation Courts indicate. Perhaps this was only to comply with the law, for the Catholic Estmond family continued to marry and have their children baptized in the church. The threat of invasion by France and then by Spain, with its Armada, must have alarmed the inhabitants of the village. The warning beacon on Beacon Hill was probably used to warn of coastal raids from early times but it is known to have been part of the chain of beacons refurbished at this time (see Map 12), and which were designed to alert the County Militia quickly.

The Protestation Return of 1641, designed to protect the Protestant religion from Catholic influence, with its list of the men of the parish was duly sent. The Civil War and its consequences could not have failed to make an impact on the village. In May 1644, John Spring, a soldier who died at Tytherleigh House and had probably been involved in the siege of Lyme Regis that had just been relieved, was buried in the Churchyard. Whether he died as a result of war wounds from that bloody conflict is not known. Also involved in the siege was John Parris of Chardstock, a Lieutenant in the King's army where he was in charge of 20 men. He later had his estate sequestrated for £150. In 1641, his estate had been contracted to be bought by Gamaliel Chase, Rector of Wambrook. The Governor of Lyme Regis considered Parris to be an enemy of Parliament and so he imprisoned Chase for the sum of £150. After many months in prison he was released and he then fled to Exeter to escape further attentions of the Lyme Regis garrison. In 1649, he was discharged, having paid his fine. In 1648, Parliament allowed Joan, the widow of John Parris, repayment of a fifth of the estate, but then reduced it to only £5. By 1664, Richard Parris was recorded as receiving a pension of £1 for loyalty to his late Majesty. John Harvey, another royalist, was compounded (fined) for £12 after the war. Tytherleigh probably saw the passage of two major parliamentary groups of forces along the road, the Earl of Essex in December 1644, who was to be shortly defeated in Cornwall and General Fairfax in October 1645, who was to capture Exeter. Also in that year, a Parliamentarian Officer, Sir Shilston Calmady, was killed in a skirmish at the gates of Ford House (below Bewley Farm) during a siege and was buried at Membury. The emergence of James Strong, the ejection of vicar John Pitts and the sequestration of the Manor, must have greatly affected the ordinary people and there was much suffering in the war.

The Hearth Tax of 1662 concerned the more affluent, but the Monmouth Rebellion of 1685 and the march of forces through Chardstock Parish (as earlier in the Civil War) must have touched everyone. The list of Monmouth Rebels includes 22 men from Chardstock. Henry Knight, Henry Rowe and Thomas Smith (the village constable who at his trial annoyed the fearsome Judge Jeffreys), were hanged. John Budge, John Pinney and Richard Spiller were transported to the West Indies. The remaining men were either pardoned or had no action taken against them. The annual observance of thanksgiving services for the deliverance of James I and Parliament from the Gunpowder Plot, for the safe arrival of William and Mary and the prayers used on each anniversary of the martyrdom of King Charles I, must have brought a realisation of how national events could affect the lives of the most humble citizen.

Improved Communications
With the coming of the turnpike roads making communication easier, the world began to close in on small rural communities. Until then, the ordinary villager would have had limited knowledge of the country beyond the immediate parish boundaries. He would have considered his family as the most important area of his life, followed by Parish affairs, as they affected his family. The adoption of the new style of calendar in 1752 appears to have passed without comment in the parish records as do the Napoleonic Wars, although French Prisoners of War were near, if not actually in, the village. Those held in Chard were reputed to have worked at Burridge. In the neighbouring parish of Membury, elaborate plans for the evacuation of the population have survived. There is no evidence of the same course of action being followed in Chardstock. In 1814, however, celebrations were held "on the conclusion of a Peace between England and France ...... when Europe was deliver'd from the most horrible tyranny ever known!!!". The festivities included ringing the bells and giving the poor a feast and entertainment. Subscriptions from the local inhabitants defrayed the cost of the exercise which amounted to £55 6s 6d. The list of subscribers concludes with the words, "Eight hundred Men, Women and Children partook of the Entertainment".

The church bells were rung to mark various national events as those recorded in the Churchwardens' Accounts for 1717 illustrate, "paid the fifth November for Ringing 12s" and "paid the King Crownation day for Ringing 3s". They were also rung many times in the long reign of Queen Victoria on royal occasions.

The improvement in educating the local children, the establishment of the College and the building of the railway also contributed to the opening up of the village. The textile industry was declining and the College must have provided alternative employment for some of the local people. The introduction of the orphans of the Crimean War and the Indian Mutiny to the school brought world events very close to Chardstock. The Inclosure of Commons came very late, not until 1856, in contrast to many other places which had experienced the loss of common grazing rights, perhaps centuries before. Nevertheless this piece of national legislation would have affected everyone in the parish. Many Acts of Parliament have obviously affected the life of the village and mention has been made of some of them in other chapters. Legislation for local government, such as the setting up of Parish Councils replacing the old vestry meetings, the reform of the judicial system and the gradual development of electoral reform have had an effect on the inhabitants of Chardstock, as they have throughout the country.

The World Wars
In recent times, the impact of two World Wars left permanent scars on the village, as they have in every community in the country. The names of the men of Chardstock who gave their lives in the two World Wars are inscribed on the War Memorial in the centre of the village. Some details about them are added below:-

1914 - 1918

John Herbert Allen	Private in the Oxfordshire & Buckinghamshire Light Infantry.
Phillip Apsey	Private in the Duke of Cornwall's Light Infantry.
George Balland Banfield	Private in the Devonshire Regiment.
Frederick Bowditch	Private in the South Lancashire Regiment.
Ernest Frederick Chubb	
Albert Thomas Cousins	Private in the Gloucestershire Regiment.
John Raymond Cousins	Private in the Devonshire Regiment.
Walter Leonard Deem	Private in the London Regiment (on active service only 3 weeks).
Arthur Edward Charles Dolling	Private in the Dorsetshire Regiment.
John Down	Private in the Somerset Light Infantry.
Frank Sidney Hull	Private in the Royal Warwickshire Regiment.
Ernest Frederick Pearce	Private in the Duke of Cornwall's Light Infantry.
C. William H. Pearce	Private in the Durham Light Infantry.
Conrad Rockett	Private in the Devonshire Regiment.
Thomas Rowe	2nd Lieutenant in the King's Liverpool Regiment.
Walter George Sparks	Private in the Yorkshire Regiment.
Reginald George Spiller	Staff Sergeant in the Royal Services.
Eli Trenchard	Gunner in the Royal Field Artillery.

1939 - 1945

Maurice John Bishop	Ordinary Seaman in the Royal Navy.
Robert Thomas Stephan Fowler	Sapper in the Royal Engineers.
Frederick Henry Hodge	Killed in the bombing of the Wilts United Dairy at Chard Junction (only civilian casualty from Chardstock).
Norman Elsdon Jones	Flight Sergeant in the Royal Air Force.
John Jenkins	Engine room Artificer in the Royal Navy.
Arthur Larcombe	Sergeant-Major in the Duke of Cornwall's Light Infantry.
Maurice Plevis Latter	2nd Lieutenant in the Royal Artillery.
Gifford Benjamin Coles Miller	Flight Sergeant in the Royal Air Force Voluntary Reserve.
William Ralph Spiller	Gunner in the Royal Artillery.
Edward Tattersall	Driver in the Royal Horse Artillery.

These wars affected everyone, especially the 1939-1945 conflict, with Air Raid Precautions, Air Raid Wardens and rationing of food. At the school, it was decided that the recent dining room would be the safest place for the children in the event of an Air Raid. It was also decided to make the room as gas proof as possible. Evacuee children from the Friern School, Peckham Rye in London began to arrive in the village. At Holy City, one lady soon left and it was reported that, "she was afraid of the cows!". Provision for a classroom was made in the Parish Room but this arrangement did not last and the children, including some from Bristol and Southampton, were absorbed into the village school. Various war projects were organised. A typical event was a concert given in St. Andrew's Hall. This was most successful in raising money for the Spitfire Fund. Gradually the evacuees returned to their homes and in 1942, Miss Wills the teacher, was recalled to London. Also in that year a certificate was presented to the Civil Parish of Chardstock to commemorate the adoption of HMMGB 40 (a Motor Gun Boat) during Warship Week, which took place in March. In May, £20 was raised for Exeter's raid victims. In 1943, Chardstock Parish Savings Group was awarded a Certificate of Honour for its part in the Wings for Victory campaign.

The Home Guard, or the Local Defence Volunteers, as it was originally known, was formed in 1940. Jack Lane was in charge of the Chardstock Volunteers. At first there were no uniforms and few weapons. Later rifles and sten guns were issued as they became available. Chardstock and All Saints belonged to the 19th (Seaton) Battalion Home Guard Devonshire Regiment and were part of Axminster "B" Company, which was commanded by Lt. Col. Sir Henry F. Cox, K.C.M.G., D.S.O. from Uplyme with Major E. Ball as second in command. Chardstock was No. 5 Platoon commanded by Lieut. P. Short. All Saints' commander was Lieut. A. E. Batten and Chardstock was under the command of Lieut. D. Eames. No. 10 Post had its H.Q. in the Cottage (now demolished) at Alston, south of Chubb's Farm. There was also a gorse hut at the Beacon. No. 11 Post was at Storridge in a shepherd's hut. Drill took place in the School Hall then known as St. Andrew's Hall. Weapon training was held at the 2.2mm shooting range at the back of Pratt's Garage, [later Burgess (Farm Industries) Ltd., then Countrywest Trading] at Tytherleigh. Patrols were organised, training took place and guard duties were performed. One of these, was to assist in guarding the Honiton Railway Tunnel during the spring and summer of 1944. Another was to report any bombs dropping, to the police. Two Log Books have survived and date from October 1940 to December 1941. Many of the entries state "Nothing to report" or involve routine matters such as the timings of patrols to and from the cottage and the state of the weather. Some of the following extracts from No 5 Platoon No. 10 post are of most interest.

1940

Oct. 15th. Single plane at 12am flying N-S This plane leaving smoke trail behind. Single plane at 12.10am flying S-N. Anti-aircraft fire at Yeovil 12am also bombs dropped in same direction. Anti-aircraft fire at Portland 12.15am.

Nov. 20th. A noise like a bomb falling in a Southerly direction at 12.15 Followed within 5 minutes by an Aeroplane going in a Northerly direction from the S.

Nov. 22nd. 1.40am Large light seen in Easterly direction possibly a plane on fire also gunfire in same direction while on patrol.

Nov. 24th. Planes crossing over from 10.25 - 11.45pm in Yeovil direction. Gunfire seen from Yeovil & Wellington. Bombs dropped in Yeovil direction.

Nov. 23rd. Heavy gunfire heard in the English Channel. Reflection of fire in the sky in Taunton direction.

Dec. 14th. Mr. Short visited. Inspected section posts. All Saints has 6" water in bottom and wire fence is down. Catmoor Cross post O.K.

1941

Jan. 2nd. Usual patrol. Heavy anti-aircraft gunfire in the direction of Yeovil and Portland, also heard bombs in the same direction.

Jan. 13th. A plane heard in Easterly direction also gunfire or bombs at 10.15pm.

Jan. 17th. Severe bombing to the direction of N.N.west, large fire from same direction.

Jan. 18th. Battery of red-torch is getting weak.

Feb. 4th. Red torch will not work.

Feb. 5th. Several planes pass over coincidence S.R. trains running as planes over head on each occasion.

Feb. 6th. A bright light showing in the direction of Axminster which kept on diminishing several times at 11.30.

Feb. 8th. Torch needs attention it let us down tonight.

Feb. 11th. P.S. (This was probably Lt. P. Short who was in command). Guard room chimney wants sweeping, can't see Sally for smoke. Have been trying to get batteries for weeks. Chimney kindly being swept by W. Skinner.

Feb. 24th. Several planes overhead, also several explosions heard in N.W. direction sounding like bombs.

Feb. 26th. 9.0 to 9.45pm Heavy sounding plane apparently circling round neighbourhood, apparently low.

Mar. 2nd. 10.55 - 11.45 Sat in car below Dommetts Farm, to be able to see further. Numerous planes about but no sound of bombs or A.A. fire. Left cottage 12.15 pm.

Mar. 4th. Please could H.G. have more pieces of flannel for pull through, for cleaning Rifles. Shells seen bursting in the direction of Bristol at 11.45.

Mar. 13th. Shortage of firewood.

Mar. 15th. Torch battery needs replacing. (If batteries of the same size unobtainable, why not supply a cycle rear lamp. It would last longer).

Mar. 20th. Very foggy several planes going East a few going West, two explosions heard at 10.25.

April 13th. About 10 bombs were dropped in the direction of Honiton at 10.30. More bombs at about 11.20.

April 14th. About 4.30am bombs dropped in Honiton direction.

April 15th. A.A. fire in the direction of Weymouth & Bristol. Aircraft going to and fro from Bristol.

April 19th. No wick in lamp.

April 23rd. Patrol to Beacon Hill. Plane flying in N.E. direction at 11.55, making very queer sounds.

Oct. 15th. Lost a pipe, owner C. A. Boraston.

Nov. 5th. Patrol to Kitbridge. Signal light flashing in Easterly direction.

Nov. 24th. Pencil missing.

Nov. 28th. No pencil. Regret I cannot obtain paper for starting fires, I must therefore ask patrols to try to bring some. P.S. (Lt. P. Short)

If the log had continued, there would no doubt have been an entry for 7th. Sept. 1943 when a Wellington bomber crashed in a field near Cotley. Three members of the crew were killed and two others, who survived, were injured. The Log Book of No. ... Platoon No. 11 Post has even fewer interesting entries.

1940

Nov. 28th. Door unlocked, no key when arrived at 10pm.

Dec. 1st. Had a visitor (The Vicar) Otherwise all quiet.

1941

Jan. 5th. Extra coal and wood in outside locker, if you have any spare newspapers at home they would be welcomed for starting fire. P.S.

Feb. 17th. Kindly sign book whenever on duty. P.S.

April 2nd. No 4x2 in hut to clean rifle.

April 12th. Enemy planes active 11pm Bombs dropped over Lyme district. Flares dropped over Honiton and Seaton district at 11.30pm Heavy A.A. fire or bombs in the Honiton area.

May 3rd. Unable to find key, Storridge O.P.

PLATE 11

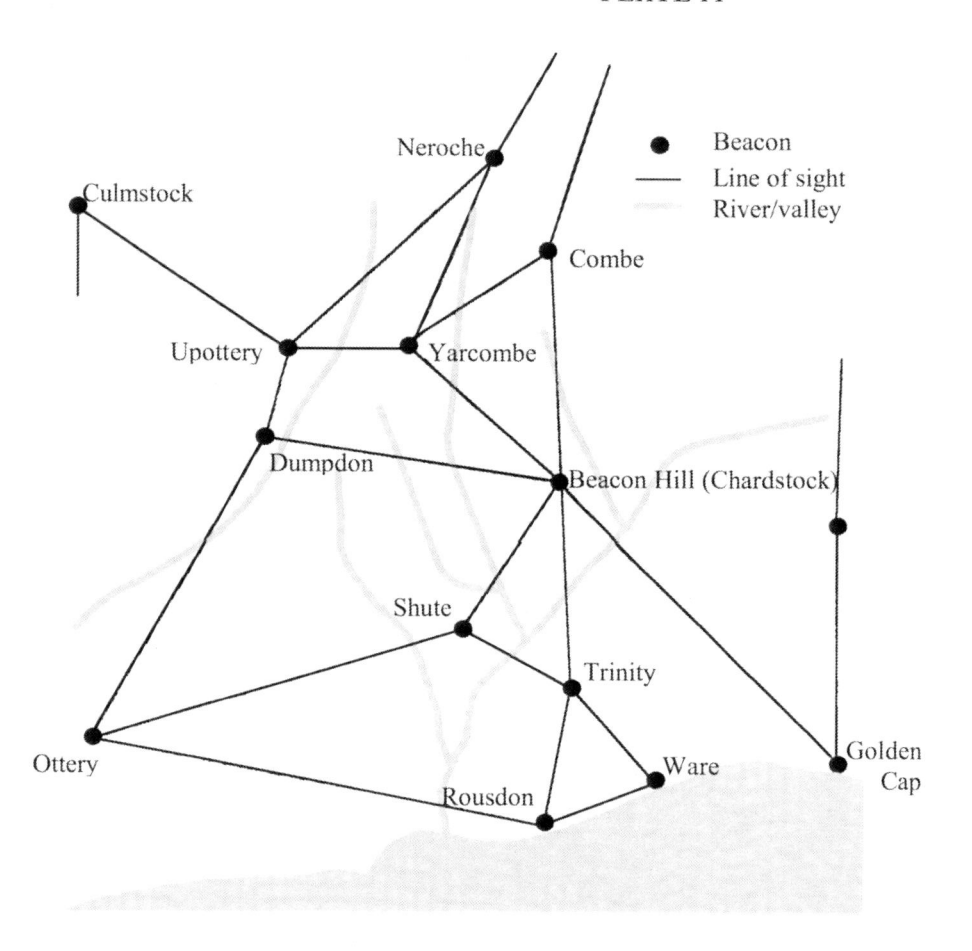

MAP 12. 16th Century Warning Beacon System, showing lines of sight

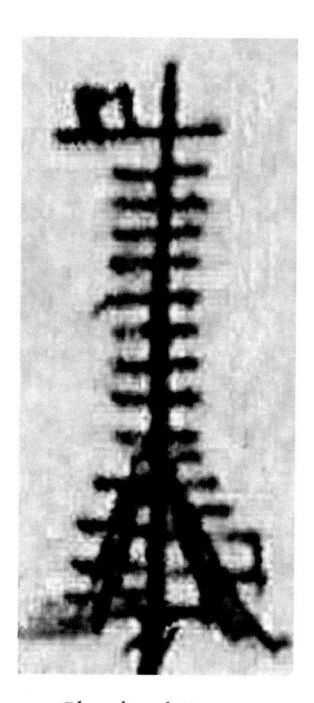

Chardstock Beacon copied and enlarged from Ogilby's Map of 1675 and showing trestle, pole, ladder and fire basket

Peter Wood at Chardstock Beacon

PLATE 12

1/2 MILE TELEPHONE AT TYTHERLEIGH

TELEPHONE IN MACHINERY HOUSE IN BROOM QUARRY

SIGNAL BOX AT BROOM CROSSING

MAP 13. Details from a Home Guard Map of the Chardstock Section of the WW2 Stopline

CATTLE UNDERPASS

AXE CROSSING SIGNAL BOX AND CATTLE UNDERPASS

S23A
S24A
S25B
S26C

RAILWAY
ROAD
ANTI-TANK TRENCH
PILLBOX
ROAD OR RAIL STOP BLOCKS (No.5 HG)
PILLBOX OCCUPIED BY No.5 PLATOON HG

RIVER AXE

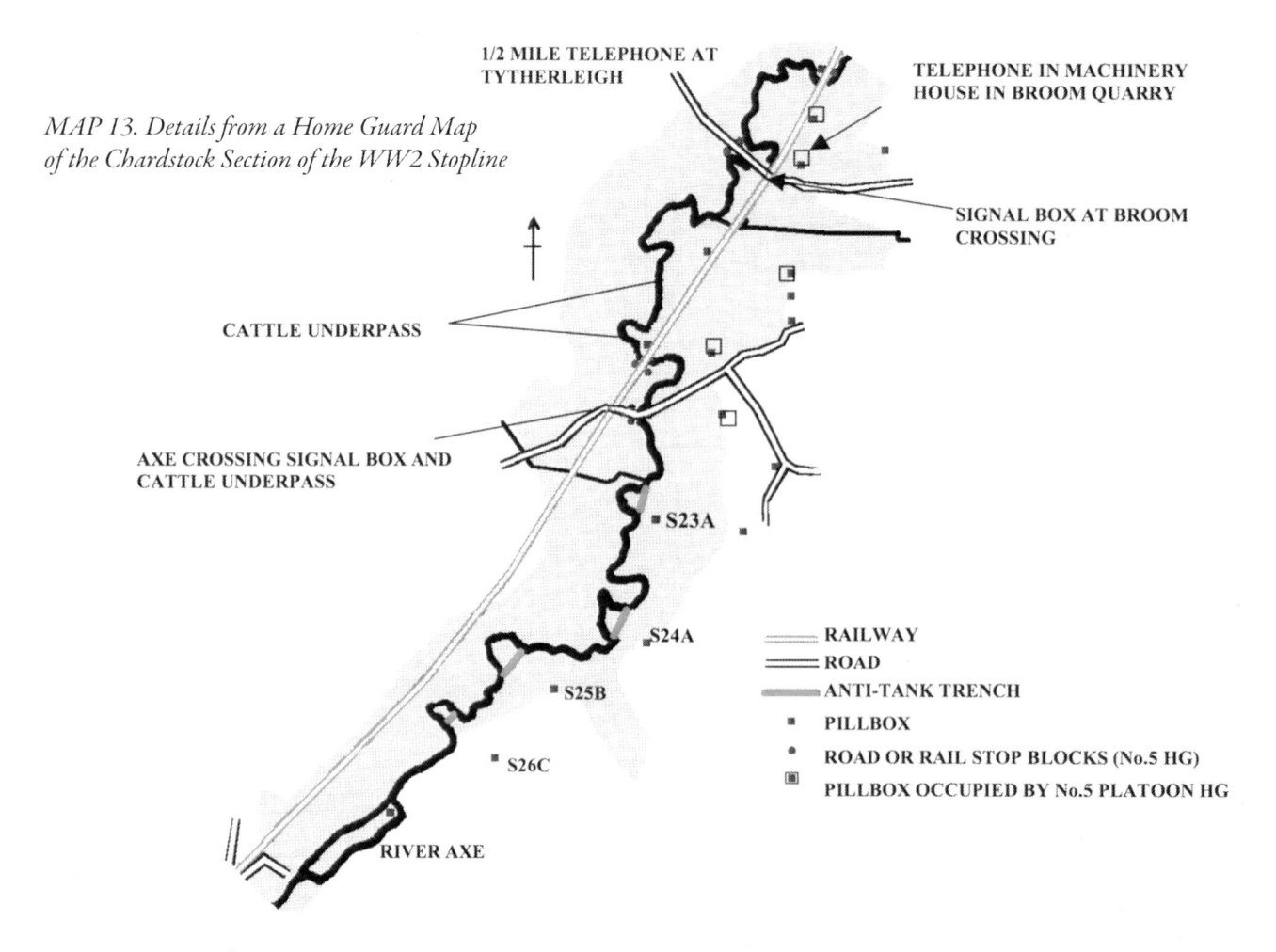

ARP Wardens

Home Guard

Left: Two Pillboxes at Broom, the nearer having Breezeblock Camouflage
Bottom Left:
Part of the Broom Bridge Road Block
Below: Easter Greetings to the WW1 Troops from Chardstock

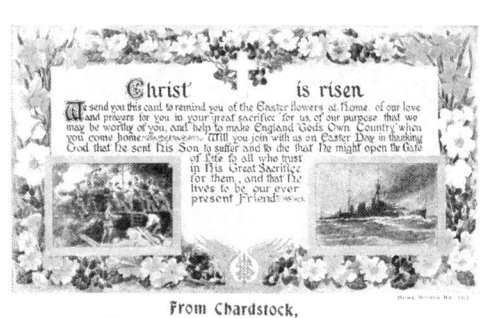

War Memorial

May 6th. Planes over big explosions Taunton district gun fire Axminster district.
June 13th. Planes active. Our own with Hitler's rations.
July 9th. All quiet, persistent light in Axminster bottom.

The Chardstock Home Guard had no responsibility for the defence of any of the pillboxes on the "Stop Line" built along the east bank of the Axe and running north to cut off the Devon/Cornwall peninsula. The purpose of this was to hinder the advance of any German forces that had landed to the west. It consisted of strategically placed pill boxes armed with machine guns or light artillery, anti-tank ditches, "dragons teeth", stanchions, and demountable railway barricades. Map 13 shows the section adjacent to Chardstock which was probably largely unmanned. This invasion nearly happened but eventually the Home Guard was "Stood Down" on 3rd. December 1945, thanksgiving religious services being held in Honiton, Axminster and Seaton. If the Stop Line had been reached or over-run, then the Secret Army would have come into action. Auxiliary Units was the name given to the secret underground resistance formed in 1940 to counter a German invasion. One hideout was built by The Royal Engineers in the garden of Major Ingrams' house on Bewley Down. There were two small rooms, one for living area and storage, the other with a concealed entrance was the radio room. Access was underneath the outside toilet and down a 10 foot (3m) ladder. Aerials went up under the bark of an adjoining Scots Pine tree. Messages and observations were collected from a messenger system, put into a tennis ball and dropped down the drainpipe, hidden in the hedge, which ran into the radio room. The recruits were trained as saboteurs and, had the Germans landed, it was planned that the members of this secret army would have emerged behind enemy lines to blow up roads, railway lines and bridges. This force would probably have had a life of two weeks or less.

A powerful searchlight with generator and ack-ack (anti-aircraft) gun was installed in the field next to Snowdrop Cottage at Kitbridge. Associated with the site were three huts on the opposite side of the road. A Nissen Hut (still there) was the sleeping accommodation for the army unit of approximately 20 soldiers. As far as is known, the gun was never fired in anger and only once by accident when being cleaned! At the end of the war, V.E. Day was celebrated with a thanksgiving service and a bonfire, upon which was burned a giant Squander Bug (a wartime propaganda symbol that had served its purpose of helping to conserve national resources). Songs and games formed part of the programme and there was general rejoicing throughout the village. The sight of soldiers and aeroplanes, the sound of guns, the evacuees and blackout and the proximity of bomber aerodromes and the Stop Line had all served to break down any form of parish isolation that had survived into the 20th Century. Now, with radio and television it is virtually impossible to remain in ignorance of national and world events.

Sources
Chubb, Mrs. K., information re. the two World Wars memorial inscription.
Churchwarden's Accounts, op. cit.
Eames. D. verbal information re. Home Guard.
Home Guard etc., War Office Library.
Home Guard Log Books, private collection.
Ingrams. D. verbal and written information re. Auxiliary Units.
Quarter Sessions Records, Dor. R.O.

Chapter Twenty One
VILLAGE ORGANISATIONS

Bowling Club
This club began in May 1957 when the present green was constructed from an old stone quarry. Members, including Jack Lane, Harold Pratt and Jack Withers, levelled the ground and the turf was laid. In 1966, the green was extended and the pavilion was erected. Until this time, the club had shared the use of the cricket pavilion. Also in 1966, the club became affiliated to the Devon County Association and the English Bowling Association. There are now about 80 members although in the past, the membership has reached 100.

CADS
The Chardstock Amateur Dramatic Society was formed in 1990 when their first production was the pantomime Aladdin. Since then, the annual pantomimes, one act plays and a variety show, have been produced.

Community Hall
For many years, meetings and social functions were held in the school hall which was originally the hall of St. Andrew's College. The possibility of providing a purpose built hall for the village had been discussed for a considerable time but nothing had been done. It was not until 1972, when there was a serious threat that the school would be closed, that the matter became urgent. The village could not afford to buy the school buildings and as a result, a number of local people together with the chairman of the Parish Council, decided to call a Public Meeting in May 1973. At this meeting it was agreed that there was a need for a hall and ten people were elected to form a committee to look into the feasibility of building a village hall. In January 1975, the committee reported that the project would be viable as a suitable site had been offered by the Milford family at a peppercorn rent. It was therefore, decided to proceed.

The first step was to get together committees with the necessary structure to apply for charitable status and to be acceptable to funding bodies. This was done with the help of the Devon Community Council. A management committee was constituted within the terms of the trust deed of the Chardstock Community Hall Trust. This committee consisted of one representative from each of the fourteen clubs and societies in the village and not more than thirteen other members of the public. The management committee was to take final decisions but to delegate the main tasks to sub-committees. The importance of the contribution of volunteers with relevant skills and the co-operation of official bodies and statutory authorities, was clear from the start. The President of the Trust, Mr. M. G. Milford, a local solicitor, undertook much of the legal work concerned with the trust deed and charitable status. Devon Community Council contributed in many ways, especially with invaluable advice during the early stages of the scheme. From the planning and drawing stage onwards all the work on the hall, except for plastering, glazing and laying the bitmac for the car park, was carried out by volunteers. They included an architect, a member of a building firm, an electrical contractor and five building tradesmen. Work was concentrated on Mondays and Wednesdays after working hours, using floodlighting where necessary, and at weekends. Those who had retired, or who could spend time during the day, assisted in such tasks as unloading materials, treating timber and decorating. A local quarry provided hard-core, the building trade either gave or supplied materials on favourable terms and all the kitchen units were donated. Local farmers loaned tractors and trailers, while much of the building machinery used was loaned by local firms.

Many fund-raising activities took place involving the whole village community. From July 1975 to March 1978, about £5,850 which was just under a quarter of the total cost, had been raised through these activities. Donations, loans and grants provided other sources of finance. Building work started in the spring of 1976 and the first function in the hall was held on 10th December 1977. The official opening was scheduled for 3rd June 1978. This date was kept, despite 14 weeks of rain in the spring when no work could be done. In fact, the car park was still being marked out on the morning of the opening day.

As time passed, the demand for the use of the hall for many varied activities grew and it soon became evident that an upgrade of the facilities was necessary. A stage, with changing rooms, a new committee room, improved toilets, especially for the disabled and a new kitchen, to meet contemporary regulations, were amenities that were lacking. A Public Meeting was called in January 1993 when the plan and a model of the proposed improvements was discussed. By an overwhelming majority it was decided to give a full mandate to the Management Committee to build an extension to the hall. Fund-raising was increased and a number of grants, donations and interest free loans were made available. A combination of voluntary workers, with the aid of professional expertise and skilled building contractors, ensured that the project was brought to a successful conclusion. The opening ceremony of the extension took place on 1st. July 1995, when it was agreed by those present that the Chardstock Community Hall would be a benefit to the whole village and the envy of all.

Cotley Harriers

The Cotley Harriers were formed in 1797 by Thomas Deane. As the name implies, hares were hunted until Boxing Day, after which, the fox was the quarry. On the death of Richard B. Eames, the fox became the main quarry but the green coat of Harriers was retained. In 1836, an outbreak of rabies spread to the hounds and the whole pack had to be destroyed, with the exception of one bitch which was not with the pack at the time. From her, a new pack of the distinctive lemon and white hounds was formed. In 1855, the Harriers passed to Thomas Palmer Eames of Broad Oak, Wambrook who was the grandson of the founder, and continues in the family, the present Master being Edward Eames.

Cotley Hunt Races

In 1840, this event was advertised as "Cotleigh Hunt Diversions" and took place on two days in May. The races which were called Sweepstakes attracted prizes of "two sovereigns with 15 added" for all horses not thorough-bred and never having won a Prize. The winner to be sold for 50 Guineas if claimed within a quarter of an hour after the Race. Other races were for a Purse of twenty Sovereigns for horses regularly hunted with Mr. Deane's Harriers and a Ladies' Plate of Ten Sovereigns. No one was allowed to follow the horses or cross the Course at the time of running. All dogs seen on the course were to be destroyed. In 1839, after dense fog had cleared, it was said that more than 6,000 people were present when the races began at 1pm.

Cricket Club

Chardstock has been a "cricket village" for well over a century and the club is now in its 110th year (in 1999). Organised cricket was played for over 30 years prior to the club's formation, with games being played by the Chardstock College side at least from the 1860s, and it is highly probable that the rustic version of the game was played well before that time. The first properly recorded game was against Thorncombe in 1887, a year after the closure of the College. Chardstock had a big advantage over many local clubs, namely, the benefit of a properly laid out cricket square, inherited from the redundant college which had its ground specially prepared and had played the game to quite a high standard. Most small clubs of that time had to be content with a pitch cut in a local landowner's field, and the outfields were very often left uncut. It was almost impossible to amass big scores on such grounds and even in 1954, there were still several villages whose outfields were not cut until haymaking time! This is a far cry from the smooth surfaces that players enjoy these days. The local newspaper described Chardstock's ground as splendid and indeed it was for those days. Against this background the club was started and, apart from the two war periods, has flourished ever since. Thorncombe were visitors on the first day when Chardstock were able to record their first victory. A hundred years later, the two clubs were again playing each other. Thorncombe have now ceased playing, hopefully only for a while.

The Club's policy has always been to give local lads a game and this is still the case today, despite the competitiveness of local league cricket. Several of the players of the 19th century have left their names enshrined in the record book and their descendants continue to uphold the tradition of a family club. There are still names going into the score books whose ancestors were local legends in their time, Parris, Hutchings, Strawbridge, Larcombe, Eames. The four brothers, Ed., Frank, Walt., and Bert. Larcombe all played from the 1920s - 50s. Their nephew, Frank Huddy played for 40 years and now his son Wesley is in his 20th year with the club. Today, even absent players, such as Paul Strawbridge, drive many miles to play for the club, a shining example of loyalty to what is a family club. Other family names spanning the years are the Goff brothers, Albert, Don and Sid, the Hulls, Pearces, Bevisses, and many more.

After the First World War, the ground changed to the field adjacent to the present one. This was less impressive and had several large rocks that made fielding difficult! Nevertheless, many exciting matches were played there, especially the local ones against Chard, Perry Street and Axminster. Perhaps the club's greatest rivals were All Saints and it was the ultimate disgrace to lose to them! An incident which illustrates the fierceness of the competition was when in the 1920s, Perry Street won a last ball victory, Chardstock's last man being stumped by Gilbert Hoare. As he left the field he was whacked across the shoulders by a lady spectator! After 1946, Alick Lisle-Smith allowed the move to the present ground, having been a previous player himself. During the last 43 years, cricketers from all over the world have played on the sloping ground, featured in the BBC's TV documentary, "And it's Chardstock to Bat". In its centenary year, the club celebrated with a cricketing tour in Spain, playing four matches, all of which Chardstock won. Since then, the club has been forced by lack of fixtures, to enter the East Devon League, which has Saturday matches, but it still continues Sunday friendly games. Standards have improved, so that earlier complete innings scores of about 50 can be compared with occasional present day personal scores of 100+, the first of these at Chardstock being scored by John Pratt. Now, many new names appear in the score books but the distinctive village succession also continues.

Girls' Friendly Society

For young women and girls over 14 years of age. The lending library was free to its members. In 1917, they met monthly in the upper college buildings. In the 1940s, Mrs. Medway (the vicar's wife) ran a Girls' Club, Drama Group and Bible Study Group, all at the Vicarage.

Guides
The All Saints' Guides celebrated their 21st Bithday in 1957 with a church service and entertainment in the Hall. Mrs. Lench was their Captain and she continued as such for many years. During the 1960s, there was also a Girl Guides group in Chardstock led by Mrs. Cross, who also formed a group of handbell ringers from the school children of the village. The successor group was formed in about 1984 and was led by Mrs. Verplancke who was also in charge of the Brownie pack. The Guides met first in the George Inn and in the Community Hall on alternate weeks.

Football Club
The re-formation of a Chardstock Football Club, after a period of some forty years, took place in the Parish Council Rooms on 2nd June 1967 when a group of villagers formed Chardstock A.F.C. The elected officers were Mr. Pryse-Jenkins (President), Mr. C. Lane (Chairman), Mrs. Daisy Hutchings (Secretary), Mr. M. Hunt (Treasurer) and Mr. J. Newbery (Coach and Trainer). The club entered Division III of the Perry Street League, playing its first match against Millway Rise on 2nd September 1967. The result was an encouraging win for Chardstock, 6-0, at home on the sloping pitch near Stockstyle Farm, between Chardstock and Hook. At the end of the first season the club was promoted, having finished as Runners Up in Division III. Dick Parris was the top scorer with a tally of 41 goals including 6 which he scored in what was to become the highest scoring match in the club's history. This was played at home on 14th October 1967 against Chard Youth Club Reserves, Chardstock winning 14-0.

The club had lost its charismatic secretary, Daisy Hutchings, who tragically died at the age of 49, before its treble winning season in 1970/71. In this season Chardstock won Division II League, Division II Cup and the Arthur Gage Cup. Robert Glentworth from Chard becoming the Club and League top scorer for the season, netting a total of 58 goals, including 7 in a 13-0 win against Drimpton Reserves on 12th September 1970. John Newbery took over as Secretary after Daisy's death with Adrian Goff as assistant secretary. The 1970/71 season had also attracted an influx of players from outside the village thus enabling a reserve side to be formed.

The club had now moved its ground to Cotley. The new ground was rented by the club for a nominal fee from Col. Eames of Cotley House. The Club's biggest home crowd of the season saw Chardstock beat Chard Town 1-0 in the first round of the Chard Hospital Cup, on 6th April 1971. The only goal was scored by another Chard import, Ben Dennis. In honour of Daisy Hutchings, the club donated a trophy to the Perry Street & District League Committee. This trophy is known as the Daisy Hutchings Cup and is still played for today in the League. The club also started a youth team for the 1974/75 season to play in the under fifteens of the Taunton Sunday League. The Perry Street League started its Premier Division, in which Chardstock was included, for the 1972/73 season. Flagging fortunes on the pitch saw the first team relegated at the end of the 1978/79 season. Long serving player and the club's top scorer, Barry Hutchings, took over as Chairman in 1977 after Cyril Lane had moved to the Channel Islands. The club tried a succession of player managers, namely Brian Male, Barry Nicholls and Nick Cleal, but the team continued to struggle and after being relegated to Division II quit the Perry Street League in the early eighties. The club was fined £8 by the League Committee as it was unable to fulfill its fixtures. It has now been disbanded and is not likely to be reformed in the foreseeable future.

Lending Library
Chardstock Lending Library operated, in the early 20th Century, in one of the College rooms called the Reading Room and opened every Sunday between 4.00 & 5.00p.m. The rules taken from a surviving book were that the borrowers paid ½d. per book which could be kept for two weeks. Overdue books were also charged ½d. Losses had to be made good by the borrower.

Masonic Lodge
In September 1847, Worshipful Brother William Tucker of the Axminster Lodge, Virtue and Honor, proposed that a new lodge should be formed in Chardstock. This was warranted as Rural Lodge No. 802. On 8th August 1848, the lodge was consecrated by W. Bro. Tucker and W. Bro. Sir John George Reeve de la Pole of Shute was installed as the first Worshipful Master. A service was held at St. Andrew's Church attended by 100 masons. A banquet followed and a collection amounting to £21 9s 7d was donated to the school. Meetings were held in a room at the school (see details of the ceiling decorated with masonic symbols in Appendix A). The lodge existed until 1855, when it was deleted from the list of lodges. During its comparatively short life, nine Masters had been installed. The dissolution followed closely upon the dismissal of W. Bro. Tucker from his office of Provincial Grand Master.

Maternity Society
This was run by the Vicar's wife, Mrs. Lewis, in 1911 but nothing more is known.

Mothers' Union
There has been a branch of the M.U. in Chardstock since about 1912, when the Parish Magazine for that year reported that members had an outing to Wayford Manor. The exact date of the founding is unknown but it would probably have been set up by the Salisbury Diocese through the initiative of a group of ladies in the parish. In 1914, it was called the Women's Union and met quarterly. There was also the Mothers' Meeting mentioned in 1883, and was being run by the Vicar's wife, Mrs. Lewis, in 1911. This was held at 2.30pm every Wednesday in the Parish Room.

Discounts were given on all materials sold to members, for example, 2s. off a pair of blankets costing under 10s 6d. Perhaps these three organisations eventually joined together to become the Mothers' Union. In the 1970s, the All Saints' and St. Andrew's branches amalgamated and continue as one organisation. A Young Wives Group (section) was formed by Mrs. Hamblen (the Vicar's wife) in the early 1970's but it only continued for a few years.

Pigeon Club
This met at The George during the 1960s and held shows in St. Andrew's Hall. Guinea pigs, rabbits and mice were also shown.

Scouts
Very soon after General Sir Robert (later Lord) Baden-Powell inaugurated the Boy Scout Movement in 1908, Scouting began in Chardstock. On 30th September 1910, a Public Meeting was held in St. Andrew's Hall when it was decided to set up a Scout Group. This would have made the troop one of the first to be formed in the country. The idea was introduced by Miss Eggar and Mr. George Spiller was elected Scoutmaster with Mr. Case as Assistant Scoutmaster. The group was run by a committee with the Vicar, the Revd. A. Lewis, acting as Chairman. In November 1912, Mr. Woodroffe, the District Commissioner, inspected the Scouts at Corner House Cottage (the site unknown). He was most impressed by what he saw. He commended Miss Eggar for her work and presented her with a special badge of distinction. Unfortunately, the following year the Scouts lost their headquarters when Corner Cottage was damaged beyond repair in a gale. A new start was made in November 1913, when Mr. Jane became Scoutmaster. With the outbreak of the first World War and the enlistment of many of the young men of the village, probably including Mr. Jane, it is likely that the troop was closed.

There follows a huge gap in the records and at present no more is known until 1950. In March of that year Mrs. Briscoe of Tytherleigh Cottage formed the 1st Chardstock Cub Group in the Army Hut (now demolished) at Kitbridge, with Miss Mary Larcombe from Castlewood, Wambrook as her assistant and with 10 Cubs. In 1953, according to the quarterly Parish Magazine, "The Shield", the Group consisted of a Scout Troop and a Cub Pack. That summer, the Scouts joined with the 1st Chaffcombe Troop to camp near Abergavenny. The Troop was about to outgrow its clubroom at the Vicarage and no more recruits from either All Saints or Chardstock could be accepted until after the camp. The Cubs were taking part in the Devon Jamboree while the Scouts were camping and had been invited to join in a Jungle Dance to be performed before the Chief Scout, Lord Rowallen. In 1957, the Scouts camped at Charmouth together with a troop from Hertfordshire and "The Shield" reported the sudden death of Mrs. Briscoe, the Cubmistress. Again it is not known when the Group closed but during the 1970's, boys were joining the Hawkchurch and Axminster groups.

Skittles Teams
Skittles has been played in Chardstock for many years, although Skittles Leagues are comparatively modern. The Tytherleigh Inn is known to have had an alley in 1954 when Anthony and Avice Apsey were landlords. Six teams, including a Ladies' team played there. A local league was in operation at The George Inn soon after World War II in 1945. This was eventually superseded by the Axminster League.

Territorials and Army Cadet Force
In 1911, there was a detachment of Territorials under the command of Serg. J. Pratt. During the celebrations to mark the coronation of King George V and Queen Mary, they attended the church service and marched through the village. When they reached the square, a salute was fired and military drill carried out. The Army Cadet Force was in being during the 1940s under the command of George Early. He was assisted by Jim and Victor Russell, who later took over the running of the Force. The cadets met in a hut at Kitbridge until the late 1950s.

Welfare Clubs (See end of Chapter 16. The Poor of Chardstock).

Women's Institute
The Chardstock W.I. was formed in 1922 and appears to have met fortnightly at first in the Parish Room, which is now used as a classroom. The National Subscription was 2s. a year and the members of the Chardstock Branch paid 2d. a month. Golden Anniversary celebrations were held in 1972 when Mrs Hodge, a founder member, performed the cake cutting ceremony. Sadly, ten years later the branch was wound up.

Young Men's Club
The earliest reference is a list of rules dated 1933, when the Vicar, the Revd. S. M. Whitwell was the Chairman. After operating for several years, the club was closed but was restarted again in September 1946. The original rules, with some modifications, were adopted. There was to be a Junior and Senior Section, and the club was opened in November of that year for five nights a week during the winter season, in the College Buildings. The club continued in existence until 1957, when it finally closed, and in 1971 the remaining funds were distributed to the school, Football Club and the Cricket Club.

Youth Club
This club was formed in the late 1970s in the College Buildings but as the venue was unsuitable, the club closed until the new Community Hall became available. It is now flourishing once again in its new home.

Sources
Brooks. R., verbal info. re. the Community Hall.
Chubb. Mrs. K., verbal info. re. the Women's Institute.
Goff, A., verbal info. re. the Football Club.
Gosling. G., And it's Chardstock to Bat, 1887-1987 obtainable from Club members.
Huddy. F., June 1997 personal account of Cricket Club.
Moore. M, verbal info. re. the Scouts.
Page. A., verbal info. re. the Masonic Lodge.
Parmiter. Miss H. M. T., verbal info. re. the Cotley Harriers.
Rogers. R., August 1997 personal account of Bowling Club.
Scouts and Guides, Chardstock Parish Magazine.
Wellington. Mrs. J., verbal info. re. the Mothers' Union.

Chapter Twenty Two
MEMORIES

The Village Shop
Life in Chardstock in the 1930s-50s was far more self supporting than it is today. The village shop, run by Mrs. Hodge and her family, supplied most of the groceries. These were all kept in large quantities loose in bins or tins, and were weighed out to customers' requirements. Sugar went into thick blue bags, flour into thick brown bags and sweets into cone shaped white bags. Cheese was cut with a wire from a large slab and salt came in bars from which you cut the required amount when cooking.

Delivery Men
Milk was provided from various farms. During the war, it was supplied by Vic Edwards who owned a smallholding at Symes Cottage. Presumably he dipped what was needed from a churn. I believe the first bottled milk was delivered from Clifford Churchill (whose sons still farm at Chilson Common) in the 1950s. My earliest memory of a delivery man is of a fishmonger who lived at Chard. He used to call on my Grandmother. He rode a bicycle which had a wooden box fixed to the back which contained the fish. There never seemed to be any cover and I wonder now how his customers avoided food poisoning! One of his hands was missing and in its place he had a steel hook from which he suspended a spring balance with its hook stuck through the fish. Fish and fresh fruit and vegetables were later delivered by Jim Pinney, also from Chard but this time by van. Later, there was Gerald French who dispensed with the fish, then came Fruity Fred (Sweetland) from Axminster and now we have Ted Patterson from Whitford. Grocery orders were delivered once a week for many years by Harold Rogers who drove the Co-op van from Chard. He was an amusing character known for his expertise with the xylophone at social functions. International Stores also delivered, sending someone to collect orders a few days in advance. Clothing and household items were obtained from Raffles of Yeovil and McNeils of Axminster. Payment was by instalments which a man called each week to collect. Bread was still baked in the village by the Miller family and delivered by their son Bill. When Mr. Miller retired and closed the bakehouse in the 1950s, Gills of Axminster delivered bread until they closed some 10 years later. After this, we had to collect our bread that Mayo's of Axminster delivered to Mrs. Hodge's shop 3 times a week. Meat was delivered by V. Purce & Son of Tatworth, Stuart of Axminster and Board of Chard Junction. Purce and Board still deliver.

Births and Deaths
Babies in these times were normally born at home with the assistance of Nurse Ellen Early who had her practice in Chardstock when my brother was born in 1941. She finally retired in 1960. When the time came for funerals, the village had its own grave-digger. In 1948, it was Sid Hankins who was also the railway crossing keeper and signalman at Broom. Later, Bill Bond did the task for many years. Coffins were made by Tom Parris, who was also landlord of the George Inn and who also had a wheelwright and carpentry business behind the Inn. When he retired, Len Clymo became the landlord and Jack Apsey, who had worked there for many years, took over the carpentry business. They made my grandfather's coffin in 1953. The Vicar made the funeral arrangements with the family and coffin bearers were chosen from relatives and friends. Soon after death, the body had to be prepared for burial. For many years, my grandmother was sent for, "to lay them out" for their final journey. The body was usually kept at home until the funeral or taken to rest overnight in the church on the eve of the funeral.

Washing, Lighting & Cooking
Many of the larger and more modern houses had electricity and water laid on but many of the cottages were without amenities of any kind. Water was fetched from a well or piped spring, and had to be carried in metal buckets. Most houses had a lean-to wash house on the side of the house, which contained a "copper" (brick furnace with a fitted metal bowl for water) to heat the water for washing or bathing. A galvanised steel bath hung on the wall and did service as a container for soaking on wash days as well as its intended purpose. Grown-ups braved the cold and bathed in private but the children bathed indoors in front of the fire. Lighting was provided by paraffin lamps and candles. Later, we had an Aladdin Lamp which had an incandescent mantle (like the later gas lights) which still burned paraffin but gave more light. Cooking was done on kitchen ranges which were kept clean by rubbing with "black lead" (actually a soot mixture and very messy). Some used paraffin stoves with wicks which were rather smelly but still produced food that tasted very good. Primus stoves, which had pressurised paraffin jet burners, were also used for the rapid heating of kettles or saucepans. Food was protected in the larder. This was situated in the part of the house furthest away from the sun. It had a tiled shelf to keep butter and cheese cool and the milk usually stood in a jug of cold water. Meat was stored in a cool shady place outside in a "safe". This was a cupboard which had open sides covered with fine mesh (such as perforated zinc sheet) which let the air circulate but kept the bluebottle flies out. Many people, if they had room, kept a pig which was partly fed on waste food and when it reached maturity, was slaughtered for meat. On flower show days, one of the side-shows was that of skittling for a piglet provided by a breeder. Chickens were also kept on a large scale with often a couple of geese for the Christmas Dinner. Turkeys were rare in those days and were certainly not available frozen!

Waste and Drainage

Answering the call of nature meant that whatever the weather, a trip to the little upright shed built at the back of the house or in a corner of the garden, often discreetly hidden by a large bush, was necessary. Night time relief was provided by using the potty under the bed. No waste removal service was available and this had to be buried in garden areas not in use.

Entertainment

A Radio or "Wireless" was an enormous thing powered by two dry batteries and an accumulator. The accumulator had to be charged up about once a week and this was done by Percy Spiller at Tytherleigh Garage and cost 6d. Two were usually kept so that one could be used while the other was charging. There was great danger of the power failing while a favourite programme, such as Dick Barton - Special Agent, was being broadcast. Another entertainment was to go to the cinema at Axminster. Stan Wakely of Membury ran what was locally called "the picture bus" that was timed to arrive for the first showing of the film programme. Any young man who wanted to see his girl friend home at Axminster had to catch the National Bus and walk from Tytherleigh because Stan's bus returned earlier.

Council Houses and Employment

Many of the villagers living under the foregoing conditions were rehoused when the Westcombes and Green Lane council houses were built. The eight Westcombes houses were built on a field that was part of the tenancy of Henry Pilton of New House Farm (opposite the Hall). It was owned by Alick Lisle-Smith (Chardstock Court) who provided the land for the benefit of the village. The first tenants arrived in 1945. The land on which the Green Lane houses were built was for many years the village vegetable allotments, and was not purchased from William Beviss of Wambrook until 1947. Prior to this it was presumably rented. These houses were built by G. T. Chubb & Sons, a village business, and were built over a period of time. The architect was Freddy Kett of Axminster. The tenants of the first four facing Westcombes were occupied in 1948. Many of the men who lived here were employed in the village. Some worked on farms. Chubbs builders, employed quite a lot and another builder, Fred Summers of Burridge, also employed two or three. Some men worked at Wilts United Dairies and at Yonder Hill saw mills.

J. R. Pratt was probably the largest employer, having quarries first at Broom and then at Kilmington and used a fleet of lorries to carry the sand and gravel. Broom was dug by hand until the first drag-line excavator came in 1937. His first lorries were serviced in the yard on which is now built Medway, The Walnut Tree and Holly Cottage. This was before the garage at Tytherleigh was built, although this was earlier than I can remember. The garage was sold to E.C.C. Quarries Ltd. and is now owned by Burgess Norringtons farm supplies. During the winter, Pratt's three threshing machines travelled from farm to farm, processing the stored wheat. My father and Sid Bowditch worked on one of these machines which differed from the others in that it not only threshed out the wheat grain but also bundled the straw into a suitable size for use in thatching. The machine was towed to the farms by tractor which had a drive wheel on its side that could be connected to the thresher by a large flat belt. If the farms were far away, a small wooden hut on wheels was also attached for the men to live in until the job was done. They travelled to Bridport, Seaton, Crewkerne, Yeovil, etc. By the 1940s, Mr. Pratt had provided Austin Seven cars to take the men home each night, even though the common means of transport in those times was by bicycle. The machines were overhauled during the Summer while their operators helped at the quarry or more often at the yard where breeze blocks (cemented clinker) were made. Another machine operated by two men was owned by Arthur Pratt. J. Lane & Son also employed many people in the 1950s-70s.

School in Wartime

Children came to Chardstock School from Cotley Wash, Burridge, Holy City, Burchill and the Tytherleigh area. They all had to walk in those days, but we Tytherleigh children were later allowed to ride in the morning on the bus that came to collect the pupils for Axminster Secondary School. I began school during the war years but remember little about it except for seeing the convoys of lorries and tanks passing our house on Tytherleigh Hill. Each time an aeroplane passed over the school, our teacher called "rabbits" and we all dived under our desks. We received food parcels from Australia which were divided among us. I remember taking home some jelly crystals among other things. We also had some sort of savings scheme at the school for which we were awarded prizes of books. At one time I collected most, thanks to my father who was helped by his friends and acquaintances and I got the biggest book. At times there were many evacuees attending our school. Three of my uncles were in the Forces and sadly one died in Belgium and another went to work in Wales as a "Bevin boy" (the alternative to National Service was to be sent to the coal mines under Ernest Bevin's scheme). My father's work at this time brought him into contact with many "land girls" Mary Bindon and Mrs Albert Harris were two who married local men. My father and uncle (who lived next door) were both in the Home Guard, as was also Jim Gilpin who lived in the cottage above us. After the war, when the BBC began broadcasting programmes for schools, our school was presented with a radio and loudspeakers by Beryl Griffin's grandfather who owned a radio shop in Bournemouth. We had annual school outings. One lovely day was at Lyme Regis and a disastrous one was at Weston-Super-Mare when the tide was out! The annual School Sports Day was held in the cricket field. Most children also attended the Sunday School run by Mrs. Margaret Briscoe, who lived at Tytherleigh Cottage. This was at 10am and the morning service followed at 11am when most of us at some time sang in the choir.

PLATE 13

Early's Garage, then..and now

Primrose Farm, then..and now

The Laurels, then..and now

Bewley Farm

Cart at Holy City

Social Events
The two main events of the year were the Tytherleigh Gymkhana and the Flower Show. The Gymkhana took place in the field directly opposite to the Tytherleigh Arms. People came from miles around both as spectators and to take part. There were classes for all ages, from children on ponies to seasoned riders. There were also carriage drawing competitions. Local farmers brought their large working horses, all groomed and dressed in their best brasses and harness. At that time, horses were still very much used on the farm. There was also a fun fair, and a large marquee which served as a tea tent during the day, and was the venue for a dance in the evening. It was at one of these dances that my parents met in 1933. The show continued to be held at Tytherleigh until the late 1950s or early 60s. It then moved to Monkton Wylde for a while, and is now held at Cotley.

The Flower Show was held annually in the Summer, and has had various sites in the village. It began in Holy City, then it transferred to a playing field in Chard Lane, and took place at Honey Hill, in a field next to the Tytherleigh to Chardstock road. The show was staged in a marquee with sideshows arranged around the rest of the field. There were always swinging boats and coconut shies which belonged to "Plucky" Huish of Chard and which were hired for the day. Also there was a Spinning Jenny, "Skittling for a Piglet" and fancy dress competitions. Another event was the arrival of the Flower Show Queen in a decorated, horse-drawn cart. One year, there was a knobbly knees competition for the men, who had to roll up their trouser legs and sit on a bench together. A committee lady judged the event, presumably by feeling their knees. One contestant caused great hilarity when he took a "please do not touch exhibits" notice from a show bench and placed it on his knees. He was passed by!

On Coronation Day, the older generation were invited to the Village Hall for a ham and salad lunch served by the W.I., and to watch the ceremony on a large television rented for the occasion (TVs were a rarity then). The rest of the village people were at the cricket field for games, sports and a tea party. The school children were given a commemorative mug. In the evening, the pubs were full and there was dancing outside. Social evenings and dances were held on other occasions, especially Friday nights, often with nothing stronger than tea to drink! A Christmas Whist Drive would be held in the Parish Room. In the 1940s, weekly film shows were held in the Hall and once a travelling company staged a variety concert. For the church, the St. Andrew's Day Sale was a big annual fund raising event as was the Christmas Bazaar which was originally a sale of work by the parishioners.

Source
Chubb. Mrs. K., written on the basis of personal memories.

PLATE 14

Smallridge, from the South

All Saints' Church

All that remains of the Army Cadet Hut

Strong's Cottage

Friendly Society Certificate and Regalia

Fête Parades in 1906 and 1907

109

PLATE 15

William Bond, a 20th Century Chardstock Shoemaker, as shown in Chard Museum

Fireback (?) Thomas Pitt or Thomas Palmer of Lodge

An early, oil burning Chardstock street lamp

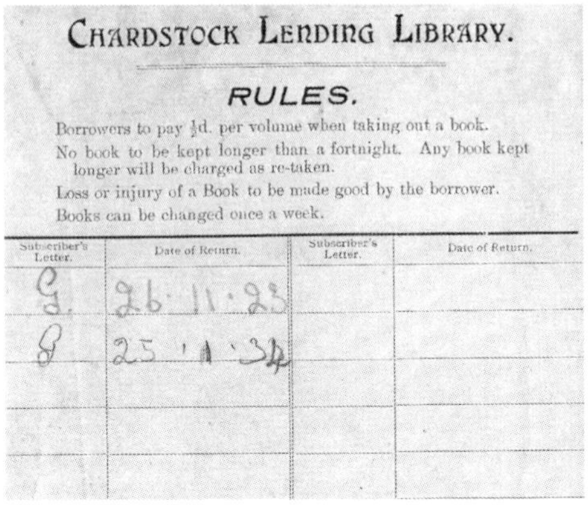

Track across the Common to Chardstock Mill

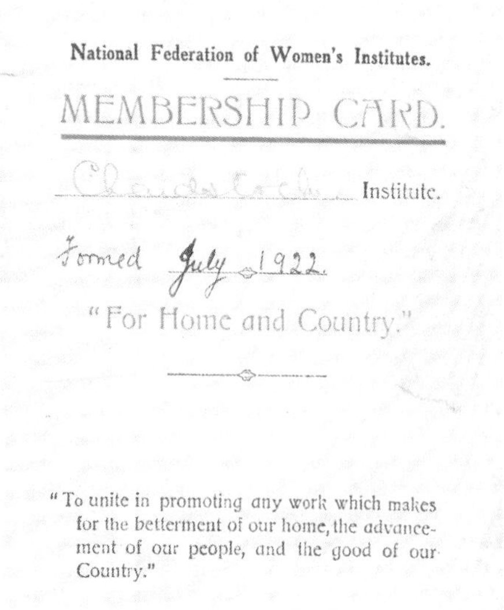

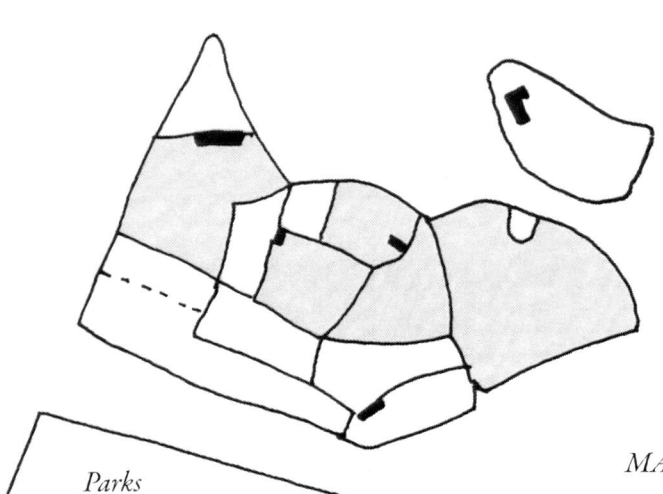

MAP 14. *The Cuckolds Pit Commons Settlement in 1840 (shaded areas denote orchards)*

Appendices
APPENDIX A - BUILDING SURVEYS

The following information was mainly researched by Mr. R. G. Gilson during the 1980s. His full reports and plans are deposited in the Somerset Record Office. Some buildings have since been modified and, in some cases, resurveyed.

Battleford ST3062 0080
This house is situated in the border area near the Axminster boundary. It is rubble built with 4 rooms in line in the main part of the house. It has been much altered and, as it stands now, is mainly of the 17th Century but insufficient detail has survived to be more precise. When it was rebuilt, some medieval timbers were available for re-use, which suggests that they may have come from the house which predated the present one. The re-used common rafters and a number of thatch battens are smoke blackened, whereas the trusses and the main structure are not. The house is unusual with its 4 rooms in-line layout, and in view of the known early occupation of the site, is clearly of somewhat higher than average status.

Bonds Cottage, Burridge ST3128 0630
This house has walls mainly of rubble with a small patch of cob visible at the back within a lean-to. It appears to date from the earlier 16th Century at which time it had an open Hall with 2 bays and a 2 storeyed, jettied, one bay inner room. At the former jetty, there is some evidence of a wattle and daub partition. There is one surviving jointed cruck which, with the associated timbers, is smoke stained. There was probably a cross-passage which has now disappeared. The Hall fireplace and ceiling date from the later 16th Century. There was a very long third room, which has become an entry area and a room. It is very probable that this was the byre and that this building was a longhouse, the byre converted in the 17th Century to an entry and a kitchen. It would seem that the house continued as a farmhouse into the 17th Century and at some later date became two cottages.

Bridge Meadow, Crawley ST2579 0814
This house is cob built with a thatched roof to the older part. The exterior gives the impression that it is a small house to which a rubble built extension has been added. The internal evidence shows that this is not so but that half of a good quality medieval house, once occupied by a Yeoman, survives, the rest being totally re-built. There would have been a cross-passage, a Hall, an inner room and a service room. The re-built passage and service room now contain an oven with an iron door cast locally, probably at Foundry Farm, by J. Bonfield and dated 1858. The Hall ceiling is framed in six panels and is moulded. It was inserted in the late 16th Century, as was the fireplace so clearly associated with it, built (unusually) in the centre of the former open Hall. The roof has a smoke blackened jointed cruck and post and truss, the upper part of which is still filled with wattle and daub. One roof-slope retains its medieval wattle work under the thatch, heavily smoke blackened. The Inner room was originally jettied into the Hall and this jetty was removed when the ceiling was inserted. The presence of a jetty in a Hall-house indicates that the Inner room was of two storeys from the start. There was probably a stair of some sort from the Inner room rather than a ladder stair from the Hall.

Burridge Pound ST3126 0632
The Tithe Map gives it as Barton Plot and shows a barn-like building and small barton. By 1896, the whole was roofed over and called Pound. It has now been recently re-roofed. Other buildings adjoin it but otherwise it is little altered. The "barn" had a large flared doorway facing west and a northern third is separated by a dividing wall with doorway and is raised in level.

Chardstock Court ST3088 0434
The fabric of Chardstock Court is of early 14th Century origin with 15th and 16th Century alterations. The building fell into disrepair in the 20th Century and has been largely rebuilt around the original features and a new roof added. There are various medieval fragments including a two light mullion window. Other features include a cinquefoil blocked circular window and a stair tower with a quatrefoil window. The detached range of buildings which had a 15th Century roof, was destroyed c.1930. Other sources describe this as a barn but are uncertain of its original purpose. It measured 70 by 17 feet and stood 20 foot to the wall plate. There were traces of square turrets on the east side and it originally had a first floor and a suggestion of three upper rooms. The roof had curved ribs, collar, purlin and purlin braces.

Coaxden Manor ST3110 0084
The house is sited in a small narrow valley running east to west. The sides of the valley rise close to the north and south of the building. The walls are of squared rubble and there are a number of ovolo moulded windows. The plan is L shaped with the end of the rear wing truncated and is said to be the result of an 18th Century fire. A second wing, inferior in construction to the main house, has been added to the north end making the house U shaped. The main block is entered through a front doorway whose porch may well be of a later date. The centre room is large and extends up through 2 storeys but it is almost certain that a floor/ceiling has been removed. This was probably a 19th Century modification

to form an open hall and gallery from a quite ordinary two storeyed building. Many of the rooms in the rest of the house have also been modified over the years. The south room has been extended into the wing which has lost at least one room from its east end. The south room was a Parlour and old engravings show it to have been panelled. The room above it is also of high quality. The wing room has unusual timberwork. Two large octagonal posts support beams which in turn support a timber framed wall in the room above. This has a blocked range of windows, a continuous series of ovolo moulded wooden mullions originally with 11 lights above re-set linenfold panelling. There may not have been a wall between the octagonal posts indicating that the lower area was open to the courtyard. There are 6 jointed crucks in the house and 3 in the wing. These, and the many ovolo mouldings, indicate a date in the 17th Century. The jointed cruck, however, is an obsolete form soon after 1600, particularly in a house of quality such as this and so the date of the building cannot be much after 1600. It is probably c.1590, bearing in mind that Sir Simonds D'Ewes was born there in 1602 and baptised in the gallery. It is interesting to speculate that this gallery was the room supported by the octagonal posts.

Cotley ST2992 0686
This house is situated in the north of the parish within a complex group of farm buildings. In front of it is its successor, a farmhouse probably datable to the 17th Century and further to the south is the 19th Century house. A barn is continuous with the first house and, although of a different width, shares its east gable. In this wall is a blocked doorway originally giving access to the house implying that the occupier was a working landowner. The house, built of local chert, was always two storeyed with a two room plan, both on the ground and first floor levels. There is a wide cross-passage and three jointed crucks, one of which has wattle and daub filling. In the west room there is a large fireplace almost the width of the house. There must always have been a fireplace as none of the timbers show signs of smoke blackening. It has an oven with an iron door bearing the name Wightman & Denning, Chard which makes it probably late 18th Century. The 2 rooms on the first floor, as those on ground level, are unequal in size. The east room has one window, a fireplace probably inserted, and evidence of blocked doors in the walls. The west room has 2 windows in the front and a small blocked one at the back. Beside the massive chimney from the room below is an inserted fireplace. The status of this building is of considerable interest. It is clearly more than a Yeoman holding, seeming to be a small manor house probably of the late 15th Century. The barn is, partly at least, of an earlier date, although possibly not greatly earlier. This is a fine structure built in the local chert stone with a slate roof. It has porches on both long walls with the roof continued down over them. The building is over 20 feet wide inside and has an interior length of about 80 feet. There are 7 raised jointed crucks but it is difficult to establish which is the oldest part of the structure. Regardless of which portion of the barn is the earliest, it certainly pre-dates the house.

Churchill Farm ST3008 0232
This farm lies in the south of the parish and adjoining a possible deserted medieval settlement. The three roomed house faces south and is rubble built with a modern tiled roof. It is set on a hillside platform with the ground falling away steeply beyond the west end of the house. This makes it very probable that the present room at this end, which has been rebuilt, was the byre of a long house. A cross-passage runs between this room and the Middle room, or Hall, and backs onto a large fireplace with an oven on one side and a circular stair space on the other. The Middle room had a nine panelled framed ceiling and a six light wooden window on the north side. A stud and panelled partition separated it from the third room which had a fireplace in the wall at the opposite end. In the thickness of this wall at first floor level is a narrow recess, with a door frame, perhaps a small Garderobe, but unfortunately the details are lost. This is a house of late medieval or early 16th Century date. The smoke blackening of the roof is not heavy which indicates that the open Hall with its hearth was not in use for a very long period. The Hall partition is probably of the same date as the house. It is in the same plane as one of the jointed crucks and the blackening of the stake holes in that truss indicate its use as a partition in the early period. This must mean that the third room was two storeyed from the start. The Hall ceiling and fireplace were probably inserted in the late 16th Century.

Farway (a cottage) ST3008 0497
Now a sunken shed, this cottage is interesting in that it represents many, if not most, of the types of habitation to be found in the small enclosures on the Commons and must be a rare survival. It is a two room, single storey, structure with central chimney and large fireplace. There is some suggestion of a half upper sleeping floor next to the central stack. The cottage may have been the subject of a newspaper article in the 1930's, although the illustration accompanying the article shows a two storey cottage. In spite of the thatched roof being in an advanced state of decay, it was still occupied as there was no place for the tenant to go.

Farway Farm ST3145 0230
A much modernised farmhouse of 3 bedroom, cross-passage plan, remote from the main part of the village. The lack of smoke blackening in the roof indicates that the date of the house is 16th Century rather than medieval. The east part of the house, situated on the falling slope of land, shows indications of a rebuilt byre end of a longhouse.

Fordwater ST3163 0243
The house, near the crossing of the river Kit, is facing the Chard to Axminster road and separated from it by a small front garden. It was built of cob and is a long, thatched jointed cruck house dating from the later 16th Century. At that time it was probably of 3 unit cross passage form with the kitchen to the south-west and the hall and inner room beyond the passage. There is no smoke blackening.

Gilletts Farm ST2627 0746
This fine, large farmhouse is situated in Crawley. Its walls are of chert rubble and some cob. It is a Yeoman's house of typical plan, 3 rooms and cross-passage but here with the addition of 2 wings possibly in the 17th but more likely in the 18th Century. The original building was an open hearth Hall house which still retains smoke blackened jointed crucks, some plank like common rafters and some wattle work under the thatch. The fireplace was probably inserted in the late 16th Century. The farm buildings include a barn which still has its wooden threshing floor between modified opposed doorways.

Higher Fordwater Farm ST3145 0230
The house is almost opposite Fordwater but set well back from the road and on the further bank of the river Kit. It is L shaped and generally of 18th Century date, although there is evidence of earlier work in the 17th Century fireplace of the south-east room. Some medieval work exists in the stud and panel partition on the first floor and a smoke blackened piece of a principal rafter was re-used as a doorway lintel in the wing room of the house. Neither of these features need necessarily be from this house and there is no other early evidence.

Hook Farm ST3085 0554
Refurbishment revealed this to be a cruck beamed longhouse originally open to the roof which had a smoke hole. Lowering the floor revealed a cobbled surface and below this was pottery identified at Exeter Museum as indicating an earlier 11th Century habitation site.

Hoopers Farmhouse ST3075 0447
This is a small mid. 17th Century house, probably of Yeoman status, situated to the west of the village, almost opposite the old vicarage. There is a cross passage with original flagstones, a Hall room and a service room. The house has been much altered, the floor lowered and the frontage rebuilt in the 19th Century. There is a stud and panel screen opposite the hall fireplace which backs onto the cross passage. The screen is chamfered on the living side and is probably in its original position. The fireplace is unusual and probably original. It has small square openings on either side which may have been used for rush lights. The roof structure has oak mortise and tenon trusses with wood pegs. The tie beams are rough and the purlins unremarkable. The roof is modern thatch owing to a major fire in the 1940's. The front facade and the above features were preserved.

Keates Farmhouse ST3220 0303
This formerly thatched small farmhouse has unblackened jointed crucks which indicate a building date in the second half of the 16th Century. Other details suggest that it was changed to a gable chimney, unheated centre room plan during the 17th Century. The fireplace at the north-west end of the house has a re-used ceiling beam lintel with TH 1748 (Timothy Hoare?) cut into it. An uncertain possible smoke hole in the masonry of the left side of the hearth suggests a curing chamber. It is thought that some of the stone has been re-used and that it came from Tytherleigh Manor House which was allowed to fall into disrepair.

Knights Farm ST3050 0146
This farmhouse was situated on the edge of South Common. The plan of 3 rooms and cross passage with a small added wing (possibly a dairy) at the back remains largely as it was when first built, though the front wall was completely reconstructed in 1837. It probably dates from the end of the 16th Century and from the start had 2 storeys and fireplaces that still exist. The centre room or Hall has a large fireplace backing onto the passage and a stair in the traditional position. Between the Hall and the inner room is a heavy stud and panel partition similar to that separating the cross passage and the Kitchen, which has a fireplace with brick lined oven and an iron door. There may also have been a curing chamber here but this cannot be proved.

Lower Ridge ST2994 0595
This very long building is on a slope in two distinct parts. The south-east end is higher and has a range of ovolo moulded mullioned windows on the ground floor and mixed ovolo moulded windows on the first floor. The entry is in the lower part which has an added wing and is a plainer building with wooden windows and no fine external detail. At the south end of the house is the Parlour which has a fireplace with an arched stone lintel. The inside of the fireplace is painted in a design of black triangles. The next room, which may have been a Buttery, has stairs in a turret behind the rear wall. The third room was the Hall with a fireplace backing on a cross-passage. This room has the remains of a jetty indicating that it was always of 2 storeys and open to the roof. It is not known if there was a true staircase or a ladder to the upper floor.

On the first floor, the room above the Parlour also has a painted fireplace, this one with a design of interlocking circles. Both paintings are of 17th Century date. The Hall may be of medieval or early 16th Century in date. The Parlour, Buttery and stair turret are part of a 17th Century modernisation of the original longhouse.

Masonic Hall ST3091 0449
A false ceiling has now been inserted into this room and all masonic decoration of presumably 1847 date, is above this. There is a central wicker lamp with bottom shade and tassels. Roof timbers have a running decoration in red on a self coloured background. The original ceiling consisted of three panels, one facing downwards and two at 45°, plus the two gable ends. The background colour is pale matt blue and the symbols are in gold. These are, north and south end - alpha and omega, top panels - crown or star alternately, west panels from the south - cross keys, St. Andrew's cross, apron and wheatsheaf, chalice with vapour, east panels from the south, axe, saw, obscured, destroyed, all side panel symbols have a scribe's quill pen above them.

The Old Farmhouse, Burridge ST3147 0626
This is a house of late medieval to mid 16th Century date which was modified in the 17th Century and later. These changes make the earliest plan (probably 3 rooms and a cross passage) no longer discernible. The walls are of rubble and the roof has two jointed crucks, one of which is somewhat discoloured. The rest of the roof is clean except for the ridge timber which is heavily smoke blackened.

The Old House, Chard Street ST3104 0456
This is a roughcast, white painted, thatched house, facing in a south-easterly direction onto the road. It has brick chimneys and wooden windows. The plan has 3 rooms in line, with an outshut behind one of them. The house is small and must, therefore, be considered to be a cottage. The accommodation was simple, with a large kitchen/living room and a small parlour, with rooms over and a service outshut. The room at the south-west end of the house is the largest, having a spacious fireplace with a brick lined oven. The house lacks positive dating evidence but very probably dates from the later 17th or more likely from the early 18th Century. However, on the 1781 Henley Estate Map the house appears as a barn or shed.

Old Orchard (previously known as Whitehouse) ST2946 0523
This house, on a north-south axis and situated at right angles to the road, is built of chert rubble with stone dressing. It has a thatched roof and ovolo mullion windows of Beer stone. The original building was a 2 bay, open-hall structure, the central truss of which has considerable smoke blackening. The main block consists of 3 ground floor rooms with a cross passage. The north room and cross passage separating it from the other 2 rooms, were added to the earlier building. The outer walls of the 2 bay sections were raised to accommodate a second storey and a semicircular staircase was built. Stone mullion windows and 2 moulded stone fireplaces were installed in the first floor rooms. This work appears to date from around 1580-1620. Later, a half-hipped wing with lower walls and an early wooden mullion window, was added to the west of the 2 bays. The present northern room appears to be a more recent addition, although, from the inventory of 1731, it was the kitchen of that date.

Pinneys Cottage ST3080 0402
This is a small, originally thatched house, the front wall of which has been rebuilt. The house now has a garage and room over on one end. The plan is of 2 rooms facing south-east. There is a stud and panel partition between the 2 rooms, one of these having an inserted fireplace. Possibly there was a third room, which was either rebuilt or added to the south-west of the present two. This would have given the quite common 3 room cross passage plan with the Hall, an unheated Parlour (or perhaps Dairy), the lost part of the kitchen and cross passage. It is possible that this was a longhouse in view of the steeply sloping site and the fact that a room has been lost. There are two jointed crucks in the roof structure giving a possible late 16th Century date. On the first floor a fireplace has initials and an 18th Century date on its lintel. On the same lintel, but perhaps of a different period, is a well preserved religious text (also painted), including the Lord's prayer.

Rose Cottage, Burridge ST315 063
The house, built mainly in rubble, is aligned with the slope of the ground. There are 3 rooms and a cross passage. The Inner room is at the upslope end and cannot be dated. Down one step is the centre room or Hall with a fireplace, possibly inserted in the late 16th Century, backing onto the cross-passage, which is down two steps. Down a further step is the third room which has no early detail. In the roof is a jointed cruck evenly, but not heavily, smoke blackened. This is a small farmhouse of, probably, early 16th Century date, originally single storeyed with an open hearth. It is probable that the area north of the cross passage was one open room. The siting of the house down the slope and the lack of early detail in the third room, makes it possible that this room is the modified and perhaps shortened, byre of a longhouse.

Springhayes (in the village) ST309 043
Very little early details survive of this stone built, thatched house. The plan was originally of 2 rooms, only the larger being heated. Evidence of the 17th Century exits in the lintel of the fireplace and the beam over the partition between the two rooms.

Strongs (in the village) ST3115 0428
This building was formerly a farmhouse and then later a general shop in the centre of the village. It has chert rubble walls and was roofed with thatch. The windows are wooden, some with small panes and irregular old glass. The plan has been altered by the conversion of the house to a shop creating no less than 5 external doorways, including that to the shop. This suggests that the accommodation may have been divided. It faces north-east directly onto the road which is above the level of the house. The room at the north-west end has a large fireplace, the remains of an oven and probably a meat curing chamber. It has extremely narrow stairs, some of the treads being only about 3 inches (7.6cm.) wide. The centre room was the shop. The room at the south-east end formerly had a large fireplace and stairs which have now been removed. In the 19th Century, this fireplace was adapted to provide a large bread oven, identified as a "Govin" oven 1850-1860. This was used for baking bread which would have been sold in the village. On the left of the oven, a domestic range was added at a later date when the room ceased to be a bakery. On the first floor, 4 partially surviving jointed crucks can be seen. They are tall, so there has been no need to raise the roof, this indicating that this was a two storeyed house from the start. This supposition is confirmed by a total lack of smoke blackening. The most likely pattern of development, therefore, is a 2 storey, half hipped house built in the 16th Century with one main fireplace somewhere within the building. It would have been altered in the 17th Century with fireplaces and chimneys fitted into the end parts of the house and the layout replanned. The layout was again changed in the 19th or early 20th Century to accommodate the bakery and shop. After being empty for several years, the cottage has now been completely restored. As far as possible, the original features have been retained, while the accommodation has been brought up to modern standards. The Strong Family Association of America look on the cottage as part of their heritage and have taken an active interest in the recent restoration of the building which is classified as a listed building. The Chardstock Estate has carried out a two year programme of renovation and the cottage is now let to a tenant. A special meeting of the Court Baron was convened in 1995 for the particular purpose of presenting to Jarvis Strong, on behalf of the Strong dynasty, a certificate confirming "full and free license and authority to visit the tenement known as Strongs, lying within the Parish of Chardstock, according to the custom of the manor".

Symes Cottage, Back Lane ST3105 0423
This house has white painted, rubble walls with some cob at the end in a lean-to. The roof is thatched and was half hipped at both ends before the construction of the lean-to. It faces north-east and is almost end-on to the lane. The plan is unusual with 3 rooms but no cross-passage. The centre room has a large fireplace and a brick lined oven. The only good dating material, apart from the roof, is the early 17th Century beam and fireplace of the centre room. This indicates that the house was built in the late 16th or early 17th Century and modified in the late 17th Century to provide its present appearance.

Whitehouse (previously part of what is now Old Orchard) ST2957 0518
The thatched house is aligned almost north/south down a slope with the upper end cut into the hillside in the classic longhouse style. There is, however, no sign of a byre construction at the downslope end. Perhaps it is a 16th Century complete re-build of a somewhat earlier longhouse. The plan was three rooms and a cross passage, now part of the kitchen. The centre room, the hall, has a blocked fireplace with a stair beside it, the chimney above being a timber framed structure with tall rod and daub panels. In the rear wall, a door leads to an apparently recent extension but this appears to be a rebuild because the door frame shows cuts on both sides to allow large barrels through. This seems to indicate the provision of a buttery beside the hall in an outshut, now rebuilt. There are 3 late jointed crucks but no smoke blackening, thus indicating a date in the later 16th Century.

Woonton Farm ST2924 0544
The farmhouse is set on an elevated habitation site of some considerable age, north-west of the village. The house area is encircled by what may be a moat or at least a broad ditch. The house is imposing with its tall front in rubble stone and dressed quoins. Its roof, originally thatched, is of double roman tiles and is fully hipped at both ends, with chimneys of cut stone slabs with moulded caps. All the windows were originally stone mullioned and transomed but some on the ground floor and all on the upper storey have been replaced by sash windows. The plan is an L shaped main block with a further building added to form a U shape and with farm buildings closing the top of the U to form an enclosed rear courtyard. The present house was probably built at the turn of the 17th Century, in fact within a few years either side of 1700, possibly to replace an earlier building. In 1810, when William Bently was tenant, a sale of 100 beech trees was held in the Great Hall of Wotton Farm House (see Chapter 5). The barn at Woonton Farm is of brick construction on a stone base. This particular style and the bricks themselves, suggest a late 17th or early 18th Century date, that is, about the same time as that of the house. The interior of the barn was divided regularly into bays, 2 at each end with 4 in the centre, these 4 bays being separated from the 2 ends by through doors, thus giving a double barn with 2 threshing floors.

Yard Farm ST2958 0306

Yard is situated to the South of the village. It is one of the oldest mentioned farms in Chardstock but the original dwelling is unlikely to have survived. The present house is a small medieval open-hall house with floors and ceilings inserted in the late 16th or very early 17th Century to form a two roomed cross-passage house with Hall and service room. No third room can have existed because of the rising land north of the Hall. There is one jointed cruck visible and the old part of the roof is heavily smoke blackened, indicating an original open fire in the Hall. To the downslope end of the house has been added a small barn with opposed doorways and thinner walls. This was clearly a corn barn as the doors are well above ground level and too small to accommodate wagons. Between the doors, a wooden threshing floor still survives. Beyond the barn is a two storeyed portion of indeterminate usage, the whole probably being of 18th Century date.

Sources
Dallimore. J. House Survey Reports, Som. R. O.
Gilson. R. G., House Survey Reports, Som. R. O.
Hutchins, History of Dorset.

MAP 15. FIELDWORK FEATURES

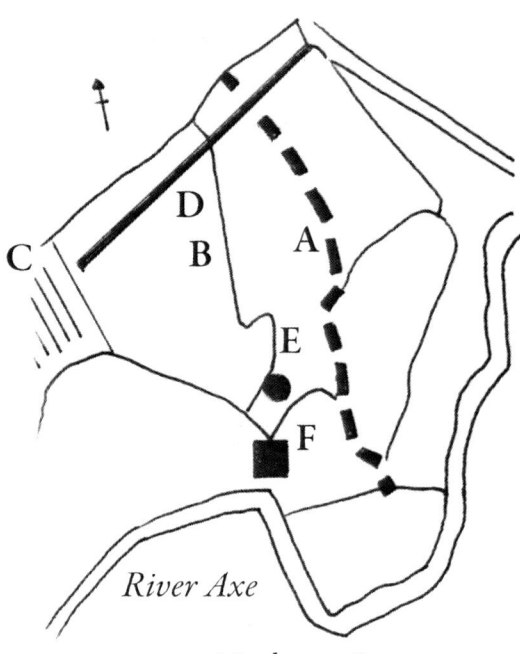

Meadows at Broom
The area was water meadows and the irrigation channel D and furrows C, could still be seen. A possible causeway A and bank C are on the 1781 map as "land". A mound E and platform F beside the old river channel are of unknown age or function.

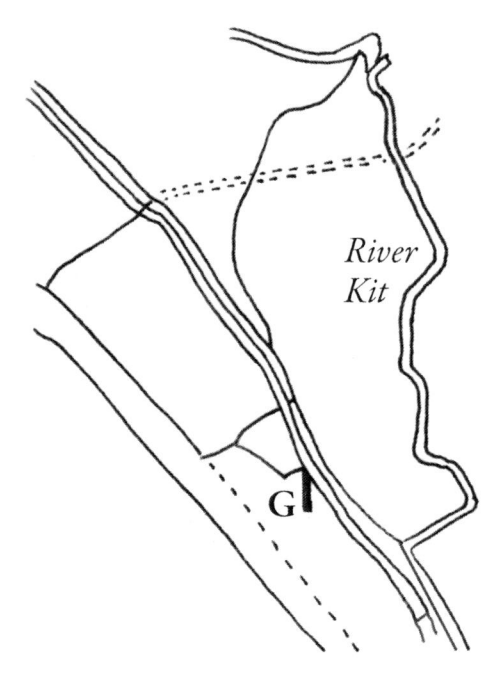

Cotley Wash
The sheepwash was filled from a river diversion and was stone lined. Adjacent is a fold and building. It is probably of 19th century date but is now being buried under rubbish.

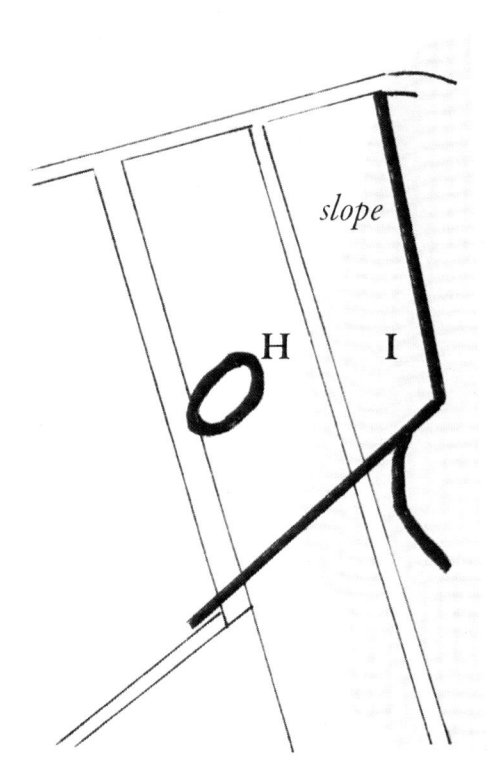

Pulman's Circle
George Pulman (Book of the Axe) said that there were three circular banks, one with Bronze Age pottery. Only H, and some related banks I, were found.

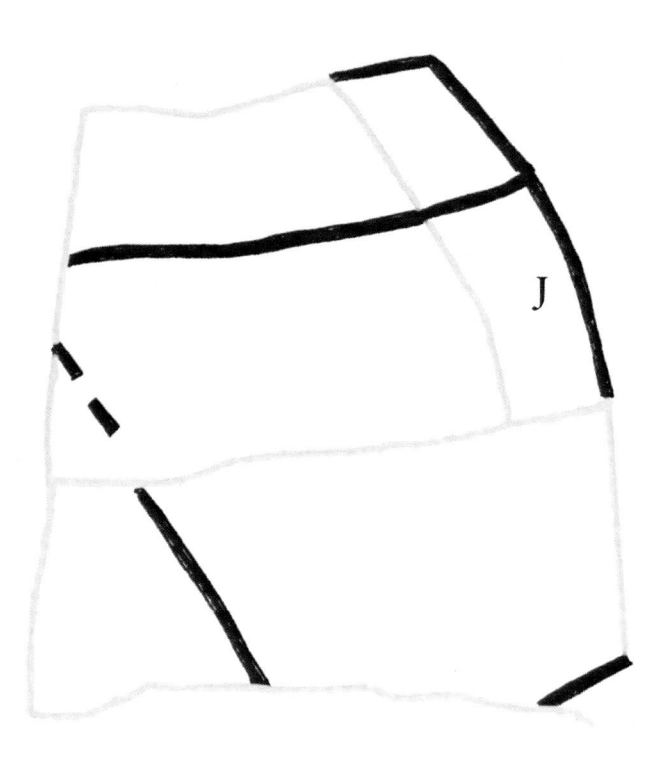

Vulscombe Field
Gerbert de Percy mentioned this small stripfield in 1155. Something of its shape can be realised from the remaining hedgebanks and low banks J in the present fields.

APPENDIX B - CHARDSTOCK PARISH CHECKLIST

*KEY: H = Henley Map   F = fieldwork   O = 1896 6"Ord. Survey   L= literature

Feature	Name/type	Source*	O.S.Grid ST East	North	Detail/comment	Illus.
arch	with Tytherleigh arms plaque	HF	3181	0324		Plate 3
bank	Half Moon (ringwork?)	F	2830	0525	unfinished/damaged? 1.5m bank, 0.5m ditch	
bank	field system	F	2834	0662	next to Bronze age settlement	
bank	lynchet boundary	OF	3172	0378	to 3220 0687	Map 4
bank	boundary	OF	3220	0687	to 3116 0752, next to Iron age site	Map 4
banks	field system	F	2650	0740	Medieval earthworks	
banks	field system	F	2700	0750	Medieval earthworks	
banks	field system	F	2790	0530	Medieval earthworks	
banks	field system, Broad Croft	OF	2810	0570	Prehistoric/medieval earthworks	
banks	field system	F	2870	0550	Medieval earthworks	
banks	field system	F	2920	0710	Medieval earthworks	
banks	field system	F	3000	0225	Medieval earthworks/settlement	
banks	field system	OF	3020	0515	probably was Vulscombe Field	Map 15
banks	field system	F	3050	0127	Medieval earthworks	
banks	field system	F	3060	0595	Medieval earthworks	
banks	field system	F	3080	0110	Medieval earthworks	
banks	field system	F	3130	0086	Medieval earthworks	
banks	field system	F	3150	0124	Medieval earthworks	
barrow	Burrows Mead	HF	3070	0125	not found	
bridge	abutment & holloway	F	2560	0820	near Crawley bridge	
bridge	Crawley	OF	2566	0810	modern, 1814 bridge washed away	
bridge	Farway	HF	3036	0525		
bridge	at Stockstyle	HF	3040	0498		
bridge	foot, over leat	HF	3048	0455		
bridge	at Mill	HF	3055	0440		
bridge	at Kit Bridge	HF	3080	0390	foot/horse, 2 arch	Plate 3
bridge	Gozzleford foot	HF	3104	0338	modern	
bridge	Ford Bridge	HF	3158	0232	undated, 3 arch	Plate 3
bridge	foot & ford, Charn Bridge?	HF	3195	0162		Plate 3
bridge	with ford at Axe Bridge	HF	3224	0170		
bridges	Broom	OF	3258	0248	2 arch & a modern steel	Plate 3
building	College Gas Works & Holder	OF	3080	0454	gone	
building	smithy at Coaxdon	OF	3110	0040	gone	
building	Shambles	H	3099	0443	site of	
building	Cadet Hut	F	3076	0386	concrete sign remains	
building	College, site of rear buildings	OF	3091	0453	parchmarks	
building	Soper's	H	3058	0444	site of	
building	Dye House	H	3058	0442	site of	
building	Auxiliary Unit Bunker	F	2814	0505	underground	
building	smithy, Tytherleigh, site of	O	3184	0325		
charcoal	Colliers Plot/Brickfield	HF	3040	0570		
charcoal	Coalpits	FT	3100	0105	workings & leat	
dip, sheep	Cotley Wash	OF	2956	0630	leat & buildings	Map 15
ditch	& bank, Grey Ditch	OF	2754	0550	to 2837 0449	Map 3
flint	arrowhead, petit tranchet	F	2832	0490	Neolithic	
flints	flakes	F	2895	0490	Neolithic	
ford	at Millway	OF	3124	0312		
hoard	coin, Money Pit Lane	O	2700	0680	1833, Roman coins & site now lost	
hoard	coin	O	2976	0690	1865, Iron Age coins now lost	
kiln	lime & pit	OF	2747	0557	wood arch, wings face SW	Plate 5
kiln	lime & limestone pit	OF	2886	0654	wings face SW, good condition	Plate 5
kiln	lime	OF	2934	0543	wings face SE	
kiln	lime & pit	OF	2982	0708		
kiln	lime, & chalk pit	OF	3062	0718	wings faced SW, gone	
kiln	brick, & waster dump	OF	3070	0386	levelled	
kiln	lime, & pit	OF	3076	0604	kiln gone	
kiln	lime, & pit	OF	3096	0600	kiln gone	
kiln	lime	HF	3124	0506	no wings, was W facing, gone	
kiln	lime	HF	3136	0520	wings faced E, gone	
kiln	lime, & chalk pit	OF	3156	0537	gone	
kiln	lime	OF	3188	0410	gone	
kilns	4 lime & pit	OF	3100	0046	no wings, faced SE	Map 7

*KEY: H = Henley Map   F = fieldwork   O = 1896 6" Ord. Survey   L= literature

Feature	Name/type	Source*	O.S.Grid ST East North	Detail/comment	Illus.
leat	to Hares Farm	OF	2700 0810		
leat	with pond, to Hares Farm	HF	2735 0747		
leat	to Bewley Farm	OF	2760 0560		
leat	irrigation?	OF	2990 0242		
leat	to Coaxdon	OF	3110 0082		
leat	mill, & sluice	OF	3130 0290	to 3105 0332	Map 8
leat	& sluice	OF	3216 0136	to 3194 0162	
leats		OF	2990 0590	to 2956 0630	
leats	water meadow	OF	3040 0104		
leats	water meadow	OF	3172 0112		
leats	& sluice	OF	3180 0190	to 3160 0228, irrigation?	
leats	water meadow	OF	3220 0240		
memorial	war, parish	F	3099 0443		
mill	wheel pit, leat & sluices	OF	3070 0386	clay pug mill for brick works?	Map 8
mill	& leat, Miller's Green	OF	2580 0814	wheel gone	Map 8
mill	& leat at Crawley Farm	OF	2704 0806	levelled	Map 8
mill	& leat at Woonton	OF	2945 0537	to 2920 0586, only leat	Map 8
mill	Lodge Mill	O	2950 0730	corn, pond & leats	Map 8
mill	?, at Farway	OF	3012 0494	only leat	Map 8
mill	?, at All Saints	OF	3029 0112	suspect building	
mill	Hook Paper	HF	3096 0548	later corn	Map 8
mill	at Hook	HF	3100 0560	wheel gone	Map 8
mill	Millwell/way	OF	3110 0312	only leat and possible building	Map 8
mill	leat & wiers at Coaxdon	OF	3113 0038	to 3142 0060, wheel gone	Map 7
mill	Minson's, site of	H	3054 0518		Map 8
moat?	Wootton manor house	F	2924 0548	obscured by quarrying	
mound	broken stone	F	2626 0736	now levelled	
mound	Beacon, ditch & bank	OF	3001 0283	16th. cent.? good condition	Plate 11
mound	Sansom's Knap	OF	3066 0200	mound not found	
mound	broken stone	OF	3110 0206	levelled	
mound	Roundabout Close	F	3215 0687	not found	
mound	with causeway	F	3240 0242	& water meadow	Map 15
pit	chalk marl	OF	3154 0528		
pit	gravel	OF	2674 0746		
pit	saw	OF	2918 0535		
pit	stone or chalk	OF	2930 0550		
pit	stone	OF	2975 0482		
pit	chalk marl	OF	2980 0690		
pit	chalk marl	OF	2980 0708		
pit	chalk marl	F	2980 0770		
pit	tone	OF	2996 0492		
pit	chalk marl	HF	3014 0600		
pit	ballast, iron ore?	OF	3016 0250		
pit	chalk marl	HF	3027 0596	marked "Mle Pit"	
pit	Pitt Land	HF	3054 0534		
pit	James' Close Pit	OF	3057 0740	chalk	
pit	Spillers Pit	OF	3060 0450		
pit	Whitham Ball Pit	OF	3060 0720	chalk marl	
pit	chalk	OF	3065 0585		
pit	Combehays Pit	OF	3070 0710	chalk	
pit	gravel	OF	3074 0320		
pit	marl	HF	3077 0604	marked "Mle Pit"	
pit	marl	HF	3078 0640	marked "Mle Pit"	
pit	& road	OF	3080 0713		
pit	marl	HF	3094 0603	marked "Mle Pit"	
pit	Marlepitt Close	HF	3100 0250		
pit	chalk marl	OF	3104 0546		
pit	limestone	OF	3106 0060		
pit	Marle Pitt Head	HF	3116 0384	Chalk marl	
pit	chalk marl	OF	3123 0544		
pit	& road	OF	3128 0274		
pit	chalk	OF	3132 0652		
pit	chalk marl	HF	3140 0570	marked "Mle Pit"	
pit	Gravel Pit Close	HF	3144 0212		
pit	gravel?	OF	3146 0734		

*KEY: H = Henley Map   F = fieldwork   O = 1896 6" Ord. Survey   L= literature

Feature	Name/type	Source*	O.S.Grid ST East North	Detail/comment	Illus.
pit	chalk marl	OF	3148 0456		
pit	gravel	OF	3160 0730		
pit	stone	OF	3166 0630		
pit	chalk marl	OF	3184 0460		
pit	stone	OF	3187 0664		
pit	?	OF	3188 0224		
pit	stone	OF	3220 0687	& 3116 0753?	
pit	saw	OF	3224 0305	good condition	
pit	? illustrated	HF	3024 0608		
pits	Pit & Quarry Closes	HF	3020 0510		
pits	clay?	OF	3030 0360		
pits		OF	3038 0126		
pits	marl	HF	3088 0609	marked "Mle Pits"	
pits	gravel	OF	3106 0077		
pits	clay	OF	3112 0120		
pits	Chilpitts	HF	3124 0506	chalk	
pits	Withypitts	HF	3136 0520	chalk	
pits	Marle Pitts	HF	3147 0458	chalk marl	
pits	Bloody Pitts	HF	3175 0436	chalk	
platform	house, Walcroft	HF	2650 0715		
platform	farm building?	OF	2818 0534	levelled	
platform	house in Lo. Wambrook	F	2966 0763		
platform	smithy at Churchill	OF	2990 0242		
platform	& barton	OF	2990 0290		
platform	house at Farway	OF	3010 0506	see settlement 3008 0503	
platform	smithy, village	OF	3098 0444	levelled	
pond	Pool Close	HF	2775 0600	gone, 14/15th. cent pottery	
pond	Pond Close	HF	2920 0463		
pond		HF	2922 0442	marked "pond"	
pond	Pond Close	HF	2954 0483		
pond	Pond Close	HF	2972 0355		
pond		F	3016 0736	dry	
pond	Pool Close	HF	3020 0650		
pond		HF	3042 0658	marked "Pd"	
pond	bathing pool	OF	3057 0457	gone	
pond	village?	HF	3101 0420	gone	
pond	Hook Pond	OF	3106 0574	dry, watercress?	Map 8
pond	& leats	OF	3137 0262	purpose unknown	
pond	by House's Linney	OF	3164 0738	als. Burridge Wood Stall	
pottery	tile scatter, Roman	F	2960 0540		
pottery	Roman, 1 sherd	F	3110 0738	2/3rd. cent., New Forest ware	
pottery	in levelled bank	F	3140 0610	12/13 cent.	
pottery	scatter	F	3140 0655	14/15 cent.	
pottery	in bank	F	3189 0324		
pottery	Old Orchard	F	2943 0525	see Appendix 1	
pound	parish	HF	3097 0434		
pump	village, plaque of site of	F	3094 0446		
road	holloway	OF	2626 0738	to 2643 0794	
road	Casse Lane	HF	2724 0710	causeway, N/S earthwork seen	
road	holloway & ford	OF	2945 0628	to 2987 0642	
road	holloway	OF	2992 0288	to 2924 0332	
road	holloway	OF	2995 0254	to 3007 0282	
road		OF	3050 0230	to 3025 0325	
road	Fosse Way	OF	3086 0019	line followed by ditch	
road	holloway, Stockstyle?	OF	3090 0472	to 3050 0515	
road	access to common	OF	3124 0630		
road		OF	3140 0126		
road		OF	3184 0366		
road	holloway	OF	3210 0175	to 3180 0280	
road		OF	3272 0284		
road block	Broom Bridge	F	3258 0248		Plate 12
ruin	Bewley Farm	OF	2744 0564		
ruin	cottage	OF	2870 0658		
ruin	?	OF	2917 0656		
ruin	Old Twist Farm	OF	2924 0332	burnt down	Plate 6

120

*KEY: H = Henley Map   F = fieldwork   O = 1896 6"Ord. Survey   L= literature

Feature	Name/type	Source*	O.S.Grid ST East North	Detail/comment	Illus.
ruin	smithy at Sycamore	OF	2952 0606		
ruin	Pewit Cottage	OF	3017 0364		
ruin	Huntley Barn	OF	3072 0640	Med. window, once a larger building	Plate 6
settlement	ringwork at Hares	F	2673 0758		
settlement	ringwork on Bewley Down	F	2832 0664	found by Pulman, see Book of the Axe.	Map 15
settlement	deserted, Garns Pit	OF	2874 0474		
settlement	commons, Sycamore	OF	2910 0590	& 2864 0624	
settlement	shrunken, at Whitehouse	F	2946 0518	Wilmington?	
settlement	shrunken, at Churchill	F	2995 0228		
settlement	ringwork, at Churchill	F	3000 0225		
settlement	commons, at Cuckolds Pit	OF			Plate 15
settlement	ringwork, Cold Harbour	OF	3110 0744	Iron Age?	Plate 1
settlement	shrunken, at Burridge	OF	3120 0610		
settlement	ringwork at Burridge	OF	3130 0624		
settlement	shrunken, ringwork	OF	3150 0110	Sandford?	
slag	& Crawley Foundry	F	2658 0756	& smithy	
slag	iron	F	2870 0550		
slag	iron	F	2920 0490		
slag	bronze?	F	3180 0320		
sluice		HF	3160 0230		
sluice	weir & leat	HF	3195 0162		
sluices		HF	3140 0268	marked "Hatches"	
stone	mile, Chard 5 / Honiton 8	OF	2570 0806	not found	
stone	boundary	OF	2620 0862	not found	
stone	mile, Chard 5 / Axminster 2	OF	3110 0126	plates gone	Plate 3
stone	mile, Chard 4 / Axminster 3	HF	3173 0272	plates gone	
stones	Stapleway?	OF	3166 0628	were these the staples?	
strip	Great Ernest	HF	3280 0286	¼ acre, wharf site?	
tree	Three County Tree	HF	3289 0282	a young oak remains	
trough	water	OF	3050 0105	brick	
wall	Old Wall	HF	2800 0540	not found	
well	Selah	OF	2814 0505	with top mechanism	Plate 6
well	Crabb's Well	OF	3200 0317	a spring	
yard	Vineyard	OF	3110 0430	viticulture unconfirmed	

APPENDIX C - FIELD AND PLACE NAMES

*source numbers are from the tithe map

Name	Source*	Earliest Spelling	Year	Possible Origin	Possible Meaning
ALL SAINTS	MAP	----------------	----	----------------	ALL SAINTS CHURCH (dedication 1840)
ALLER MOOR	1189	LE ALLERS	1422	ALOR	ALDER TREES, PROBABLY COPPICED
ALSTON	MAP	ALEWOLDESTONE	1201	AELFWEALD'S TUN	PERS.NM + PRINCIPAL FARM
ALSTON FARM	DOC	----------------	----	----------------	RICH.CHARD (copy) FORMERLY BOWDITCH'S
ASSH	DOC	----------------	1332	AESC	ASH TREE - unlocated
AXE BRIDGE	MAP	----------------	----	----------------	REPAIRS 1603
AXE CROSSING	MAP	----------------	----	----------------	RAILWAY CROSSING
AXE FARM	MAP	AXE	1332	----------------	MARG. SEWARD WID. OF GODWIN (copy)
AXE LANE	DOC	----------------	1596	----------------	TO AXE FARM
AXE MEAD, GREAT	782	AXMEDE	1426	MAED COMMON	MEADOW BY THE RIVER AXE
AXE (RIVER)	MAP	AXAM	693	ISCA	GUSHING
BAGLESS, LONG	625	BAGLESS	1537	BAG LEES	STRIPS USED FOR SHEEP PASTURE
BALLYRAG GREAT MOOR	403	----------------	----	BALLY	STRIP WITH HILLOCKS (obscure)
BARLEY AIRISH	1175	----------------	----	ERSC	BARLEY STUBBLE GRAZING
BATCH, GREAT	1	----------------	1582	BAEC	LOW RIDGE
BATTLEFORD HALL	MAP	BAKELFORD	1333	?	? FORD
BAYCRAFT	823	----------------	----	BAY	WALNUT ORCHARD?
BEACON HILL	MAP	BEKING	1552	BEACN	SIGNAL FIRE (& see Toterygg)
BEER MEAD	605	BEREMEADE	1599	BEARU	MEAD NEAR BEER
BENNETS MEAD	759	BENETESIMEDE	1422	BEONET	MEAD WHERE BENT (a grass) GROWS
BERE	DOC	----------------	1155	BEARU	ENCLOSED WOOD PASTURE (unlocated)
BERRE FURLONG	DOC	----------------	1566	----------------	FURLONG NEAR BEER (unlocated)
BEWLEY DOWN	MAP	BELEDONNE	1426	----------------	SEE BEWLEY FARM & DOWN
BEWLEY FARM	MAP	BEILEGE	1202	BAEL LEAH	HALF WAY CLEARING
BEWLEY FARM	MAP	BEWLYE FARM	1582	----------------	RICH. DEAN (lease)
BEWLYE LANE	DOC	----------------	1582	----------------	NEWLY CONSTRUCTED 1582
BEWSPIT FURLONG	DOC	----------------	1566	----------------	ON BEWLEY DOWN?
BIRCHILL	MAP	----------------	1598	BIRCE	BIRCH TREE
BIRCHILL FARM	MAP	----------------	----	----------------	INCLOSURE (1850) FARM (late name)
BIRD FURLONG	DOC	BIRDFURLAG	1155	BRID	UNCERTAIN
BLACK ALLER GROVE	MAP	----------------	----	----------------	SEE ALLER
BLACK MOOR	MAP	----------------	----	----------------	BLACK OR BACK MOOR
BLOODY PITTS	976	B(F)LUDDYE PYT	1582	BLODIG	SLAUGHTERING HOLLOW ?
BOARFEILDE	DOC	----------------	1598	BAR	BOAR FIELD
BOOLES LOWER MEAD	215	BULLSACRE	----	----------------	BULL, IRON BLOOM, PLANK (obscure)
BOTTOMS, LONG	1393	----------------	----	----------------	BOTTOM HEADLANDS
BOUNDS LANE	MAP	----------------	----	----------------	SEE BOUNDS ORCHARD
BOUNDS ORCHARD	1399	----------------	----	----------------	BY PARISH BOUNDARY
BOWHAYS, LITTLE	1332	----------------	----	BOGA	HEDGED, CURVED STRIPLANDS
BOX, GREAT	1501	BOX	1432	BOX	BOX TREES OR ISOLATED LAND
BOYMANS	DOC	----------------	1598	----------------	PERS.NM.? BOYMAN
BRAMBLECOMBE COPSE	MAP	BRAMBLECOMBE	1599	BREMER	BRAMBLE
BRAYLANDS	1317	----------------	----	----------------	SEE BRIMLAND
BREACH	MAP	----------------	----	BRAEC	RECLAIMED LAND
BRIDGE MEAD	783	----------------	----	BRYCG	MEAD IS ACROSS THE RIVER AXE
BRIMLAND	1606	----------------	----	BRIM	EDGE OR TOP LAND
BRINSCOMBE LANE	MAP	BREINELCOMBE	1599	BREMEL	BRAMBLE
BROAD CRATE, GREAT	33	BRODECROFT	1422	BRAD	SEE BROAD CROFT
BROAD CROFT	MAP	----------------	----	----------------	BROAD ENCLOSURE HAVING SPECIALISED USE
BROADE MEADE	DOC	BRODEMEDE	1422	----------------	BROAD MEADOW
BROADE MEADE LANE	DOC	----------------	1596	----------------	AT TYTHERLEIGH
BROADEFEILD	DOC	BROADEFEILD CLOSE	1598	----------------	ROAD FIELD
BROCKFIELD, GREAT	1227	----------------	1582	BROC	BADGER OR BROKE(N) FIELD
BROCKHOLE LANE	MAP	BROKCHYNELL	1422	BRECAN	BROKEN HILL (quarries)
BRODE LACHE	DOC	----------------	1155	LAECC	BROAD BOG
BROMEKOMBE	DOC	----------------	----	BROM	BROOM COMBE - UNLOCATED
BROOM BRIDGE	MAP	----------------	----	----------------	TITHERLEIGH BRIDGE 1781
BROOM CROSSING	MAP	----------------	----	----------------	RAILWAY CROSSING
BROOM LANE	MAP	BROMEHYLL	1540	----------------	IN THORNCOMBE
BROWNASHE MEADE	DOC	BROUNASHE	1427	----------------	BROWN ASH

* source numbers are from the tithe map

Name	Source*	Earliest Spelling	Year	Possible Origin	Possible Meaning
BUDDILY HILL	813	BOODDLEMEADE	1598	BOODLE	CORN MARIGOLDS OR CLEANSING PLACE ?
BUGGE CLOSE MEADE	DOC	BUGGE CLOSE MEADE	----		BOG HAUNTED (UNLOCATED)
BURCHILL COMMON	MAP	----------------	----	----------------	SEE BIRCHILL
BURGATS ASH, LOWER	969	BOUREGORE	1422	BAR	BOARS' MUDDY PLACE
BURRIDGE	MAP	BUUDIHC	C13	A BUFAN DIC	CURVED DITCH
BURRIDGE COMMON	MAP	----------------	1582	----------------	SEE BURRIDGE
BURRIDGE CROSS	MAP	----------------	----	----------------	NO EARLY MENTION
BURRIDGE FARM	MAP	----------------	----	----------------	
BURRIDGE HOUSE	MAP	----------------	----	----------------	
BURROWS FARM	MAP	----------------			INCLOSURE FARM (1850) - PERS.NM.
CALVEN LEASE CLOSE	DOC	----------------			TRIPS USED FOR CALF RAISING
CAMEL LEARS	361	----------------	----	LEASOWS	CROOKED PASTURE FIELD
CAP CRATE	184	----------------	----	CAEPPE	CAP SHAPED CROFT
CARPENTERS SQUARE	774	----------------	----	----------------	"L" SHAPED
CARTER'S ORCH. PLTN.	MAP	----------------	----	----------------	PERS.NM.- PARSON CARTER?
CASSE LANE	MAP	----------------	----	CAUSEY	CAUSEWAY (to Longbridge ?)
CATMOOR CROSS	MAP	CAMOORE	1648	CATTE MOR	CAT MOOR
CATMOOR FARM	MAP	----------------	----	----------------	INCLOSURE FARM (1850)
CAUSEWAYE	DOC	----------------	1582	----------------	PROBABLY JUST S. OF KITBRIDGE
CHALLENGER GATE	MAP	----------------	1822	CEALD	HANGRA- BY CHALLENGER FARM
CHAN CRATE	808	CHARN BRIDGE	1588	CYRIN	CROFT BY CHURNING WATER
CHARD LANE	MAP	----------------	----	----------------	OLD DIRECT ROUTE TO CHARD
CHARD WOOD SIDE	1400	GT. CHARD WOOD 1	646	----------------	BESIDE CHARD WOOD
CHARDSTOCK	MAP	CERDESTOCHE	1086	STOC	LACE. OF CHARD OR OF THE COMMON
CHARDSTOCK HOUSE	MAP	----------------	1898	----------------	ORIGINALLY PARADISE HOUSE (PRE 1840)
CHARNE BRIDGE	DOC	----------------	1598	----------------	SEE CHAN, OCCURS AT FORD AND AXE
CHELLKHULL	DOC	----------------	1422	CEALC	CHALKHILL, NEAR CHILPIT?
CHETFELD	DOC	----------------	1426	CETO	OPEN SPACE (DISCUSSED IN CHAPTER 1)
CHILL PITS	MAP	CHELPITT GATE	1598	CEALC	CHALK PITS
CHILL PITS LANE	MAP	CHELPITT	1598	----------------	SEE CHILL PITS
CHILPITS, LOWER	1129	CHELPITT	1598	----------------	SEE CHILL PITS
CHUBBS FARM	MAP	----------------	----	----------------	PERS.NM. CHUBB 1597
CHUBBS MEAD	575	----------------	----	----------------	EE CHUBBS
CHURCH HAYE	DOC	----------------	----	----------------	CHURCHYARD
CHURCHILL FARM	MAP	CHATTOSHALE	1422	HALE HILL	SPUR, PREFIX OBSCURE
CHURCHILL LANE	MAP	----------------	----	----------------	TO CHURCHILL FARM
CHURCHWEY	DOC	----------------	1422	----------------	TO CHARDSTOCK OR ERROR FOR CHURCH HAYE
CHURCH/CHICK LAND	30	CHICKLAND	1582	CICEN	DIALECT FOR CHICKEN, CHICKWEED, CHURCH?
CLAPPER GATE	MAP	CHURCHILL GATE	----	CLAP	GATE SMALL HORSE GATE
CLAYLANDS	1522	----------------	----	CLAEG	HEAVY STRIPLANDS
CLEALDS	1622	----------------	----	CLUD	CONTAINING ROCKY OUTCROPS
CLEEVE WOOD, LITTLE	MAP	----------------	----	----------------	WOOD ON A STEEP SLOPE
CLEEVEHILL LANE	MAP	LIVE	1155	CLIF	STEEP SLOPE
CLOADS	845	CLODES	1645	----------------	PERS. NM. CLOAD 1605
COALPIT CLOSE	727	----------------	----	COL	CHARCOAL KILN SITE?
COATE	224	----------------	----	COTE	ALLUDING TO THE SHAPE
COAXDEN	MAP	COCHESDENE	1155	COCC'S	PILES (of wood?) OR WOODCOCK'S VALLEY
COAXDON, HIGHER	MAP	----------------	----	----------------	NO INFORMATION
COAXDON, LOWER	MAP	----------------	----	----------------	NO INFORMATION
COAXDON COMMON	MAP	----------------	----	----------------	NEXT TO COAXDON
COAXDON HALL	MAP	COAXDON	----	----------------	
COAXDON MEAD	DOC	COXDEN MEADE 1598	----	----------------	COAXDON COMMON MEAD
COAXDON MILL	MAP	----------------	----	----------------	AT ONE TIME WAS A FULLING MILL
COCK CRATE	1105	----------------	----	COCC	HILLOCK OR WOODCOCK CROFT
COCKMEADFEILD	DOC	----------------	1612	COCC	UNCERTAIN - MEAD BY THE FUEL PILES?
COCKROADFEILD	DOC	----------------	1631	COCC	UNCERTAIN - ROAD TO THE FUEL PILES?
COLD HARBOUR	1424	----------------	----	CEALD	HEREBERWE COLD SHELTER
COLLIERS PLOT	1228	----------------	----	COLYER	CHARCOAL BURNER'S SITE?
COLMANS	1310	----------------	----	----------------	PERS.NM. COLEMAN 1525
COLMERS MEAD	1394	----------------	----	CEALD	MERSC COLD MARSH

*source numbers are from the tithe map

Name	Source*	Earliest Spelling	Year	Possible Origin	Possible Meaning
COLSTON COMMON	MAP	----	----	----	COXEN COMMON 1781, NEAR COLSTON FARM
COLSTON CROSS	MAP	----	----	----	NEAR COLSTON FARM
COLSTON FARM	MAP	COLTESTHORN	1340	COLT'S THORN	THE ANIMAL OR A PERS.NM.
COLTFURLONGE	DOC	----	1566	COLT	STRIPS USED FOR HORSE REARING
COMBEHAYES PIT	MAP	----	----	----	SMALL VALLEY ENCLOSURES
COMBHAYS	1301	----	----	CUMB	SMALL VALLEY ENCLOSURES
COMMON MEAD	841	----	1645	----	MEAD HELD IN COMMON USE
COOKS MEAD	822	----	----	----	PERS.NM. COOK 1569
COOMBS PLOTT	1045	----	----	----	PERS.NM. COOMBS 1569
COPSE STILE	MAP	----	----	----	STILE INTO CHARD WOOD
COTLEIGH DOWN	1425	----	----	COTTE LEAH	WOOD DWELLING
COTLEY	MAP	COTTELEGH	1201	COTE	SHELTER WOOD
COTLEY LANE	MAP	----	----	----	LANE TO COTLEY FARM
COTLEY WASH	MAP	COTLY WASHE	1582	WAESSE	SHEEP WASH SITE
COURT FARM	MAP	COURTE FARME	1645	----	CHARDSTOCK MANORIAL FARM
COURT HAYE	DOC	----	1598	----	ENCLOSURE BELONGING TO COTLEY
COWLEAZE	882	----	----	----	ARABLE PASTURE
COX MOOR	1255	----	----	----	SEE COXEN
COXEN COMMON (Crawley)	MAP	----	781	COCC'S	ILES (of wood?) OR WOODCOCK'S VALLEY
COXES CLOSE	1312	----	----	----	PERS.NM. COX 1569
CRABBS FARM	MAP	----	----	----	PERS.NM. CRABB 1624
CRABBS WELL	MAP	----	----	----	SEE CRABBS FARM
CRADDOCK HILL	1228	----	----	----	OBSCURE, CROFT TOP?
CRAMMERS	1398	----	----	----	OBSCURE, CONVERGING STRIPS? APPLE?
CRAWLEY	MAP	CRAULAUEE	1150	----	CROW WOOD, See Chapter 6
CRAWLEY, HIGHER	MAP	----	----	----	SEE CRAWLEY
CRAWLEY, LOWER	MAP	----	----	----	SEE CRAWLEY
CRAWLEY BOTTOM	MAP	----	----	BOTM	BOTTOM OF TURNPIKE HILL 1815
CRAWLEY BRIDGE	MAP	----	----	----	CROWLEY BRIDGE 1781 (50m N of A30)
CRAWLEY COMMON	MAP	----	----	----	SEE CRAWLEY
CRAWLEY DAIRY	MAP	----	----	----	EE CRAWLEY
CRAWLEY FARM	MAP	CRALLEWEYE	1332	----	SEE Chapter 6
CRAWLEY FOUNDRY	MAP	----	1827	----	SEE FOUNDRY FARM
CREWKERNE TURNING	MAP	----	----	----	TITHERLY CROSS 1796
CRUFF	1567	----	----	----	DIALECT - CROFT
CUCKOLDS PIT	MAP	----	----	----	OBSCURE
CULVERFIELD	924	----	----	CULVER	PIDGEON FIELD
CURST CRATE	949	----	----	----	? CROFT (OBSCURE)
C(R)OCKERS MEAD	353	----	----	----	PERS. NM.? NO POTTERY FOUND.
DADELBED	889	----	----	ADDLE ?	OBSCURE - DUNG BED?
DALLEYS	DOC	----	1645	----	PERS. NM. DALLEY ?
DAME SHELLS	1252	----	----	DAMASK	CLOTHLIKE SHELVES
DAWBNEYS MEAD	771	----	----	----	PERS.NM. DAWBNEY 1622
DENEWORTH	DOC	DENFORD	1065	DENU WORTH	VALLEY CLEARING
DENINGS MEAD	524	DENNINGS	1645	----	PERS.NM. DENNING 1604
DEW STILE	259	----	----	----	DEWY STILE
DIRKS	MAP	----	1822	----	PERS.NM.DURK 1731
DOR.B.L.L&C WORKS	MAP	----	----	----	OWNED BT Wm.WHEATON IN 1865
DOTTE	1632	----	----	----	A BOIL (REFERRING TO THE SPRING)
DOWN	1250	----	----	DUN	LEVEL HIGH GROUND
DOWNEND LANE	MAP	----	----	----	REFERS TO BEWLEY DOWN
DRAYTONS MEAD	430	----	----	----	PERS.NM. DRAYTON 1728
DROVE	768	----	----	----	STOCK ROUTE
DUKES CLOSE	856	----	----	----	PERS.NM. DURK? 1731
DUMMETS DOOR	502	----	----	DOR	REFERS TO GATE ONTO BURCHILL COMMON
DUMMETTS	MAP	----	----	----	PERS.NM. DUMMET 1597
DYEHOUSE MEAD	1073	DYEHOUSE	1598	----	SITE OF DYE HOUSE
EALES MEAD	541	----	----	HELDE	SLOPING
EAST FIELD	DOC	----	1582	----	UNIDENTIFIED
EASTCOMBS	DOC	----	1566	----	UNIDENTIFIED
EASTER WAY	1320	----	1582	EOWESTRE	TO THE SHEEPFOLD

*source numbers are from the tithe map

Name	Source*	Earliest Spelling	Year	Possible Origin	Possible Meaning
EASTHAM	DOC	HOSTHAM	1426	----------------	EAST ENCLOSURE
EDENCOTE FARM	MAP	----------------	----	----------------	UNIDENTIFIED
EGG MOOR LANE	MAP	----------------	----	----------------	19th. CENT. NAME
EGGMOOR COMMON	991	EGGEMORE	1155	ECG MOR	EDGE MOOR
ELY PIT	1391	----------------	----	----------------	SEE EALES
ENGLANDS ORCHARD	041	ENGLAND	1582	INLAND	NEXT TO FARM OR PERS.NM. ENGLAND 1613
ERNEST	897	ANESTATHES	1155	AN STAETH	SEE "TRANSPORT"
EVERGRASS FIELD	292	----------------	----	----------------	ALWAYS GRASS
FARTHING	1300	----------------	----	----------------	FURLONG, SEE FURLONG
FARTHING LANE	MAP	----------------	----	----------------	NEXT TO FARTHING, BURRIDGE
FARWAY BRIDGE	DOC	----------------	1600	----------------	REFERS TO FOOT OR PACKHORSE BRIDGE
FARWAY FARM, HIGHER	MAP	FARNEIE	1155	FAER WEG	16th.CENT. LONGHOUSE
FARWAY FARM, LOWER	MAP	----------------	----	----------------	POPULAR WAY
FARWAY MARSH	MAP	FAREWAYE MARSH	1596	----------------	AREA NAME
FENNEY LANE	DOC	----------------	1598	----------------	WET LANE
FERNHAM	MAP	----------------	201	FEARN	FERNY ENCLOSURE (ALSO FEARNEHAYES)
FIELD, LITTLE	DOC	----------------	1598	----------------	UNIDENTIFIED
FISHERNE WELL	DOC	----------------	1582	----------------	OBSCURE - FISH STORE SPRING?
FLAX PLOT	724	----------------	----	----------------	FLAX CROP SITE
FLUDDY PYTT	DOC	FLODYPUT	1422	FLOD	SHEEPWASH? (SEE BLOODY)
FORD CAUSEWAY	DOC	FORD CAUSEY	1601	----------------	AT BEWLEY FARM
FORD FARM	MAP	----------------	----	----------------	SEE FORDWATER, HIGHER
FORD WATER	944	FORDE, LA	1537	FORD	FORD SITE
FORDWATER FARM		----------------	----	----------------	16th. CENT.
FORDWATER FARM, HIGHER	MAP	----------------	----	----------------	EE FORDWATER
FOSSE WAY	MAP	----------------	----	FOSS	DITCH BY THE WAY (SEE WALWAY)
FOUNDRY FARM	MAP	FOUNDRY	1827	----------------	JOHN BONFIELD'S FOUNDRY
FRANKS MEAD	1532	----------------	----	----------------	PERS.NM.?
FREEKS PARKS	412	FREAKES PARKS	1671	----------------	PERS.NM. FREKE 1597, WAS STEWARD
FURLONG, GREAT	120	----------------	----	FURLANG	BLOCK OF STRIPS
FURSEHAM	DOC	----------------	22	FYRS	FURZE ENCLOSURE
GALLYGANDERS PLOTT	1626	----------------	----	GALLY	FIERCE GEESE
GANNETTS MOORE	DOC	----------------	1597	GEMAENE	see GARNSPIT
GARNSPIT ORCHARD	145	GERMANUESPUT	1422	GEMAENE PIT	USED BY THE COMMUNITY
GILLETTS CLOSE	1153	----------------	----	----------------	PERS.NM. GILLET 1614
GILLETTS FARM	MAP	----------------	----	----------------	PERS.NM. GILLET 1614
GILLS	DOC	----------------	1645	----------------	PERS.MN.GILL?
GOATHILL, GREAT	373	GOTEHILL	1582	----------------	GIRT OR GREAT HILL OR GOAT PASTURE
GOLDSMITH'S LANE	MAP	----------------	----	----------------	PERS.NM.GOLDSMITH?
GOSSIPING CLOSE	127	----------------	----	GAT SHIPPEN	OBSCURE. GOAT SHED OR GOD BLESSING
GOZLEFORD	MAP	GOSSEFORD	1598	GOS	GOOSE/GOSLING
GRABHAMS MEAD	817	----------------	----	----------------	PERS.NM. GRABHAM 1603
GREAT CLOSE	DOC	----------------	1598	----------------	UNIDENTIFIED
GREEN LANE	MAP	GREENEWAYE	1582	----------------	SEVERAL IN CHARDSTOCK, DROVE WAYS?
GREEN LANE FARM	MAP	----------------	----	----------------	SEE GREEN LANE
GREENHAMS CLOSE	1009	----------------	----	----------------	DERIVATION NOT KNOWN
GREENHAYS FOOT	MAP	----------------	----	----------------	SEE GREENWAYS FOOT
GREENWAYS FOOT	925	----------------	1598	----------------	END OF GREENWAY
GREGHAMS FARM	MAP	----------------	----	----------------	PERS.NM. GRABHAM? - 1603
GUPPYS MEAD	545	GUPPIES	1645	----------------	PERS.NM. GUPPY 1598
HACK FURZE, LOWER	796	----------------	----	----------------	GORSE FOR FUEL OR FODDER
HADDERS	390	----------------	----	----------------	HEATHER, ADDERS OR COWPATS? SEE HODDERS
HAKES	MAP	HAKE	1427	----------------	PERS.NM. ?
HALEWELL	DOC	----------------	1422	HALE	SECLUDED WELL
HALF MOON	MAP	----------------	----	----------------	REFERS TO SHAPE OF EARTHWORK?
HALFENDALE	603	----------------	----	DAL	HALF PORTION OF MEADOW
HALLBROOKS MEAD	1030	----------------	----	----------------	PERS.NM.? SEE HAYLEBROOK
HALLSHARDS	549	HALLSHORD	1781	----------------	OBSCURE, HOLLOW POTS OR HOARD
HAM MEAD, GREAT	132	----------------	----	HAMM	RIVER LOOP
HAMMOND BREACH	784	----------------	----	----------------	PERS.NM.?
HANDCOCKS, GREAT	450	HANCOCKS WOOD	1582		PERS.NM. HANDCOCK 1599

*source numbers are from the tithe map

Name	Source*	Earliest Spelling	Year	Possible Origin	Possible Meaning
HANGING BACH	11	----------------	----	BAECE	RIDGE WOOD
HARES FARM	MAP ---	----------------	----	----------------	Pers. Nm. HARE 1362
HARESTONE	1130	HAWSTONE	1598	----------------	HOAR (GREY) STONE
HART RIDGE	DOC	HERT RYGGE	1332	HEORT	HART RIDGE
HARVEYS GREAT MEAD	258	----------------	----	----------------	PERS.NM. HERVEY 1425
HASTLEY	4	----------------	----	HAEST	BEECH WOOD
HAUNTLEY PLOT	1275	----------------	----	----------------	SEE HUNTLEY
HAVERLAKE	550	----------------	----	HAEFER	LACU GOAT STREAM
HAVILAND LANE	MAP	----------------	---	HEFIG	HEAVY SOIL
HAWKINS FIELD	273	----------------	----	----------------	PERS.NM. HAWKINS 1653
HAYES, THE	DOC	BEILHEYE	1202	----------------	MOST OF BEWLEY FARM
HAYLEBROOK MEAD	1496	HALEWELL	1422	HEALH	BROOK IN A GULLY
HEADCROFT, SOUTH	662	----------------	----	HEAFOD	CROFT AT HEAD OF STRIPS
HELLIARES MEADE	DOC	----------------	1645	----------------	PERS.NM.OR OCCUPATION, HELLIER?
HERNCROFT, GREAT	705	HURN	1332	HYRNE	CROFT AT CORNER OF STRIPS
HODDERS HILL	391	HURDER	1577	----------------	PERS.NM. HODDER 1651 OR HERDER
HOLDYCHE MEADE	DOC	----------------	1549	----------------	LANDS HELD IN ~~. IN THORNCOMBE PARISH?
HOLE MEAD	810	HOLEWELL	1426	HOLH	MEAD IN A HOLLOW
HOLECROFT	831	----------------	----	HOLH	CROFT IN A HOLLOW
HOLLY FARM	MAP	----------------	----	----------------	CROFT IN A HOLLOW
HOLY CITY	MAP	LA HOLE	1422	HOLH	HOLLOW (CITY refers to deserted village)
HOME FARM	MAP	----------------	----	----------------	HOME FARM OF TYTHERLEIGH MANOR
HOMECLOSE LANE	MAP	----------------	----	----------------	RUNS BY HOME CLOSE, HUNTLEY
HOMELEA FARM	MAP	----------------	----	----------------	MODERN NAME
HONEY HILL	MAP	HONEYELL	1422	HUNIG	STICKY SLOPE
HONEYLANDS	832	HONNEY LEA	1422	----------------	STICKY PASTURE
HOOK	MAP	LA HOCHE	1155	HOC	HOOKED CULTIVATED AREA
HOOK CROSS	1152	HOOKE CROSS	1598	----------------	CROSS ROADS, SOUTH OF HOOK
HOOK FARM	MAP	----------------	----	----------------	See HOOK
HOOK FIELD	DOC	HOKE FEILD	1582	----------------	PRESUMABLY THE COMMON FIELD OF HOOK
HOOK HILL	DOC	HOOKEHILL	1582	----------------	SEE HOOK
HOOK HILL COMMON	MAP	----------------	----	----------------	NOW FIELDS, WAS BY BROCKFIELD
HOOK MILL	MAP	----------------	----	----------------	FLOCK MILL 1822
HOOK PAPER MILL	MAP	----------------	----	----------------	HOOK SOUTH MILL
HOOK POND	MAP	----------------	----	----------------	MILL POND WAS AT S. END OF BURRIDGE COM.
HOOPERS MEAD	146	----------------	1582	----------------	PERS.NM. HOOPER 1609
HOORES	MAP	HURESCOME	1598	HYRSE	MARE'S VALLEY
HOPYARD, OLD	874	----------------	----	----------------	BEER HOPS
HORSE CRATE	1628	----------------	----	----------------	CROFT FOR HORSES
HORSEHORD	549	----------------	----	HORD	? HOARD
HOWCRATE	813	----------------	----	HOH	CROFT ON THE HILL SPUR
HULLS MEAD	867	----------------	----	----------------	PERS.NM. HULL 1787
HUNTLEY 4 ACRES	1304	HUNTLEY FIELD	1426	----------------	SEE HUNTLEY FIELD
HUNTLEY BARN	MAP	HUNTELEGE	1155	----------------	HUNT CLEARING
HUNTLEY FARM	MAP	----------------	----	----------------	FARM AT HUNTLEY
HUNTLEY FIELD	DOC	HUNTLEYFELD	1426	----------------	COMMON FIELD AT HUNTLEY
HUNTLEY LANE	MAP	----------------	1598	----------------	AT HUNTLEY
HUREL CLOSE	1577	HURESCOME	1598	HYRDEL	VALLEY WITH HURDLES
HUSK	923	----------------	----	HYRST	WOODED HILL
HUTCHINS ORCHARD	596	----------------	----	----------------	PERS.NM. HUTCHENS 1667
JAMES CLOSE	1432	----------------	----	----------------	PERS.NM. JAMES 1695
JAMES CLOSE PIT	MAP	----------------	----	----------------	BY JAMES CLOSE
JAMES LANE	MAP	----------------	----	----------------	REASON FOR NAME NOT KNOWN
JAMES LANE	DOC	----------------	1598	----------------	SEE JAMES LANE, CRAWLEY
JAMES LANE CROSS	MAP	----------------	----	----------------	AT THE TOP OF JAMES LANE
JEFFERYS PLOTT	1285	----------------	----	----------------	PERS.NM. JEFFERY 1768
KEATES FARM	MAP	----------------	----	----------------	PERS.NM.KEAT 1671
KILN CLOSE	1128	----------------	----	----------------	LIME KILN
KIT RIVER	MAP	KITTENOFER	1422	OFER	BANK OF THE KIT
KITBEER, GREAT	1465	----------------	----	BEARU	ENCLOSED WOOD NEAR R. KIT
KITBRIDGE	MAP	KYTBRIDGE	1582	----------------	REFERS TO FOOT OR PACKHORSE BRIDGE

* source numbers are from the tithe map

Name	Source*	Earliest Spelling	Year	Possible Origin	Possible Meaning
KITE MOOR	948	KITTEMOR	1422	CYTA	KITE (BIRD)
KNIGHTS HOUSE	DOC	----------------	1598	----------------	PERS.NM.KNIGHT 1711
KNIGHT'S FARM	MAP	----------------	----	----------------	CALLED JUST FARM UNTIL 1822
LADDER STILE	1587	----------------	----	----------------	A TYPE OF STYLE
LADYEHAYE	DOC	----------------	1602	----------------	SEE LIDDYHAYE
LANCE ORCHARD	1530	----------------	----	HLINC	LYNCHET
LANCEND	372	----------------	----	----------------	LYNCHET END
LAND CRATE	892	----------------	----	----------------	CROFT BY THE HEADLAND
LANGDONS	1276	----------------	----	----------------	PERS.NM. LANGDON C19th
LANULETS	1236	----------------	----	----------------	LYNCHETS
LAURENCE CLIFFE	DOC	----------------	1582	----------------	MEANING NOT KNOWN
LEWIS THORN	1226	----------------	----	HLAEW	HILLOCK OR BARROW, THORN
LIDDYHAYE	DOC	----------------	1602	----------------	NEAR GREENWAYS FOOT, SEE LIDGEATE
LIDGEATE	DOC	NEXT TO COMMON	1598	HLID-GEAT	SWING GATE (TO CONTROL CATTLE)
LODGE FARM	MAP	LOGGE	1332	LOGE	TEMPORARY DWELLING
LODGE HOW	1473	----------------	----	----------------	HILL BELONGING TO LODGE
LODGE MILL	MAP	----------------	----	----------------	MILL IN LODGE MANOR
LONGLAND	DOC	GREAT & LITTLE	1598	----------------	STRIPS LONGER THAN USUAL
LOOM CRATE, HIGHER	1590	----------------	----	----------------	CROFT WHERE LOAM WAS DUG
LYDDYE LAKE	DOC	LYDDYE LAKE	1601	HLITH LACU	THE PARK GUTTER
LYNHAY	125	----------------	----	----------------	STORE, POSSIBLY FOR FLAX
MAGS ACRE	999	----------------	----	----------------	PERS.NM. MAGGS 1610
MANLANDS	312	----------------	----	GEMAENE	STRIPS NEXT TO THE COMMON OR BOUNDARY
MARE, GREAT	109	----------------	----	MAERE	BOUNDARY
MARKET WAY	DOC	----------------	1597	----------------	PROBABLY NEAR HUNTLEY
MARKS MEAD, HIGHER	1011	----------------	----	----------------	PERS.NM. MARKES 1651
MARKS OATLEY	1165	----------------	----	----------------	SEE OAKLEY
MARLE PIT, GREAT	1495	----------------	----	----------------	PIT WHERE CHALK MARL WAS DUG
MAYNE PONDE	DOC	MAYNE	1332	GEMAENE	BOUNDARY (was at POOL CLOSE)
MEADHAMS	DOC	MEDHAM	1422	MAED HAMM	RIVER BEND MEADOW
MILL, TUCKING	DOC	TUCKING MILL	1582	----------------	MILL USED FOR FELTING CLOTH
MILL BRIDGE	DOC	----------------	1598	----------------	PROBABLY FOOTBRIDGE BELOW CHARDSTOCK
MILLERS DOWN	607	----------------	----	----------------	PERS.NM. MILLER 1649
MILLERS GREEN COMMON	MAP	----------------	1781	----------------	CRAWLEY MILL
MILLWAY	MAP	----------------	----	----------------	TO THE MILL AT MILWELL
MILLWAY, GREAT	913	----------------	----	----------------	PROBABLY A CORRUPTION OF WILWAY
MILNEHALE	DOC	----------------	1201	MYLEN HALH	MILL HOLLOW, NOW MILLWELL
MILWELL FARM	MAP	----------------	----	----------------	FARM AT MILWELL
MILWELL HILL	442	MILLELL SLADE	1566	----------------	HILL SLOPE ABOVE THE MILL
MINSONS	MAP	----------------	1822	----------------	SEE MINSONS PLATT
MINSONS PLATT	1185	----------------	----	----------------	PERS.NM. MINSON 1695
MONEY PIT LANE	MAP	----------------	----	----------------	AN OLD COIN HOARD FOUND?
MOOR LANE	1151	MOOR, LA	1332	MOR	WET PASTURE
MORE FURLONG	DOC	----------------	1422	FURLANG	BLOCK OF ARABLE STRIPS NEXT TO MOOR
MORLESWOOD	DOC	----------------	1556	MOR LEAH?	WOOD NEXT TO LE MOOR?
MOTWEIA	DOC	----------------	1327	GEMOT	WAY TO THE MEETING PLACE (NR. BURRIDGE ?)
MOW FURLONG	DOC	----------------	1566	MUGA	ARABLE STRIPS USED AS MEADOW
MYRTLE FARM	MAP	----------------	----	----------------	19th.CENT.NAME
NAPPY CLOSE	213	----------------	----	HNAEPP	ANT HILLS
NARFORDS	MAP	----------------	----	----------------	NAME FOR FORD BY COTLEY WASH ?
NELLS, LOWER	849	----------------	----	----------------	PERS.NM.?
NEW HOUSE FARM	MAP	NEWEHAWLLE	1582	HALL	NEW HOUSE
NORTH CROFT	769	----------------	----	----------------	AT NORTH OF THE FARM
NORTHMOOR	1150	NORTHMOR	1545	----------------	MOOR TO NORTH OF VILLAGE
NOSTERS SHELLS	1350	NOTEAYSSHE	1422	SCYLF	PERS.MN. NOSCITER 1636, HIS LYNCHETS
OAKLEY MOOR	117	OCELEGH	1422	AC	OAK WOOD
OAT ARISH	1212	OTELOND	1426	ATE	OAT STUBBLE
OCELGHELIS	DOC	OKELOGHELIS	1422	HLITH	OAK SLOPE BY LODGE
OKELOGHELIS HALEWELL	DOC	----------------	1422	----------------	SECLUDED SPRING NEAR OKELOGHELIS
OLDELAND FURLONG	DOC	THE OLDELAND	1422	----------------	OLD ARABLE (STRIPS)
OSMOOR (IN DENEWORTHY)	DOC	OSMER	1332	MOR	PERS. NM. OSINERE (HAWK KEEPER) MOOR

*source numbers are from the tithe map

Name	Source*	Earliest Spelling	Year	Possible Origin	Possible Meaning
OVERLEAZE	137	OVYLOND	1422	----	FORMER MANORIAL STRIPS
OXEN LEAZE	287	----	----	----	GRAZING STRIPS FOR OXEN
PADDLE	508	----	----	----	PADDLE SHAPED (CURVED)
PARADISE	557	----	----	----	WET OR UNPLEASANT
PARADISE HILL	MAP	----	1781	----	MEANING A HIGH PLACE?
PARISH MEAD	878	----	----	----	FOR SUPPORT OF NEEDY
PARK, GREAT	405	PARROKE	1317	PEARRUC	DEER PARK
PARKS	MAP	----	----	----	PARK, NOW SUB-DIVIDED
PARKS, OLD	DOC	OLDER PARK CLOSE	1566	----	THE OLDER PARK ON STORRIDGE HILL
PARKWEYE	DOC	----	1422	----	UNLOCATED
PARSONAGE	DOC	PARSONAGE HOUSE	1598	----	NOW THE OLD VICARAGE
PARSONAGE LAND	DOC	PARSONNES HAM	1598	----	PARSON'S LAND NEXT TO RIVER
PASSCROFT	226	PESECROFTE	1422	PISE	CROFT FOR PEAS
PEARCES MEAD	982	----	----	----	PERS.NM. PEARCE 1497
PETERS CLOSE	1407	----	----	----	PERS. NM.?
PINNEYS CLOSE	864	----	----	----	PERS.NM. PINNEY 1497
PITCHERS CLOSE	175	PICHES	1645	----	PERS.NM. PITCHER 1607
PLAISTERS, HIGHER	1297	----	----	PLEG STOW	SPORTS AREA
PLATT	875	----	----	PLAT	PLOT
POLDONS	DOC	POLDONS HOUSE	1598	----	PERS.NM.?
POOL CLOSE	20	POLDONE	1645	POL	POND
POTTERS MEAD	1209	----	----	----	PERS.NM. POTTER 1741
PREBENDAL MANSION	DOC	----	1646	----	TURNED INTO A BARN, NOW DEMOLISHED
PROUTLEY	801	PROUTE	1332	PRUT	PERS.NM. PROUTE 1340
PUDISHAYS	DOC	PURDYES HAY	1604	----	PERS.NM.
RACHAELS PLOT	1288	----	----	----	PERS.NM.?
RACK CLOSE	737	----	----	----	CLOTH STRETCHING RACKS, SEE COAXDON MILL
RAG, LONG	1176	----	----	----	LONG NARROW FIELD, TEMPORARY WAY
RANSOMES FARM	MAP	----	----	----	RANSOME'S FARM
RANSOMS PARKS	402	----	----	----	PERS.NM. RANSOME 1676
READS HILL FARM	MAP	----	----	----	REDSHILL 1822
RED LANE	MAP	----	1603	----	RED - REASON UNCERTAIN
REW, HIGHER LONG	1157	LONG REWE	1582	RUH	ROUGH
REXEY CLOSE	1512	----	----	REX	REEDY
RIDGE	MAP	LA RIGGE	1155	HRYCG	RIDGE
RIDGE, HIGHER	MAP	----	1822	----	FARM AT RIDGE
RIDGE, LOWER	MAP	----	----	----	FARM AT RIDGE
RIDGE HILL	MAP	RUDGHILL	1582	----	SEE RIDGE
RIDGE HILL FARM	MAP	----	----	----	FARM AT RIDGE
RIDGEHAY	1267	RUDGEHAIES	1582	----	ENCLOSURE BELONGING TO RIDGE FARM
RIDING, GREAT	806	----	----	RYDING	CLEARED WOODLAND
RIDLEY	590	----	----	RYDING	CLEARING
RIGLEY LANE	MAP	----	----	----	PROBABLY CORRUPTION OF RIDLEY
ROCKEY	DOC	----	1599	----	LARGE STONES
ROUNDABOUT CLOSE	1338	----	----	----	CIRCULAR FEATURE
ROWLEY	902	----	----	RUH	ROUGH CLEARING
ROWS ARRISH	581	----	----	RAW	RIDGED FORMER ARABLE
RUDS, GREAT	807	----	----	----	UNCERTAIN
RYELANDS, GREAT	129	RYCROFT	1582	RYGE	STRIPS USED FOR RYE
SALISBURY PLAIN	275	----	----	----	LAND BELONGING TO THE BISHOP
SALT CLOSE	25	----	----	----	DAISY FIELD? SALT ROUTE?
SALTCOMBE	DOC	SELCOMBE MOORE	1582	SALH	SALLOW TREES
SALTERN VERN	735	SALTERNFEARNE	1598	AERN	SALT HOUSE FERN? ASH FOR SOAP MAKING?
SANDFORD FARM	MAP	----	----	----	PERS.NM. SAMFORD 1569
SANSOMS KNAP	MAP	----	1822	----	BY SANSOMS MEAD
SANSOMS MEAD	553	----	----	----	PERS.NM. SANSOM 1636
SAWPIT PLOT	747	----	----	----	SAWING PIT
SCORES	1317	----	----	----	OBSCURE
SEALS MOOR	133	----	----	SALH	SALLOW TREES
SEAMANS	DOC	----	1645	----	PERS.NM.?
SEEDY CLOSE	19	----	----	----	"SEED" CROP eg. TURNIPS

*source numbers are from the tithe map

Name	Source*	Earliest Spelling	Year	Possible Origin	Possible Meaning
SELAH	MAP	------------	----	------------	
SELLWOODS	DOC	------------	1645	------------	PERS.NM.?
SERRYES	DOC	------------	1645	------------	PERS.NM.?
SEYMOURS CLOSE	957	------------	----	------------	PERS.NM.?
SHARKS HOLE	490	CHATTESHOLE	1422	------------	DEMON'S HOLLOW, ALSO SEE CHURCHILL
SHEEPLANDS	1120	------------	----	SCEAP	STRIPS USED FOR SHEEP PASTURE
SHOOLS	968	------------	----	SCOFL	SHOVEL SHAPED STRIPS
SHORT LANDS	1411	------------	----	SCEAT	GROUP OF SHORT STRIPS (FURLONG)
SHUTES	562	------------	----	SHOTTS	STRIPS
SLADELAND	1633	SLADE, LA	1422	SLAED	GRAZED HEADLANDS
SMALLRIDGE	MAP	SMARIGE	1086	SMAEL HRYCG	NARROW RIDGE
SNIPES	198	------------	----	SNAEP	BOGS
SOLMEDE	DOC	------------	1426	SOL	MUDDY MEADOW
SOPERS MEAD	1147	------------	----	------------	PERS.NM. SOPER 1626
SOUTH COMMON	MAP	------------	1781	------------	COMMON IN THE SOUTH OF THE PARISH
SPEEDS	DOC	------------	1645	------------	PERS.NM.SPEED 1545
SPIRL OR SPARL	DOC	SPILLERS PITT	1598	SPELL SPEACH	MAKING PLACE
STAKE GATE	704	------------	----	------------	TEMPORARY GATE
STANLEY MEAD	1633	STAMERLEGE	1155	STAN MOR LEAH	STONE MOOR WOOD
STAPLEWAY	1335	FURLONG	----	------------	WAY BY A LARGE STONE
START CLOSE, HIGHER	1479	------------	----	STEORT	CLOSE ON THE END OF THE HILL
STARVE ACRE	346	------------	----	------------	POOR LAND
STATVERS, HIGHER	513	------------	----	STOTT	YOUNG CATTLE
STEALE LANE	DOC	------------	1598	STIGOL	STEEP WAY
STEVENS FARM	MAP	------------	----	------------	PERS.NM.STEPHENS 1425
STOCKSTYLE FARM	MAP	------------	----	STOC STIGOL	CHARDSTOCK'S STEEP PATH
STOP COPSE	MAP	------------	----	------------	CORRUPTION OF BRINS TOP - SEE BRIMLAND
STOREAGE HILL	920	STORIGE	1426	STEORT HILL	AT THE END OF THE RIDGE
STORRIDGE HILL	MAP	------------	----	------------	SEE STOREAGE
STORRIDGE LANE	MAP	------------	----	------------	LANE ON STORRIDGE HILL
STOUT	507	------------	1598	STOUT	BULGING
STOWTE BEACON	DOC	------------	1781	------------	BEACON IN THE AREA CALLED STOUT
STRAP, LONG	612	------------	----	STRAP STRAP	SHAPED
STREET ORCHARD		STRETE ORCHARD	1422	STREYT/STRAET	STRAIGHT ORCHARD OR ON A STREET
STRONGS	MAP	------------	----	------------	PERS.NM.STRONG
STRONGS MEAD	574	------------	----	------------	PERS.NM. STRONG 1596
STUBBYMEDE	DOC	------------	1422	STUBB	MEADOW HAVING TREE STUMPS
SYCAMORE	MAP	SECCOMBE MOORE	1582	SECG	SEDGE VALLEY
SYCAMORE FARM	MAP	------------	----	------------	FARM AT SYCAMORE
SYMES MOOR	1015	------------	----	------------	PERS.NM. SYMES 1606
TANSEY CLOSE	3	------------	----	------------	TANSY CROP?
TEN ACRE GATE	MAP	------------	1598	------------	GATE ONTO COMMON LAND BY TEN ACRE FIELD
TERFMOOR	27	------------	----	------------	TURVES FOR FUEL
THISTLEFIELD	DOC	------------	1645	------------	COMMON FIELD, LOCATION NOT KNOWN
THOSHAM	DOC	------------	1422	------------	LOCATION OR MEANING UNKNOWN
THOUSAND ACRES	1088	------------	----	------------	VERY SMALL FIELD
THREE COUNTIES TREE	MAP	------------	1781	------------	TREE WHERE 3 COUNTIES MET
TILLYE LANE	DOC	------------	1600	------------	TYTHERLEIGH?
TIN MEAD	604	------------	----	TINDING	RECLAIMED LAND
TIN MOOR	MAP	------------	1781	------------	SEE TIN MEAD
TITHERLY COMMON	MAP	------------	----	------------	1796 TAYLOR MAP
TOLLERS MEAD	585	------------	----	------------	PERS.NM. TOLOR 1525
TOMS WOOD, GREAT	169	------------	----	------------	ERS.NM.?
TOTERYGG	DOC	------------	1327	BEACN/TOOT	SIGHTING POINT/LOOKOUT HILL
TOWNSEND	DOC	------------	1582	------------	END OF CHARDSTOCK TOWN
TRIANGLE	MAP	------------	----	------------	TRIANGULAR AREA MADE BY INCLOSURE ROADS
TURNERS LANE CLOSE	1002	------------	----	------------	PERS.NM. TURNER 1425
TWIST	MAP	LA TWYSTE	1280	------------	TURNING OR DIVIDED VALLEY
TWIST, OLD	MAP	------------	----	------------	See TWIST
TYDERLY MEADE	DOC	TYDERLY BROADMEAD	1608	------------	COMMON MEAD FOR TYTHERLEIGH MANOR
TYTHERLEIGH	MAP	TIDERLEGE	1155	TIEDRE	THIN OR COPPICE WOOD
TYTHERLEIGH FARM	MAP	------------	----	------------	FARM IN TYTHERLEIGH

* source numbers are from the tithe map

Name	Source*	Earliest Spelling	Year	Possible Origin	Possible Meaning
TYTHERLEIGH FARM, LOWER	MAP	----------------	----	----------------	FARM IN TYTHERLEIGH
TYTHERLEIGH GREEN	MAP	----------------	1781	----------------	COMMON AREA IN THE CENTRE OF TYTHERLEIGH
TYTHERLEIGH GREEN	872	----------------	----	----------------	COMMON AREA IN THE CENTRE OF TYTHERLEIGH
TYTHERLEY FEILDE	DOC	GORSGOE	1582	----------------	COMMON FIELD FOR TYTHERLEIGH MANOR
TYTHERLEY WOOD	DOC	----------------	1582	----------------	SEE THTHERLEIGH
UPHAYE FARM	MAP	----------------	----	----------------	NO EARLY REFERENCE
VERN CRATE	1640	----------------	----	FEARN	CROFT OVERGROWN WITH BRACKEN
VERNHAYS/VENNHAYS	1284	VERNEHAY	1645	----------------	ENCLOSED PASTURE WITH BRACKEN
VICARAGE	DOC	----------------	1645	----------------	SEE PARSONAGE
VINES CLOSE, LONG	474	----------------	----	----------------	HOPS CROP?
VINEYARD	MAP	----------------	----	----------------	HOPS CROP?
VINNEYS, HIGHER	493	----------------	----	----------------	POSSIBLY PERS.NM. VYNE 1624
VOLSCOMBE	200	FUGELSCOMBE	1201	FUGOL	BIRDS' VALLEY
WADHAMS	918	----------------	----	----------------	PERS.NM. WADHAM 1450
WAGGS PLOT	MAP	----------------	----	----------------	PERS.NM. WAGG 1405
WAITHILL	917	WATELAND	1423	----------------	OBSCURE, WAYED (FOSSE/WALWAY)?
WALCROFTS	MAP	WALLCRATE	1582	----------------	UNCERTAIN
WALL, OLD	27	----------------	----	----------------	DERIVATION UNKNOWN
WALLAGE PLOT	851	WALWAYES PLOT	1598	WALLAGE	WITHY CROP & ADJACENT TO WALWAY
WALLCRATE, GREAT	1615	----------------	----	----------------	WALLED CROFT
WALLEY WOOD	941	----------------	----	----------------	SEE WILWAY & SEE "TRANSPORT"
WALLIS WOOD	DOC	----------------	1645	----------------	SEE WILWAY & SEE "TRANSPORT"
WARE ACRE	843	WARETON	1426	WAER	WIER ON THE R. AXE
WARRYS CLOSE	1311	----------------	----	----------------	PERS.NM. WARRY 1652
WASGILL MEAD	593	----------------	----	WASE	MUD DITCH
WATER	DOC	----------------	1422	----------------	LOCATION POSSIBLY BELOW BEWLEY FARM
WDEMUL	DOC	----------------	1155	----------------	MILL OF OR BY WOOD
WEILDS	110	----------------	----	WEALD?	WOODED
WELTCHES	DOC	----------------	1645	----------------	PERS.NM.WALSH 1422
WESTLEIGH	834	----------------	----	----------------	WEST GRAZING AREA
WESTOFERS MEADE	DOC	WESTOFERS MEADE	1598	----------------	PERS.NM.WESTOVER 1525
WHITE HILL	1527	----------------	----	----------------	DESCRIPTIVE, DAISIES?
WHITE MOOR	1601	----------------	----	----------------	DESCRIPTIVE, COTTON GRASS?
WHITEHALL	MAP	----------------	----	----------------	POSSIBLY A RECENT NAME
WHITEHOUSE	MAP	----------------	1598	----------------	WHITE APPEARANCE OR A DAIRY?
WHITES PLOT	786	----------------	----	----------------	PERS.NM. WHITE 1608
WIATTS 2 ACRES	1237	----------------	----	----------------	PERS.NM. WIAT 1525
WILLIS	1256	----------------	----	WITHIG	WITHIES CROP
WILLS OATLEY	1164	----------------	----	----------------	PERS.NM. WILLS 1597
WILMOTS CLOSE	214	----------------	----	----------------	PERS.NM. WILMOTT 1760
WILWAY	915	WALWAYS PLOT	1598	WEALA	WAY OF THE BRITISH
WISK ORCHARD	377	WISEMEAD	1598	WISCE	MARSHY
WITHAM BALL, GREAT	1422	----------------	----	----------------	POSSIBLY, WHITE ISOLATED PIT
WITHY BEER	933	----------------	----	----------------	WITHY PATCH
WITHY PITTS	1127	----------------	1566	----------------	PITS USED TO GROW WITHIES
WOLLMYNGTON COURT	DOC	ALSTON	1598	----------------	OWNED BY WILMINGTON
WOLMINGTON MORE	DOC	----------------	1582	----------------	PROBABLY BELOW WOONTON FARM.
WOODEYESSE	DOC	WOODOVESSE	1582	EVESE	WOOD EDGE, AT THE EDGE OF PARKS
WOODGROVE	1261	----------------	----	GRAV	MALL COPPICED WOOD
WOODHILLS	857	----------------	----	----------------	COPPICE SPAR COCKS
WOODWARDS PARKS	1109	----------------	----	----------------	PERS.NM. WOODWARD 1738
WOONTON FARM	MAP	WILMINTUNA	1155	WULFHELMINGTUN	WULFHELM'S PRINCIPAL FARM
WORSTHAMS	1014	----------------	----	----------------	WEST ENCLOSURES
WYETTS	DOC	----------------	1645	----------------	PERS.NM.WIATT 1525
YARD FARM	MAP	YGERD	1332	GEARD	YARD
YARD MOOR	DOC	YEARD MOORE	1612	----------------	MOOR BELONGING TO YARD FARM

APPENDIX D - A COMMON FIELD AT ALSTON

No early maps or detailed documents have been found to support the fieldwork evidence of a former common field attached to Alston. Chubbs Farm seems to lie in the nucleus of the settlement. To the south, this settlement has spread onto the former arable strips. The boundary of the field to the west of Alston seem to be still clearly marked by footpaths, tracks or watercourses. Maps 16 and 17 show the field as it possibly was in the 12 - 13th. Centuries and as it is now. The tenants of 1781 are given below. It can be seen that the dispersed pattern of strip holdings still survived then, although hedged. The side table on map 16 shows that there are repeating patterns of tenants in the three north / south orientated furlongs. It is not known whether this reflects the original pattern of strip holdings at some time, but a similar effect has been seen at Tatworth where an early map does survive (see Carter R and Downes T, Tatworth Middle Field, Chard History Group, 1996).

The following details of tenants are as given in the Henley survey of 1781.

C	John Amor Jr. - formerly Dennings, late Warry, held with Tollers at Churchill.
D	Mary Burd - late Coombs or Hills, at Alston.
F	Richard Chard - formerly Bowditches, called Alston.
Z	(east) Moses Leaves (cottages).
Z	(west) Mary Harvey.
3C	Ealenor Briggs - late Knights at Alston.
3I	Adam Culverwell - Birchill.
3Q	Hannah Bond - once Tucker, once Chris. Bond, Darkes House.
3R	James Hoare - of Strongs.
3S	Elizabeth - now Chapmans wife.
3T	Sarah Wills (widow) - part Shutes.
(1)	Sometime Turners or Tinners.
(2)	Millers Hay.
(3)	Sometime Guppy's.

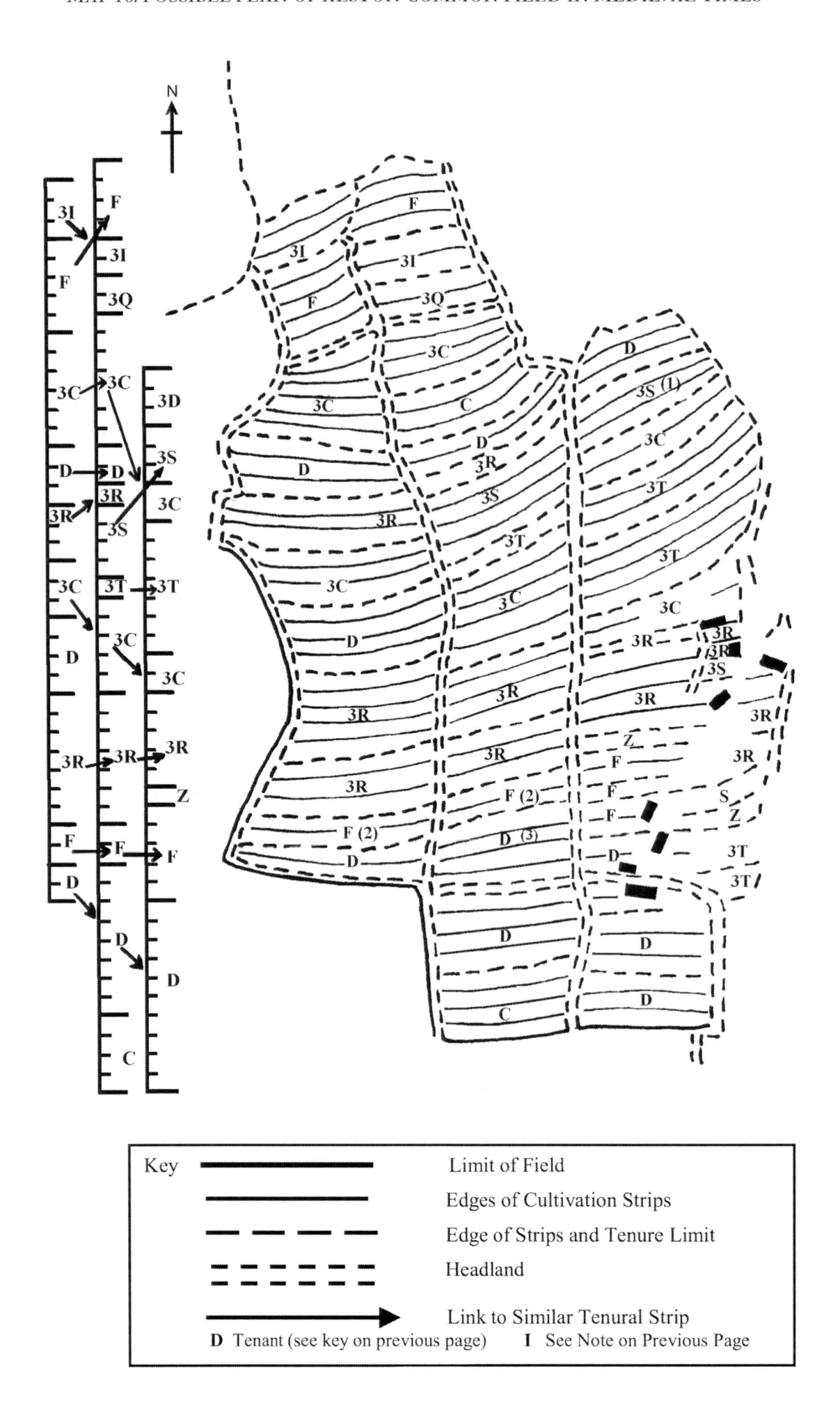

MAP 16. POSSIBLE PLAN OF ALSTON COMMON FIELD IN MEDIEVAL TIMES

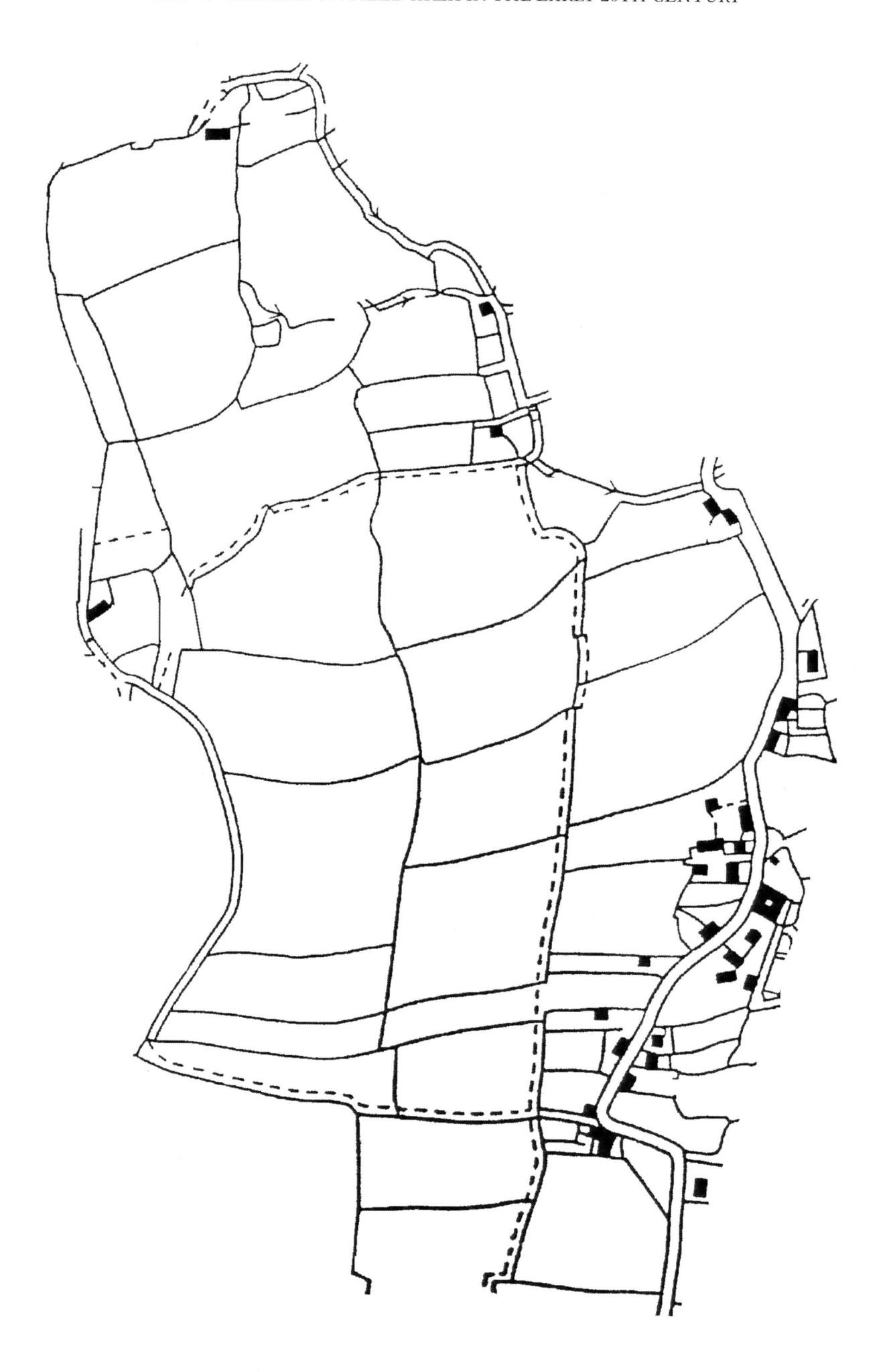

MAP 17. THE ALSTON FIELD AREA IN THE EARLY 20TH CENTURY

APPENDIX E - LISTS OF PREBENDARIES, VICARS AND CURATES

Date	Prebendary
c.1214	Abraham de Winton
c.1226	G. de Sandford
c.1284	Henry de Esse, Canon
?1309	William de Chaddleshunt, Archdeacon of Wilts.
?-1336	Raterius de Miro Monte
?1336	John Piers (filius Petri)
1348	John de Mota
1350	John Goghe
1352	Martin Monlyshe
?-1373	William de Osmundeston
1373	John Cheyne (died 1406)
1389	Richard Felde
1402	William Glym
1406	John Haket
1406	John Bathe
1415	William Werkeman, Rector of Stourton
?1426	Richard Caudray
1430	William Bothe, Archdeacon of Middlesex
1439	Stephen Booth
1441	Stephan Wilton, Archdeacon of Sarum
1442	George Nevyll, 11 year old son of the Earl of Salisbury
1457	John Lax, Private Sec. to Pope Calixtus III
?-1464	John Walbrond
1464	Robert Stillington
1474	Leyson Geffray
1475	John Dogett
1481	William Sheriff
?-1486	Ralph Heathcott
1486	Christopher Bainbridge, Cardinal Priest 1505
1489	Thomas Maddes
1501	John Hobbull, Canon
1505	Christopher Twyneho, Canon
1507	Edward Higgins
1509	Thomas Martyn, Canon
1515	Edward Finch, Archdeacon of Wilts.
1517	John Stone
1524	John Pinnock
1537	Robert Bysse
1546	Innocent Reade
1564	Robert Hooper, Rector of Fyfield
1570	Edward Dering
1576	John Swone
1613	William Osborne, Canon
1660	William Payne
1689	Robert Pierce, Rector of N. Tidworth
1707	Charles Wroughton, Rector of Codford St. Peter
1728	Richard Hele, Vicar of Britford
1756	Edward Blake, Vicar of St. Thomas', Sarum
1765	John King
1770	John Huish
1802	Edward Tew
1818	Henry Woodcock, Canon of Christchurch
1841	Hon. Charles. A. Harris, Bishop of Gibraltar 1868
1863	John Wilkinson, Rector of Broughton Gifforde
1876	John Duncan, Vicar of Calne 1865
1907	Robert C. Abbott
1913	The Venerable Eric J. Bodington
1930	E. C. Eddrupp, Vicar of Corfe Mullen
1961	George B. Gerrish
1965	John P. Hinton, Rector of Bridport
1975	P. Roberts, Rector of Dorchester
1989	(to 2004) Christopher Bryant, Vicar of Devizes
2009	Canon Harold Stephens, Rector of Dorchester Team Ministry
2012	Canon David Seymour, Vicar of Sturminster Newton

Date	Vicar
-1286	William Briton
1297	Canon William de Cerdestok
1309	William de Stratton
1318	William Dave
1321	Thomas de Axminster
1332	Thomas (again?)
?1338	Henry le Clerk
1348	James Tolie
1348	Ralph Ayshonere
1351	Richard de Weston
1361	William Gregori
1361	William Michell
1405	Roger Berewike
1420	John Berkhamsted
1429	William Weston
1461	Nicholas Kymer
1479	Walter Barbour
1481	Robert Wyot
1519	Thomas Hobbut
1546	John Cryche
1578	Thomas Barkesdale
1583	Thomas Carter
1585	William Carter
1591	William Carter
1597	Richard White
1628	Jolm Pitt
1645	James Strong (Pastor)
1648	Richard Morse (Minister)
1650	William Collman (Minister)
1654	Benjamin Mills
1661	Richard Luce
1669	James Keate
1705	John Drayton
1716	Thomas Prydanl
1717	John Gould
1729	George Balllpton
1731	William Goodenough
1734	Richard Hele
1769	Robert Stevens
1807	Thomas Carter
1830	Elborough Woodcock
1834	Charles Woodcock
1875	George H. P. Barlow
1883	Francis Parham
1906	Arthur Lewis
1919	Bishop Albert E. Jocelyne
1930	Samuel M. Whitwell
1937	John A. Furguson
1945	Leonard J. Medway
1952	Robert C. Westall
1958	Robert K. Roper
1964	Alan D. Murray
1968	William G. Revill
1970	Jolm W. F. Hamblen
1978	Henry C. O. Tate
1982	The Revd. Barrie Swift, Team Rector, Axminster Team
1983	Chardstock became part of the Axminster Team, and the title of Vicar of Chardstock became obsolete.

Date	Team Vicar in Chardstock
1983	Adrian S. Mason
1987	Geoffrey M. Walsh
1992	Anthony J. Ashwell
1996	Ruth Waring
2006	Judith Roberts (became Judith Abbott)

Date	Associate Priest in Chardstock
2014	Geoffrey M. Walsh (not resident)

Date	Curate
1769	William Palmer
1806 - 12	William Liddon
1814	A. Tucker
1820s	Thomas Babb
1823 - 29	J. C. Fanshawe
1829 - 34	Fortescue Todd
1906	William Lidden
1996 - 2004	Roger Waring (Hon. Curate)

Drawing by Frances Parry Woodcock, niece of the Vicar, in 1855 before the major rebuilding of the church in 1864

APPENDIX F - PERAMBULATION OF THE W AND NW BOUNDS IN 1672

Memorandum the 14 day of May 1672 there was a perambulation or a visiting of the Western and Northwestern bounds of this parish of Chardstoke by the Vicar and divers others the parishioners.

The Bounds against Membury are in Mr Leggs Eastcombes ten foote from the ditch where there is now a stone standing in which place formerly stood a thorne, and afterwards the bounds are in a ground called Greyditch ten foote from the banke into the said ground, and where the banke ends ten foote from the ditch, and onwards Northwest from Chelhanger gate the bounds passe into a ground belonging to Mr Daubreyes tenement ten foote within the ditch, and afterwards the bounds passe Northwestward upon Bealy downe along by the hedge of downe end tenement which hedge is in Membury parish.

And afterwards against wambrooke the bounds are at the utmost corner of Bealy farme next Deereham upon Bealydowne, where there is crosse cutt in the ground by the hedge and a stone pitcht into it, and from thence the bounds go Eastward upon the down by a ridge of stones, and so to a little stone burrow in the middle of the rode going to Crawley where there is another cross cutt in the earth, and from thence Northeastward to a marke of some stones upon top of the hill at the south side of the enclosure where one Tristram Warren once enclosed, and from thence down to a little stone burrow on the North side of a little path below the ground that Thomas Guppy Enclosed, and from thence Eastward to another stone burrow a little beyond the greene, and then presently to another stone burrow upon the top of Woollforne hill, & from thence down the hill to the corner of the wall of Bremellcombe ground to the great pitt.

	Thomas Vincent aged 62	William Warry
	William Fippin aged 78	Richard Turner
James Keate Vicar	John Welsh aged 56	Joseph Rampson
	Richard Keate	Henry Atwell
	Giles Bagwell	
		cum multis aliis

Source
Chardstock Parish Registers, Dev. R.O. 2590 A/PR2 Microfiche 2,3.

APPENDIX G - SOME OCCUPATIONS (PROFESSIONS AND TRADESMEN)

c.1700
Engraver	Phillipp Levermore
Physician	Richard Stoodley
Parish Clerk	Francis Morley

c.1780
Carpenter	William Long, Simon Larcombe, William Tucker, William Symes, John, Robert, William & Thomas Apsey, James Abbott, Thomas Trott, George Perham, John & Robert Seaward, Robert Harris, Timothy Morrey, Humphrey Long.
Cordwainer	John Searle, Robert Carter, Thomas Pearce, Joseph Seager, Robert Cook, Robert Manley, John Cousins, Thomas Deem, Edward Batstone, Joseph Crabb, William Forsey, Joel Showers.
Blacksmith	John Welch, Thomas Ellett, Thomas Banfield, David Bondfield, James Dening.
Taylor	Thomas & John Carter, William Roe.
Sheerman	Luke Pike.
Thatcher	John & Christopher Bond, John Turner.
Baker	Robert Paine.
Miller	John Leat, John Bunstone, John Helliar, Daniel Board.
Cooper	William Bond.
Shoemaker	Joseph Searle.
Papermaker	Richard Rose.
Basketmaker	William & James Newberry.
Weaver	John Hutchins, Giles Gregory, Samuel Keetch.
Woolbreaker	Henry Harvey.
Cloth Worker	Robert Plyor, William Hutchins, Moses & Thomas Forsey, William Keetch.
Surveyor	William Bond.
Sergemaker	John & Joel Bowring.
Mason	John Parris.

c.1820 (by proportion)
Labourers 37%
Dairymen 14
Farmers 10
Yeomen 6
Butchers 4
Thatchers 4
Miscellaneous 25

c.1820
Butcher	Humphrey Long, Robert Hayes, Robert Knight, Moses & John Forsey, Richard Turner.
Thatcher	John & Richard & William Turner, Richard Cook, Henry Dimond.
Baker	Robert Norman, George Welch, Jacob Larcombe.
Surveyor	William Pickering.
Soldier	Jacob Larcombe, Henry Burn, Thomas Denziloe.
Shoemaker	Richard Tutcher, John Deem, George Seagar, Samuel Dare (Tyth.), James Newberry (S.Common), William Chick (Grabhams), Alexander Mose.
Huntsman	Joseph Parsons (Cotley).
Sawyer	William Morey.
Blacksmith	Thomas Ellett, John Bowyer (Tyth.), Lawrence White.
Publican	John Young.
Victualler	John Miller (Tyth. Inn), John Apsey.
Carpenter	Robert Apsey, Jacob Perring, Samuel & William Searle, George Morley, Carolus Smith, William Keetch, Luke Seaward, Robert Harris.
Wheelwright	William Keetch, William Colling (Stockstyle), Thomas Charles.
Cooper	John Parris, Thomas Chappel.
Mason	Simeon Tucker (Cuckolds Pit), Francis Pearce.
Threadspinner	David Wakeley, John Rockett, Robert Pinney.
Cordwainer	Richard Tucker, William Newberry, Robert Summers (Furnham).
Miller	John Collyer, Thomas Guppy, Francis Dawe (Sandford).
Clerk	Andrew Tucker, Charles Fanshawe.
Tailor	John Domett (Farway Marsh), John Virgin.
Flaxspinner	Joseph Apsey (ex. Thorncombe).
Flaxdresser	Joseph Vivian.
Basketmaker	Amos Newberry (Fordwater).
Governor of Workhouse	James Perring.
Ropemaker	Robert Pinney, John Beer (Farway Marsh).
Schoolmaster	Malachi Dening.
Gamekeeper	John Fowler.
Shopkeeper	Isaac Wills (Alston), Richard Drayton.
Curate	Fortescue Todd.

c.1850

Surveyor	Robert Bondfield.
Blacksmith	John & William Bowyer, Thomas & John Ellett (Alston), Abraham Bonfield.
Miller	James Chard, Simeon Long, George Dawe (Coxdon), Thomas Habway (& a Baker), Thomas Dyer (Lodge), Robert Hallett, William Turner, James Eames (Hook), Arthur Zeally, James Lock (Lodge), Alfred King (Lodge), Abraham Bevis (Hook).
Shopkeeper	Bridget Deane, Charles Causley, Robert Deane, Robert Deem, Richard Long, Richard Larcombe.
Shoemaker	Robert Deane, George Turner, William Bond.
Tailor	Jonathan Kibly, John Virgin, Henry Parsons, John Domett, Joseph Parris, George Bearsley.
Publican	John Miller (King's Arms), John Hobbs (Alston), Abraham Follett (King's Arms), William Wiscombe (George Inn), Thomas Parris (George Inn).
Cooper	Joseph & John Parris.
Bricklayer	Samuel Pearce.
Butcher	Robert Pope, William Ellett (Alston), Thomas Forsey, Charles Pratt.
Carpenter & Wheelwright	Luke Seaward Thomas Parris, Azariah Elswood, John Perryman.
Horsedealer	Thomas Selwood, William Carter.
Grocer & Draper	William Sumption, William French (& Postmaster).
Mason	Simeon Tucker, Robert Somers.
Carrier	John Parris.
Ironfounder	John Bonfield.
Registrar & Tax collector	Robert Bonfield, John Baker.
Clerk & Grocer	Robert Deem.
Thatcher	Henry & John Diment, Robert Hull.
Carpenter	Giles & James Gregory, William Pearce, Walter Watts, James Manfield.
Milliner & Dressmaker	Eliza Hallett.
Limeburner	John & Thomas Hunt, John Grubham, William Wheaton.
Confectioner	Elias Miller.
Seedsman	George Morey.
Stonemason	Eli Trott, Eli & Luke Tucker.
Grocer	Elias White, John Woodmelish, Anna Wills (Alston).
Clock & Watchmaker	James Drayton.
Basketmaker	Amos & Thomas & Simon & Soloman Newbury,
Surgeon	John Wills (Coaxdon Hall).
Flaxdresser	Joseph Corr.
Straw Chair, Beehive maker	Nicholas Phippen.
Dressmaker	Caroline Seward.
Shoemaker & Parish Clerk	Robert Deem Snr.
Appletree grower	John Denning.
Threshing machines	Thomas Parris & Sons.
Poultry Dealer	Emmanuel Parris.
Book Binder	George Beale.
Road Contractor	Thomas Pearce, George Perham.

INDEX

Main references only are listed; there may be further references on adjacent pages.
Page numbers in italics indicate plates.

Accounts, Account Rolls	7 16
Ale houses	83
Allotments	37
All Saints	10
All Saints School	50
All Saints Church	57 *109*
Alston	6 7
Alston Common Field	131
Amateur Dramatics – see CADS	
Anti-aircraft gun battery	99
Apprentices	73
Arms and Soldiers	62
Army Cadet Force	103 *109*
ARP Wardens	95 98
Axe Farm	39
Axe, River	4
Babb, Rev Thomas	*i*
Battleford	39 111
Beacon Hill	4 93 97
Bells, church	54 55 *59*
Bewley Down	4 6 7 22 44
Bewley Down School	49
Bewley Farm	1 38 *107*
Black Death	93
Blacksmiths	29 31
Bonds Cottage, Burridge	111
Bonfield family	29 31
Boot Club	78
Bounds Lane	4 5
Bowling Club	100
Bowditch	19 *21* 87
Bricks, brick-making, tiles	4 26 32
Bridge Meadow, Crawley	111
Bridges	23 24 25 64
Briefs	81
Brockfield	16
Bronze Age	4 5 34 93
Broom Crossing	1 24
Burridge –see Bowditch	
Burridge Common	27 31
Burridge Farm	39
Burridge Pound	111
By-ways	22
CADS	100
Canals	24
Cello	*63*
Charcoal burning	16
Chardstock, Civil Parish	10
Chardstock, origin of name	6
Chardstock Court	44 111
Charities	70 79
Chubb's farm	38
Church, early	*i* 7 44 52 58 *59* *63* 135
Church, new	53 *63*
Church, All Saints – see All Saints Church	
Churchill Farm	40 112

Churchyard	56
Cider making	16 37
Civil Court – see Manor Court	
Civil War	8
Cleeve Farm	38
Clockmaking	31
Clothing Club	78
Clubs	78 100
Coaches	24
Coal Club	78
Coaxden	20 *21* 31 *33* 39
Coaxden Manor	111
Cold Harbour – see Bounds Lane	
Commons	14 36
Community Hall	00
Construction, of buildings	44
Copyhold	12
Cotley	19 *21* 39 *43* 112
Cotley Harriers	101
Cotley Hunt Races	101
Cotley Wash	*117*
Council Houses	106
Court Farm	38
Court – see Manor Court	
Crawley	6 10 *21* 23 31 39
Cricket Club	101
Cuckolds Pit	*110*
Curates	134
Customs of the Manor	12
Dame Schools	49
Deer – see Parks	
Denning, Eliezor	91
D'Ewes family	20 86
Domesday Book	6 34
Dumnonii	4 93
Durotriges	4 93
Eames family	19
Early's Garage	*107*
Ecclesiastical Court	62
Education	46
Eggmore	7
Electricity supply	30
Enclosure	36 94
Estmond family	8 86 *87*
Estrays	15
Evacuees	49 95
Fairs	27
Farms	38 *41* 42 *43*
Farway	24 39
Farway Cottage	112
Farway Farm	112
Fernie, Andrew	53
Fieldworks	117
Field Names	122
Five Bells	83 84

139

Flax	30
Flower Shows	108
Football Club	102
Ford	20
Fordwater	113
Foss Way	22
Foundry, Crawley	22
Fulling – see Mills, fulling	
Gargoyles	63
Gas supply	30
Geology	1
George Inn	15 44 84 *87*
Gilletts Farm	113
Girls' Friendly Society	101
Grey Ditch	22
Guides	102
Hall – see Community Hall	
Hall, Sir Edward Marshall	92
Health	74
Henley family	7 8 10 15 48
Heriot	12 17
Higher Fordwater Farm	113
Highways	22
Holy City, origin of name	7 24 38
Home Guard	95 *98*
Honeyhill	31
Hook	7 31
Hook Farm	113
Hoopers Farmhouse	113
Hunting	7 101
Ice Age	1 2
Industrial School for Servant Girls	46 *51*
Inns	83
Iron, iron working	1 4 16 22 30
Iron Age	4 34 93
Jones, John	2
Keates Farmhouse	113
Kitbridge	1 2 *25* 31
Knights Farm	113
Lace making	31
Land use	34
Laurels, The	*101*
Library	102 *110*
Licences	14
Liddon, Rev William	90
Lime, lime kilns	1 24 31 *33*
Lisle-Smith family	10
Lodge	*21*
Longhouses	44
Lower Ridge	113
Luce, Rev Richard	90
Manor, The	6 *21*
Manor Court	12 62 64
Manor House	8 *13*
Markets	27
Mills, fulling	18 30
Mills, milling	6 7 17 31 *35* 65

Marl, marl pits	1 14
Masonic Lodge	102 114
Maternity Society	102
Methodists	68
Milford family	10
Militia	75
Millway Farm	7 40
Monmouth Rebellion	94
Monuments, church	55
Mothers' Union	103
National School	46 48 *51*
Neolithic – see Stone Ages	
New Inn	44 84 *87*
Nonconformity	68
Norman period	6
Occupations	137
Old Farmhouse, Burridge	114
Old House, The	114
Old Orchard – see Whitehouse	
Orphan School – see St Andrew's College	
Packhorses	26
Paper making	31
Parks	7
Paupers	70
Perambulation	136
Percy, Gilbert de	7 44
Permeke, Constant	92
Pigeon Club	103
Pinneys Cottage	114
Pitt, Rev John	88
Place Names	122
Plate, church	55
Ploughs, ploughing	6 17
Police	67
Police House	27
Poor, the	69
Poor Rate	70
Poorhouse – see Workhouse	
Pottery	4
Post Office	30
Pratt, J R	106
Pratt's Garage	29
Prebend	7 58 59
Prebendaries	134
Prebendary Court	64
Professions	137
Primrose Farm	*107*
Pulman's Circles	4 *117*
Pulman, George	4
Quakers	68
Quarter Sessions	66
Railways	23 24
Ransom's Farm	38
Rational Society	78 *109*
Registers, Parish	56
Ridge	7 *21* 39
Roads	22
Romans	1 4 22 93
Rose Cottage, Burridge	114

St. Andrew's College	47 *51*
Salisbury, bishops of	6 16 27 44
Sampson's Charity	81
Saxon period	6
Schools	46
School, All Saints – see All Saints School	
Scouts	103
Shambles	27
Sheep	17
Shops	27 105 *107* 109
Skittles	103
Smallridge	*109*
Snuff making	31
Springhayes	115
Stone Ages	4 34
Stop Line	98 99
Strong family	14 27 88
Strongs, house and shop	27 30 *109* 115
Sub-manors	19
Symes Cottage	115
Tenancy	12
Territorials	103
Thorncombe Lands Charity	79
Threshing machines	29 32
Tiles – see Bricks and Tiles	
Tiling	17
Tithes	58
Toll House	23 *25*
Trade	27
Tradesmen	137
Transport	22
Travellers' Rest	83
Turners Charity	81
Turnpike Trusts	22 25

Twist Farm	40
Tytherleigh	7 20 *21* 25 52 *87* 91
Tytherleigh Cott - see New Inn	
Tytherleigh farms	39
Tytherleigh Gymkhana	107
Tytherleigh Hill	40
Tytherleigh Inn	83
Vagrants	69
Vermin	36 62
Vicarage, Old	44
Vicars	134
Visitations	62
Vulscombe Field	*117*
Wale family	10
Wambrook	6 10 39 58
War Memorial	94 *98*
Warren, right of	7
Water supply	30
Weaving	30
Welfare Clubs	77
Whitehouse	1 38 114 115
White's Charity	81
Wills, John	91
Wilmington	6 7 20 *21*
Women's Institute	103 *110*
Woodcock, Rev Charles	46 48 59 91
Wool – see Sheep	
Woonton Farm	1 4 38 115
Workhouse	73 75 76 77
Yard Farm	38 116
Young Men's Club	104
Youth Club	104

OBITUARY

Mary Parmiter 1920 - 2014

Mary Parmiter, who died in October 2014, aged 94 will be remembered for her comprehensive work on the history of Chardstock. With her parents she came to the village in the 1950s after service in the Royal Air Force and developed an interest in Local History. She loved walking with her dogs and thus got to know most of the farmers in the area. These contacts came in useful when, together with Roger Carter and Peter Wood, she "field - walked" for Parish Surveys of Wambrook, Whitestaunton and Chardstock. Her local knowledge was extensive, and her sharp eyes spotted many finds of pottery and other archaeological features. Mary read widely and had an abiding interest in local and family history, researching many Chardstock families. Together with Joan Tunstall she compiled a record of the memorial inscriptions on the tombstones in Chardstock Churchyard and worked with us on producing our book "The History of Chardstock". Her mind was always alert, she had a marvellous memory and a forceful personality. Her unsurpassed knowledge of the history of Chardstock and its people will be sadly missed.